Personality Assessment with ID37

Thomas Staller • Cornelia Kirschke

Personality Assessment with ID37

Motivation and the Ability to Self-Direct

Springer

Thomas Staller
ID37 Company GmbH, Berlin, Germany

Cornelia Kirschke
ID37 Company GmbH, Berlin, Germany

ISBN 978-3-030-53920-7 ISBN 978-3-030-53921-4 (eBook)
https://doi.org/10.1007/978-3-030-53921-4

This Springer imprint is published by the registered company Springer Nature Switzerland AG
The registered company address is: Gewerbestrasse 11, 6330 Cham, Switzerland

All I wanted to do was live the life that was inside me, trying to get out. Why was that so hard?

Hermann Hesse, Demian –
The Story of Emil Sinclair's Youth

Foreword | Practical Application

Success Through Diversity

People all over the world drink Coca-Cola. Our employees are as different from one another as are our customers. At Coca-Cola, people from vastly different cultures and religions, as well as people of all ages, have been working together for decades. Within our company, we tolerate and actively support people with different ways of life, points of view and interests. Coca-Cola is a signatory to the German Diversity Charter and is a member of the Fair Company initiative and the Alliance against Homophobia. To us, diversity means that we live out an open, fair and tolerant corporate culture every day.

We know that diversity contributes to our company's success. The promotion of diversity and inclusion is an important aspect of our corporate goals. This is reflected in part in the fact that our teams are put together in a deliberately heterogeneous way. Heterogeneity refers here not only to skill sets and cultures, but also and especially to team members' personalities. In this context, we have learned to appreciate the value of personality diagnostics instruments. The use of individual personality profiles gives us the ability to better understand each individual's motives, which in turn enables discussion of these motives. We work to ensure that our team members develop a deep and imaginative understanding of what differences and similarities mean, and that they feel comfortable in revealing these transparently. This promotes mutual respect and tolerance, and enables everyone to remain true to themselves. Cohesion and the culture of diversity are enhanced, and the quality of team results improves.

Our focus is on gaining an understanding of what is important to people, what drives them, what is difficult for them and where they can perform best by doing something close to their hearts. Many companies use personality assessment tools in their talent acquisition and development processes. We have decided to use personality assessments primarily in the context of our talent-development programs, and to offer the service to all participants as a voluntary measure. It is a helpful, widely used tool in preparation for team-development measures, when new teams are being assembled and following reorganizations. Our users talk openly about their positive experiences, piquing their colleagues' curiosity. We have seen that interest in our work with the tool is growing significantly.

Those like me who have worked for many years in the education and training sector are familiar with a wide variety of personality models that are used for different purposes. The great advantages of ID37 include its high level of precision, its empirical quality and the fact that it incorporates the most recent research in the field. The high level of accuracy delivered by its analytical results serves to mirror the personality in a highly individualized way. Comparable to a "photo taken from within," these results are meaningful, multifaceted and easy to understand. Of course, the results are value-neutral, and we always treat them in a value-neutral way.

The ID37 personality assessment supports us as human-resources professionals in helping our employees, executives and teams become more self-sufficient. For example, managers and employees can use the personality profile as a basis for discussing individual career paths and plans, with the goal of helping employees remain enthusiastic about working for the company over the long term. A personality profile is a helpful tool in allowing work to be organized more efficiently and successfully. You can learn exactly how this is done in this book.

Most readers probably won't have access to internal ID37 Masters in their companies that would allow them to use the analysis tool directly. In such a case, I can only encourage you to work with an ID37 Master, or even to sign up for a training program with Thomas Staller. I find the insights I have gained regarding motives, their significance for the personality and their contribution to the appreciation of diversity to be a great enrichment. For experienced Masters, this book offers a well-founded supplement for their professional work. The practitioners among you would be well advised to study the clearly described case studies. They inspire people to take a new look at themselves, their emotions and their behavior, and to incorporate the resulting insights into their personal-development work.

We remain committed to ensuring that our employees experience a strong sense of connection to their colleagues, the company and its brands – for that special attitude toward life with Coca-Cola. I am convinced that personality assessment instruments like ID37 support us in this endeavor. This book serves as a reference work, a source of inspiration and an invitation to engage in self-reflection.

National Sales Training Manager, Coca-Cola European Partners, BU Germany,

Berlin, Germany Clemens W. Krebs
2020

Foreword | Science

A Precise Instrument for Personal Development Processes

Personality is what distinguishes us as individuals in our daily lives, actions and interactions. Specific to one's person, it is as unique as a fingerprint. Personality significantly influences behavior and perception, in both professional and private contexts. It plays a role, for example, in a person's performance and satisfaction in higher education and at work, in their ability to withstand stress, and in the extent to which they are satisfied with life. It makes us determined and persistent. All of this has been supported over and over again by a number of relevant international research findings. In addition to shaping how we perceive our surroundings, our fellow human beings and their behavior, personality also plays a role in determining how we act – how we interact both in and with our environment. A person's personality is therefore an enormously important factor in all areas of an individual life, but also in society.

As a highly complex construct, personality is shaped by the interplay of various characteristics and processes. Despite the variety of important and established models, there is no single comprehensive collection of characteristics that can be used to describe personality in exhaustive terms. Depending on the context and objectives targeted, however, examining a subset of personality traits can provide useful and valuable insights. This is true both in terms of research and in the context of practical application, for example, with interventions. For example, in an increasingly complex society that offers more freedom and opportunities while demanding more responsibility and initiative than ever before in areas such as education, work and one's private life, a person's motives are of particular importance. As personality traits, motives represent what we strive for in life and what is important to us. They are therefore important coordinates for us in orienting our behavior and goals in specific situations that arise in daily life as well as those that mark phases of our lives. Interventions that draw upon evidence-based motives in initiating and guiding personal development processes thus provide people with a useful compass that helps them navigate the complexity of modern society, which features countless opportunities.

A goal-oriented and sustainable intervention that focuses on personality traits such as a person's motives requires an effective instrument able to assess such motives and thus make them visible. Measuring motives at the level of individual persons, which is necessary for interventions, places very high demands on the quality of a measuring instrument, which includes the need for an extremely high degree of reliability and technical accuracy in measurement. In order to be able to guarantee such things, at the University of Luxembourg, we have used the most modern test development methodology to construct an ID37 questionnaire that meets high scientific standards, incorporates the current state of motivation research and provides practitioners with an unprecedented fact base as a foundation for development processes. With the 16 fundamental motives, the ID37 personality assessment provides comprehensive insight into the personality traits that motivate a person's actions and interactions on a fundamental level.

With this intriguing and pathbreaking book, the reader is provided a practical and evidence-based introduction to the model of the 16 motives and what these motives mean for the pursuit of success and satisfaction. Thanks to the book's straightforward approach, readers without a background in psychology can easily understand the basics of personality, its relevance for one's professional work and why it is worthwhile to explore one's personality. With the help of case studies illustrating how the instrument works in application every step along the way – from taking the test to scoring it to evaluating its results with the client in the assessment session – the book offers easy-to-use guidance on how to use the ID37 personality assessment in making the 16 motives apparent. This book offers the reader a new approach to understanding people, the means to expand one's understanding of motivational psychology and the opportunity to acquire a new coaching method. This book is sure to broaden your horizon in the field of motivational psychology!

University of Luxembourg, Research Group Computer-Based Assessment,

Luxembourg
2020

Samuel Greiff
Jan Dörendahl

Preface

What is it that determines how we feel, think and act? Across the board, scientists agree that people follow an inner script. Motives – that is, the personality traits that are expressed differently in each person – are the key elements of this inner script. They are what drive us forward. In other words, they direct us in how we feel, what we think and the actions we take.

The ID37 personality assessment is a diagnostic procedure that helps people identify and understand their motives. Based in empirical science, the procedure was developed over a two-year period of research at the University of Luxembourg by an interdisciplinary team of academic experts and professionals in the science of personal development. One of the team's experts is the coauthor of this book, Thomas Staller.

The "ID37" brand name stands for our identity as human beings – "ID" is synonymous with our unique identity as individuals and "37" refers to 37 degrees Celsius, the body temperature at which we feel most comfortable.

Motives have a significant impact on our personality, reveal much about our individual comfort zone, and help explain our emotions and behavior. To be sure, the 16 motives specified by the ID37 are only part of what makes up a person's personality. They are, however, precisely those factors that are manifest in relatively constant behavior over time and across situations, and which constitute a rather stable part of our identity. In this book, we focus on these factors of our personality. We describe how they are identified by the ID37 personality assessment and what significance they have for self-direction and life satisfaction. We've organized the book's content to reflect the triad of drive, satisfaction and success – which offers a set of clear coordinates in targeting a successful life.

Our book is designed to assist consultants, trainers, coaches, executives, human-resource managers and professionals as they help their clients and employees with the support of the ID37 personality assessment. It also targets certified professionals who already work with personality diagnostic instruments such as the LUXXprofile or the Reiss Motivation Profile. The book also provides valuable insights for anyone who is interested in personal development but who has yet to engage in a personality assessment process. It will prove beneficial for anyone seeking to build their skills through self-awareness and self-direction with the help of a tool for practical application. We wish everyone on the path to improving their drive, satisfaction and success the joy of discovering useful insights throughout their journey.

On a final note, we would like to point out that we use masculine pronouns for readability purposes only. The use of such forms is intended to include all genders.

Berlin, Germany
2020

Thomas Staller
Cornelia Kirschke

Acknowledgments

Our biggest thanks go to **Kamila Joanna Laures** for her tireless dedication and commitment to this publication. Never failing to impress, her holistic approach, combined with her attentive accuracy, has made the book more accessible to a broad audience of readers. She has been a continuing source of inspiration for us and, without her this book never would have made it to publication.

Special thanks go to **Ilona Bernhart**, whose sure editorial hand and professional input helped bring the book to its final draft. For many years now, we've benefited from her profound expertise, loyalty and valuable cooperation.

We are grateful to our business partner, **Michael Kloss**, for his willingness to engage us in countless discussions and unfailingly constructive criticism. On several occasions, his input opened our eyes to things we had not considered.

We would also like to express our appreciation for the University of Luxembourg and **Professor Dr. Samuel Greiff** in particular, whose preface has enriched our book. In addition, we thank **Dr. Jan Dörendahl** for contributing his time and expertise, answering our questions, and providing us guidance throughout the process. We also thank **Dr. Christoph Kemper**, who was in charge of test development. The innovative testing procedure presented here is in large part a product of his know-how in personality diagnostics and the psychology of personality and motivation, as well as his commitment.

We would also like to thank the Springer publishing house. **Dr. Reinald Klockenbusch** supported our project from the very beginning. He introduced us to the expert **Heiko Sawczuk**, whose exceptionally friendly manner provided us ongoing encouragement as he guided us through the publication production process. We would also like to express our appreciation for the international colleagues from Springer-Verlag and their supportive assistance.

A special thanks go to **Barbara Serfozo**, who translated the manuscript with great skill, care, and enthusiasm. We would also like to take this opportunity to express our gratitude to **Anja Krahnert** for her many years of support. The energy with which she has championed ID37 cannot be overstated.

This book draws upon countless discussions and regular exchanges with our customers and partners from ID37, the LUXXprofile, and Reiss Motivation Profile. Each and every one has enriched this book and helped bring it to life with the numerous experiences, examples, and cases in application they've provided.

We owe a debt of gratitude to our valued client**, Clemens W. Krebs**, National Sales Training Manager at Coca-Cola, for the opportunities brought by fantastic projects and for finding the time to contribute a foreword to this publication. His contribution not only enriches our publication, it establishes a direct link to ID37 in practice.

Finally, we owe to you all the great joy and satisfaction that comes with the completion of this book.

Berlin, Spring 2020

Thomas Staller
Cornelia Kirschke

Abbreviations

ACO	Ant-Colony Optimization
AERA	American Educational Research Association
APA	American Psychological Association
CFA	Confirmatory factor analysis
EFA	Exploratory factor analysis
GDPR	General Data Protection Regulation
HR	Human resources
MBTI	Myers–Briggs Type Indicator
STEN	Standard tens
WOOP	Wish, outcome, obstacle, plan
ZRM	Zurich Resources Model

Contents

Personality

1

1.1 The Stranger on the Train

Imagine you are sitting on a train, and a newly boarded passenger is beginning to make a scene, because his reservation has turned out to be invalid. The train's conductor responds to the passenger politely but is receiving the full brunt of the man's fury. The man returns repeatedly to the conductor, giving his anger free rein as he renews his complaints for a second and third time. Sitting relatively close to the scene, you were previously enjoying a relaxing journey home after having successfully taken care of a business appointment. Other travelers appear unfazed, with some clearly even regarding the angry man to be in the right. However, you find the situation stressful. You have little sympathy for the man; indeed, you have trouble understanding behavior of this kind. You find him to be inconsiderate and lacking in self-control, stirring up the other passengers and treating the conductor unfairly. Your erstwhile relaxed mood has evaporated, and you consider how you might intercede to smooth over the situation.

This scene reveals much about you or, rather, about the observer on the train. The observer is most likely a peaceable person, and consequently considers the man's treatment of the conductor and the subsequent disturbance of his fellow passengers to be particularly grievous. In contrast, the person doing the complaining most likely considers it quite normal to express anger in this way.

This example demonstrates how people can experience the same situation in fundamentally different ways. Indeed, we all perceive the world differently. Observations and personal experiences are influenced by our own personality. That is to say, people behave as determined by their personality. What prompts the man on the train to return repeatedly to the conductor? What drives the observer to want to intercede? And how will the conductor react? The answers to these and similar questions depend in large part on a variety of factors specific to each individual. These answers help us successfully navigate our personal and professional lives. This knowledge helps us understand what makes other people tick, why they act the

T. Staller, C. Kirschke, *Personality Assessment with ID37*,
https://doi.org/10.1007/978-3-030-53921-4_1

way they do and what behavioral patterns they're following. It helps us understand what brings people together and what divides them. People are complex, especially in their interpersonal interactions.

Science has long sought models suited to explaining the complexities of individuals and their modes of behavior. The ID37 personality diagnostic instrument differs from other models and is characterized by the following:

- a focus on motives as a key aspect of human personality;
- it captures and describes an individual personality on the basis of 16 fundamental motivations present in every human being. These motives are particularly well-suited to getting to the core of a personality, and to explaining the causes of human behavior;
- it creates a very accurate personality profile which, to a certain degree, even enables behavior to be predicted.

At the core of the ID37 personality model is a psychological testing process that we developed jointly with the University of Luxembourg and which draws on current research by Henry A. Murray, William McDougall and Steven Reiss, among others. This theoretical foundation has been supplemented by more than 10 years of empirical science and practical experience with the Reiss Motivation Profile diagnostic instrument.

The 16 motives that are measured by means of the ID37 process comprise: CURIOSITY, SOCIAL ACCEPTANCE, INFLUENCE, STATUS, RETENTION, AUTONOMY, SOCIAL PARTICIPATION, PRINCIPLES, SOCIAL ENGAGEMENT, STRUCTURE, SAFETY, REVENGE, PHYSICAL EXERCISE, FOOD ENJOYMENT, FAMILY and EROS (Chap. 4).

The results of the analysis are presented in the form of a motives profile that separately reports each motive's intensity of expression (Fig. 4.1). With ID37, we provide users a tool grounded in empirical science that helps bring their own reality and the reality of others into clearer focus. In the professional sphere, consultants, trainers, coaches, human-resources and staff-development managers, as well as executives can use the tool to derive individual strategies and tailored personal-development measures.

1.2 What Is Personality?

There are countless definitions for the term "personality" that derive from a wide range of theoretical and research traditions. The consensus is that each person is unique, furnished as they are with a broad range of individual characteristics, and that personality must be considered within the context of the individual life.

For example, personality psychologist Jens B. Asendorpf defines personality as follows:

> A person's personality refers to the totality of his or her personality traits: individual characteristics as embodied and as expressed in regularities of behavior and experience. (Asendorpf 2015, p. 2)

Personality has no uniform definition within the field of psychology. In general, it refers to the entire sum of an individual's behavioral characteristics.

Below, we highlight some terms and phenomena that are associated with personality.

In everyday speech, the basic concepts of "person" and "individual" center on the idea of personality:

- The term "human being" refers both to the biological species of Homo sapiens, as well as its existence as a social being.
- "Individual" means a being distinct from others. The term reflects the uniqueness of each human being, as the word "individual" derives from the verb "dividere" (Latin: to divide), and literally means "that which is indivisible." The individual becomes a personality by taking possession of the achievements of the culture from which one comes; however, the demarcation of the self comes about through personal characteristics and independent action, interests and idiosyncrasies, resulting in the development of an individual identity. This implies that not every person is a personality, at least as a newborn (Simon 2006, p. 12 f.).

Despite all of one's individuality, every person is also a social being. In the view of Russian psychologist Alexei Leontiev, personality develops within society. By this, he means that personality is generated via interaction with our environment. The capacities for thought, action and feeling thus always develop under the conditions created within a specific society. Being born in a particular location and in a particular era connects each person with a specific social, economic, political and cultural milieu that influences them and the course of their lives. Throughout their lives, every person receives everything one needs through interaction with other people. This is vital in intellectual terms too, as individuals also derive their speech, knowledge and behavior norms from others (Leontiev 1975, cited by Simon 2006, p. 10 f.).

A person is thus both an individual and a social being. For this reason, personality must always be considered in context.

1.2.1 Two Dimensions of Personality: Traits and States

Personality scholarship distinguishes between traits – which are generally stable – and states, which are subject to change.

Dimensions of Human Personality

- **Traits** = are characteristic behaviors or feelings such as anxiety that are genetically determined, largely unchangeable and found across all cultures. Traits describe observable behavior.
- **States** = are temporary behaviors or feelings such as fear that are influenced by environmental factors (e.g., socialization, culture and situational conditions) and can therefore change.

It makes sense to use traits to describe an individual because they lead to behavioral patterns that remain relatively stable over the course of a person's life.

As the German neurologist Dr. Gerhard Roth has stated:

> Over the course of their lives, people exhibit consistent patterns of feeling, thinking and behavior. These patterns are not necessarily fixed; as a rule, they are dynamic and vary in how they develop and manifest themselves. Developmental and situational dynamics start to display patterns at an early stage. This is what we call a human being's personality (Roth and Ryba 2016, p. 125).

A Closer Look: Even When We Change, We Remain True to Ourselves

People change only within the construct that is their personality. People who believe they have fundamentally changed their personality and claim to have become "an entirely different person" are usually mistaken. This can be shown by assessing a person to determine whether specific or distinctive characteristics have been present since childhood. In most cases, a person's memories of the past have been overwritten by other events, or the person has learned over the years to adapt to a situation. If the gap between what a person aspires to and that which they experience on a daily basis is too wide, this can have a profound impact on the person's well-being and health. For example, a person who has chosen an entirely new profession was presumably unhappy in their previous work. Clearly, either their job, or the environment in which they worked, was ill-suited to them. When they switch career paths, they don't change their nature, they merely give stronger expression to who they actually are. According to research conducted by personality psychologist Jens B. Asendorpf, people tend to seek out environments that suit them rather than adapt themselves to specific conditions. And even when they do adapt, this takes place within the framework determined by their personality (Roth and Ryba 2016, p. 220 f).

Neuroscientist Christian E. Elger addresses in his book *Neuroleadership* the extent to which personality structures are stable or changeable:

> "Personality is in no way a permanent or rigid structure. It is a condition that is affected by internal and external circumstances. Thus, on the one hand, people are a reflection of their environment and, on the other, life itself involves ongoing change management. In each case, the brain is driven by the search for rewards, which is why current research on happiness draws heavily from neuroscience." (Elger 2009, p. 39)
>
> The idea that personality is innate was abandoned several years ago. Clearly, genes play a role here. But the extent to which they influence personality traits lies somewhere between 30% and 60%, as several studies on identical twins have shown. The rest is determined by social factors. Some scholars believe that key personality traits are set within the first three years of a child's life. Others, however, claim to be able to prove that an individual's personality is not fully established until the age of 50. Most likely, our neuronal plasticity means that we continue to change throughout our life (Elger 2009, p. 145)

Empirical studies carried out over several years have shown that the basic structure of one's personality is established in early childhood, remains largely stable throughout adolescence and, over time, grows increasingly resilient to external influences (Roth and Ryba 2016, p. 221 f.)

As a dynamic construct, personality is subject to constant change. Motives provide a relatively stable framework within which a personality changes.

Several other scientists are also convinced of the existence of persistent and relatively stable traits that influence our behavior in specific situations. As such, traits are not directly observable, but can only be inferred from behavior.

Disposition
Disposition refers to a characteristic of one's person that remains stable over the medium term, that is, for at least several weeks or months. A person's disposition can lead them to exhibit specific kinds of behavior in particular situations. (Asendorpf 2015, p. 3).

Asendorpf thus sees disposition as a pattern, that is, a tendency to act a certain way. It is not behavior per se, as this varies constantly and is directly observable. If, for example, a person is inclined to be afraid of speaking publicly, this is what we would call a behavioral disposition (Asendorpf 2015, p. 3).

The distinction between behavior and behavioral disposition is important, as dispositions help us acquire a more accurate image of a person's personality. Unlike a discrete event such as our initial contact with a person, recurring patterns of behavior give us the opportunity to assess more realistically a person and their personality.

Behavioral patterns, or a disposition, characterize a personality, not behavior itself.

The personality assessment tool ID37 provides a reliable framework for rendering individual dispositions tangible and explainable and, to a certain extent, makes it possible to predict an individual's behavior. These patterns of behavior are identified in the motives profile. For example, the motive of STRUCTURE shows differences in the tendency to structure one's surroundings in simple and consistent terms (Fig. 1.1a, b).

The ID37 personality profile sheds light on key patterns of behavior.

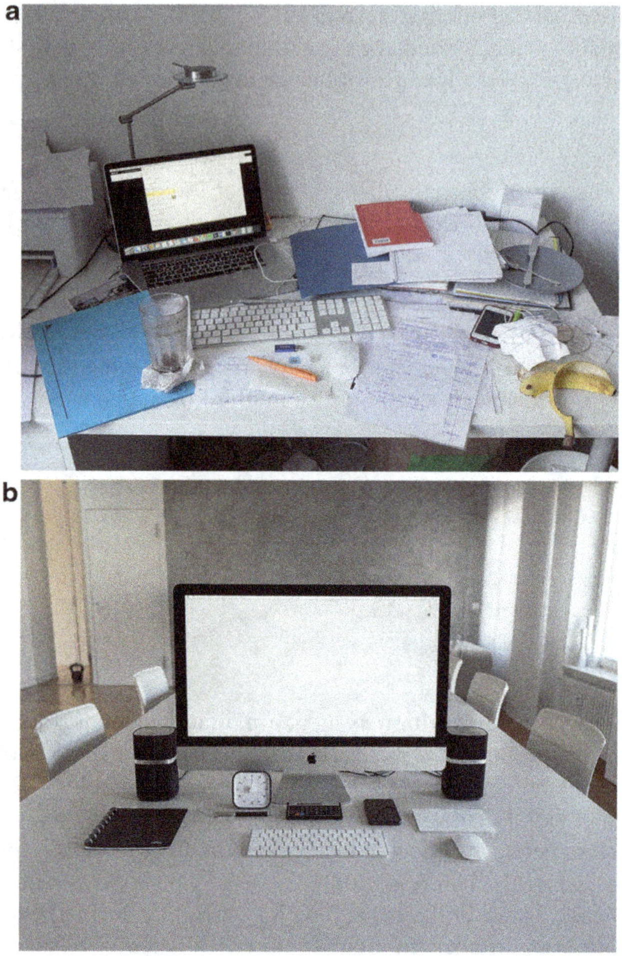

Fig. 1.1 Various dispositions for the STRUCTURE motive. (**a**) allows conclusions to be drawn from a weak expression of the STRUCTURE motive, (**b**) allows conclusions to be drawn from a strong expression of the STRUCTURE motive

1.2.2 What's "Normal"?

We speak of a "normal" personality as one that generally lines up with what's culturally accepted and expected. In other words, when patterns of experience and behavior – that is, how a person perceives the things, events and others around them, how they feel about and respond to them, how they conduct themselves or treat others – lie within the bounds of the norm, we consider this reflective of a normal personality.

But what is "the norm"? The ID37 tool offers an effective benchmark in establishing what counts as normal. Grounded in empirical science, ID37 is a standardized instrument. The results it delivers show how one's personality compares to the cultural norm. As part of its standardization process, each of the 16 traits were calibrated individually against a reference population. This is one of the tool's strengths – it describes neither types nor typologies, but the qualities that make a person unique in contrast to a representative sample of the larger population (Sect. 4.2.3).

Particularly noteworthy are those personality characteristics that deviate from the norm significantly (Fig. 4.5). These characteristics have a stronger effect on experience (e.g., joy, frustration) and observable behavior than do characteristics in the middle range. In the former case, we refer to an extreme personality, in the latter to a normal personality. For example, when a mother considers herself to be abnormal because being home every night to put the kids to bed is not a priority for her, her feeling about this is not abnormal. Her personality profile may feature a very weak expression for the FAMILY motive (Sect. 4.4.15). ID37 brings to light the various facets and characteristics of a normal personality while at the same time highlighting how we differ from each other and how unique we are as individuals.

This is demonstrated by a simple matter of math: If we assume a total of 16 personality traits with, for example, only five scale units per motive, we get nearly 150 billion different possible combinations and expressions of personality – without even having considered all other factors that influence personality.

The fact that a person with a few rough edges can be perceived as "not normal" is problem primarily associated with a lack of understanding. When people exhibit strong personality characteristics, we tend to confuse this with personality disorders or pathological behavior. These individuals may rub others the wrong way because despite being so different, they are nonetheless afforded the same treatment as others. Take, for example, the situation created by an open-plan office. Such environments are designed for conformity. However, everyone has different needs. A setting designed to treat everyone in the same manner will therefore, over time, result in discomfort, dissatisfaction and conflicts.

The limits of an ID37 personality assessment: The motives profile is not designed to distinguish between people who are mentally healthy and those who are not. In cases where someone exhibits behavior that causes personal suffering, social problems and/or brings harm to a firm, it is important to carefully consider if our expertise is appropriate for working with the individual.

> ID37 brings to light the multifaceted nuances of differences among people. At the same time, it points to specific ways in which these differences can be leveraged for positive effect. It is not intended to diagnose mental illnesses.

1.2.3 Understanding Personality with ID37

The ID37 personality assessment tool draws on 16 distinct fundamental motives to identify a person's motivational structure. These motives apply to everyone, but their expression and the extent to which they are experienced varies from person to person. Motives are useful as indicators of personality because they are relatively stable and allow us to identify behavioral patterns.

Of particular interest are those cases in which the expression of a motive deviates from that of the average population. The greater the deviation, the more intense the emotional experience of that motive is. Accordingly, it's also more likely that this particular motive will be manifest in repeated behavior.

The combined interplay of each motive results in a profile that offers us the means to understand more deeply the contours of a personality and how it influences a person's thought, emotions and behavior (Chap. 4).

The motives profile thus provides a reliable frame of reference for improving self-understanding. It helps us step out of the closed system of the self. Greater self-awareness helps us open up to people and experiences. Indeed, the more we talk about this, for example, during an assessment session with an ID37 Master, the easier it becomes.

ID37 contributes significantly to efforts aimed at understanding which motives steer a personality in a particular direction and serves as well to nudge individuals toward self-reflection. It encourages the person being assessed to examine their own self-perception from a distance and to open themselves up to input from others.

1.2.4 What Does this Mean for My Professional Work?

If there's one thing for sure, personalities are dynamic. Indeed, the contours of our personality take shape, change and develop within certain boundaries throughout the course of our lives. For our professional life, we draw on the framework provided by the 16 motives comprising the ID37 assessment tool, which describes a unique personality.

Motives refer to personality characteristics that are generally stable. As aspects of personality that accompany us over the long term, they allow us to position an individual in relation to their surroundings. They shed light on who we are, what priorities we have and, as a result, how we might achieve satisfaction.

Personal development involves us targeting change. Asking how we might change is therefore one of the most important questions we can pose. For an ID37 Master, the motives profile is the key to effective coaching as it unlocks the door to achieving the development desired by the client. In this way, we can identify the motives that influence a person's natural disposition. This then allows a person to determine whether they are able to realize these motives in a given circumstance and the extent to which they feel comfortable in doing so.

The ID37 personality diagnostics instrument is a strong place to start when it comes to personalized coaching and professional development work.

References

Asendorpf, J. B. (2015). *Persönlichkeitspsychologie für Bachelor* (3rd ed.). Berlin: Springer.
Elger, C. E. (2009). *Neuroleadership*. Munich: Haufe.
Roth, G., & Ryba, A. (2016). *Coaching, Beratung und Gehirn*. Stuttgart: Klett Cotta (e-Book).
Simon, W. (Ed.). (2006). *Persönlichkeitsmodelle und Persönlichkeitstests*. Offenbach: Gabal.

Drive

2

2.1 Motives as the Basis for Behavior

People seek to bring about events that lead to positive emotional states, either by seeking (approach) or avoiding (avoidance) something. If a person expects a positive or negative experience in their interactions with other people, things or situations, this belief will be reflected in corresponding behavior.

A Closer Look: Neurobiological Perspective on Approach and Avoidance
According to neuroscience, a person's personality is inextricably related to his brain's characteristics. For example, the brain's limbic system has been identified as the origin point of affects, feelings, motives, goals, conscience, empathy, morality and ethics. It is regarded as the area or entity in the brain that largely determines our personality, including our actions. Neurobiological processes take place there that serve as the basis of the motivation system, for example. These processes prompt the brain to repeat things and actions that have led to rewards in the past, and to avoid things and actions that have led to negative experiences (Roth and Ryba 2016, p. 137 ff.). This means that the specifics of what leads to rewards and of what is avoided varies among individuals, but that the same processes are being triggered in the brain.

Motive
A motive is an inducement to behavior in the sense of a guiding, activating, orienting force (McClelland 1985, cited by Eilles-Matthiessen and Scherer 2011, p. 18).

T. Staller, C. Kirschke, *Personality Assessment with ID37*,
https://doi.org/10.1007/978-3-030-53921-4_2

For a person in whom the SOCIAL PARTICIPATION motive has a high priority, for example, there is typically nothing more pleasurable than being with other people (Sect. 4.4.7). Because he therefore seeks this out, he often makes arrangements to meet others, attends events and goes to parties. For a person that does not ascribe a high priority to this motive, being in the company of large numbers of people is not an attractive proposition. His behavior is therefore not actively oriented toward engaging frequently in sociable situations, and he even tries to avoid too much social contact.

When we say that someone does not ascribe a high priority to a motive, this entails both a qualitative and a quantitative statement.

- The motive is an indication of why we act the way we do: What is genuinely important to this person and their view of life? What does he strive toward (qualitative)?
- The strength of the motive's expression, by contrast, is a quantitative statement: How much does the person need to satisfy the motive, and how intensively, how long in duration and how often?

To illustrate this point, we imagine a motive as a scale that forms a continuum (Fig. 2.1). Imagine you're an executive at a corporation. You are asked to evaluate the intensity of your desire for physical exercise, and to enter the appropriate level on the PHYSICAL EXERCISE scale, with options ranging from very weak to very strong. Very strong indicates a powerful desire for physical exercise. You may engage in extreme sports such as triathlons, but you don't earn your income through sport. You train rigorously and for long periods of time every day, for as much as 14 hours every week, because it is a genuinely important part of your life. You plan your day around activities involving sports and feel stressed when you have to take a break because of sickness or a densely planned business trip and can therefore not satisfy your desire for physical exercise. You would thus choose the value "very strong" on the scale.

> Motive-driven behavior can have two underlying causes: approach or avoidance. What a person strives for is an essential element of their personality.

If you are by contrast someone who doesn't have a particular need for physical exercise and can't understand why other people get excited about fitness, you would choose the "very weak" value on the PHYSICAL EXERCISE scale. You would try to avoid physical strain that you find to be unpleasant. In this regard, you would be quite flexible with regard to the amount of your physical exercise.

However, there are also motive expressions that fall between the extremes. For example, if physical activity is not of fundamental importance to you, but you do need exercise now and then, you would probably indicate a value somewhere in the middle. You would be quite flexible with regard to the amount of your physical exercise.

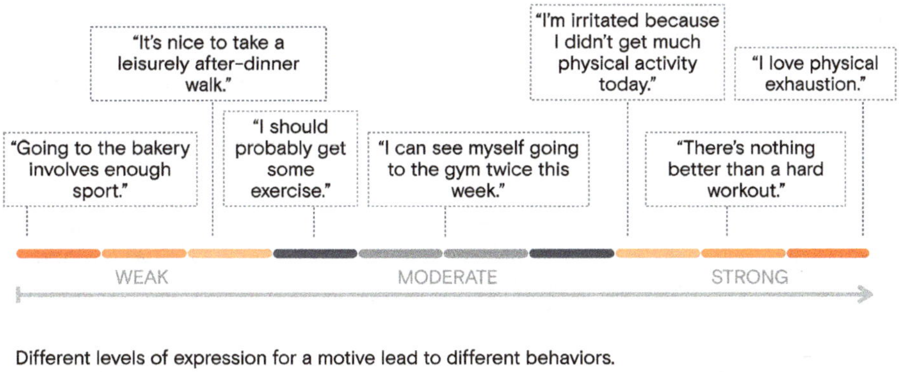

Fig. 2.1 How motives work, as illustrated by the PHYSICAL EXERCISE motive

A person whose motive expression falls into this middle area may show both tendencies in their behavior. Thus, he sometimes wants to engage actively in sports, but in certain phases also wants to relax physically. If you observe only one of the two behaviors, you risk quickly drawing incorrect conclusions, such as: goes regularly to the gym, is a person motivated by physical exercise.

This is why observed behavior, which often represents only a snapshot in time, is only minimally meaningful, whereas the measurement of motive expressions offers relatively reliable evidence. Here we can see the considerable benefit of the ID37 personality diagnostics instrument in recognizing persistent behavioral patterns, and in helping one understand an individual personality.

> By striving for or avoiding something, people want to bring about positive emotional states. People in whom motives are expressed differently also behave differently, have different emotional sensations, think differently and perceive the world differently.

Motive-based behavior is what we call "natural" behavior – for example, when a person with a very strongly expressed PHYSICAL EXERCISE motive engages in intensive sport. Regardless of whether such a person is conscious of their underlying motivation or not, he acts on the basis of an inner drive, and shows a clear behavioral tendency.

For the executive in the above example with a passion for triathlons, it is natural to go home directly after work in order to engage in a workout or train. This does not mean that the ambitious triathlete will not stay at work later if the circumstances call for it. In such a case, he must deliberately suppress his natural inclinations and act in a manner commensurate with the situation. This is possible temporarily; it becomes problematic only if the situation becomes permanent.

In the section addressing practical experience, we explain how this self-direction can be learned (Sect. 6.3).

2.1.1 Motivation

The terms "motive" and "motivation" are both derived from the Latin verb "movere" (Latin: to move, to impel).

Motivation
Motivation is an activating orientation toward a positively evaluated target state that serves to guide the momentary conduct of life (Rheinberg and Vollmeyer 2011, p. 15).

Motives and motivation are closely related, but should be distinguished:

- **Motives** are orienting, situation-independent drivers of behavior. They are rooted deep within the personality and are to some extent even genetically determined. The degree to which they are expressed will vary from person to person.
- The process of **motivating** entails the excitation of the motives, which is triggered by incentives.
- When someone is subject to this motivating process, the result is **motivation**. Motivation is a state in which motives have been activated. It triggers action that is directed toward a target state that is expected to be positive.

Prospect of Success as a Motivating Incentive
If a team member A assesses a tricky task as being soluble, he may offer to take on this task himself – impelled by a positively evaluated target state. For example, he may wish to be viewed afterward as an expert, or as "the team's savior." The person's underlying motive could be SOCIAL ACCEPTANCE, with a high level of expression.

A team member B, with a similarly strong expression of the SOCIAL ACCEPTANCE motive, by contrast sees no incentive to take on the task, because he feels it to be too difficult. If necessary, this person will even try to avoid working on this task, because he expects negative consequences to come from it, such as being regarded as a failure. There is no motivation present.

2.1.2 Where Does Motivation Come from?

Motivation arises through the perception of a target state or expectation of a reward, through the execution of an activity, or the presence of an outcome to be achieved. Thus, the incentive to act comes either from within the person or from an external source (Brandstätter et al. 2013, p. 91).

Intrinsic Motivation
If an activity is carried out for its own sake, intrinsic motivation is operating. A person is acting under his own impetus. Preferences within him impel him to do something (for example, to engage regularly in intensive sports). No external instrument of control is needed in order to carry out an activity gladly and consistently.

Extrinsic Motivation
Extrinsic motivation is aroused by external factors, such as material reward. The incentive to do something lies primarily in the consequences of the action. Extrinsically motivated behavior is often dependent on external agencies of control and is discontinued when the instruments of control cease to operate. Moreover, it has been demonstrated that external incentives not only lose their effect quickly but must also be consistently increased in order to retain their effect (Roth and Ryba 2016, p. 229).

Intrinsic and extrinsic motivation differ with regard to the origin of the incentive to act – which can come from within or be associated with a prospective external goal.

However, extrinsic motivation is also related to the motives of the person being motivated. For example, a prospective promotion and the associated gain in status might motivate a person in whom the STATUS motive is strongly expressed, but not one with a weakly expressed STATUS motive. An executive who wants to provide effective extrinsic – that is, external – motivating incentives must understand his employees' motives.

2.1.3 Motivation Depends on Contextual Factors

In addition to the personality, environmental factors such as opportunities to act and incentives play an important role in behavior. A person will exhibit behavior deriving from his specific motives only when he encounters a situation in which incentives are present that stimulate those motives and their relative expressions.

If we take the above example of the team task (Sect. 2.1.1) and change just a single situational factor – for example, say the team leader is not present at the team meeting – this can have an effect on the motivation. Team member B, for example, might show somewhat more readiness to tackle the task because he feels subject to less oversight without the presence of the leader. The situation influences how a team member evaluates the target state.

The surrounding culture or social system also influences individual behavior. This is particularly true of people whose personality profile features motive expressions of only medium strength that do not rise or fall to any extremes. It can thus be assumed that a person in a strictly hierarchical line organization will act differently than if they were in a looser network structure. This is related to the fact that people constantly learn to deal with new situations and adapt themselves to systems. This enables them to find their bearings quickly in very different worlds. This is an example of context- and situationally dependent learned behavior (Roth and Ryba 2016, p. 130).

Motives must always be considered in context. How a person acts on his motives and what motivates him depends in part on his environment.

The ID37 personality assessment helps us understand what environment people will feel comfortable in based on their personalities. For example, people with a strongly expressed SOCIAL PARTICIPATION motive tend to feel happier in situations that allow for social interaction (Sect. 4.4.7).

Learning Languages as if Automatically

A young person who has a very strongly expressed SOCIAL PARTICIPATION motive likes to make new acquaintances, because he – intrinsically motivated in this direction – finds this to be fun. Because this teenager grows up by chance in a neighborhood with many international peers, he will very probably make considerable effort to improve his English language skills rapidly, for instance by watching original-version English-language series, or by learning new vocabulary. If he was not fortuitously growing up in this environment, or if his SOCIAL PARTICIPATION motive was more weakly expressed, he would be less motivated – at least based on this particular driver of behavior – to acquire the English language.

Where does motivation come from? The motivation for a certain type of behavior derives from the interaction of:

- Factors within a person, including needs, motives, interests and goals;
- Factors within the environment, including opportunities, requirements, incentives and their interactions.

2.1.4 Self-Motivation

When experiencing intrinsic motivation, a person wants to engage in the activity for as long, as often and as intensively as possible, because it is perceived as being rewarding. This is the motivation that does not slacken. An intrinsically motivated activity can provide its own energy for long periods of time, because it positively serves a variety of internal needs, motives, feelings and goals (Martens and Kuhl 2004, p. 155). The activity is experienced as self-congruent, or in keeping with itself. For this reason, projects initiated at a person's own impetus are as a rule more successful than projects driven from the outside. Internal drive and emotional gain are demonstrably greater in the former case (Roth and Ryba 2016, p. 230). In a similar context, Mihály Csíkszentmihályi (2005, p. 11) coined the concept of flow as a particular form of the subjective experience of an intrinsically motivated activity. A person here finds themselves entirely wrapped up in the activity; the experience is perceived as being unimpeded, and everything seems to be happening "in flow" (Sect. 5.1).

If one attributes self-motivation to motive-based drivers of behavior, it can be seen why motives are considered to be inner resources. By this, we mean everything a person can repeatedly rely on within themselves in order to activate behaviors that promise a positive result and an emotional benefit.

Self-motivation very often takes place unconsciously. This is an advantage, because it functions even if a person does not need to be aware of it (Martens and Kuhl 2004, p. 104).

> People cannot be sustainably motivated by external forces. Only self-motivation is lasting, because an activity is experienced as both suitable and satisfying.

2.1.5 What Does this Mean for My Professional Work?

The goal of personal development is to enable people to motivate and manage themselves on a conscious basis. In so doing, they become independent of external circumstances and happenstance. This requires that they come to know themselves better and come to grips with their life circumstances. What stimuli do they respond to, what do they prefer in life, and what environments do they create for themselves or need in order to feel comfortable?

The ID37 personality assessment provides us with access to the individual motives. Motives affect self-motivation, the willingness to achieve, and satisfaction. Thus, it rapidly becomes clear what resources can be activated, and what aspects fit the person's life priorities.

Our task as a coach, consultant, executive or human-resources manager is to create the conditions in which people can act and work in a self-motivated way. We can help people gain self-awareness. We can support them in becoming experts in the subject of themselves, and in learning how to act with confidence. In an ideal case, the person learns to rely on their own resources, and in the future no longer needs either the coach's advice or their boss' praise.

The better we are able to understand the process of self-motivated behavior, comprehend personality and context, and develop personally tailored strategies, the more sustainable the person's success.

2.2 Motivation-Driven Action

As previously shown, the person and the situation are the decisive factors in the realization of an action. The assessment of the emotional benefit promised by a situation can trigger an action or not. This represents the basic schema for the sequence of motivation processes as described in the work of motivational psychologist Heinz Heckhausen (Fig. 2.2).

Example from the Working World
If a product owner in an agile team places a task in the "to be expedited" task pool (that is, tasks must be handled with a higher priority), this can lead a team member to exhibit a high level of readiness to act. This impulse could be triggered by a strongly expressed SOCIAL ACCEPTANCE motive. For a person motivated in this way, the identification of the task by the product owner could itself constitute an incentive to deal with the task, in expectation of positive consequences to the action (e.g., praise) that he associates with positive emotions (e.g., joy). The motivation that arises through cognitive and emotional processes is expressed in an action – in this case, the high level of effort shown by the team member. Subsequent to the action, the person will engage in retrospective processes of self-evaluation – "Did I do that well?", "Why did I do that?" – as well as emotional reactions (e.g., pride) appropriate to the situation. The result of this self-assessment will in turn affect the next situation.

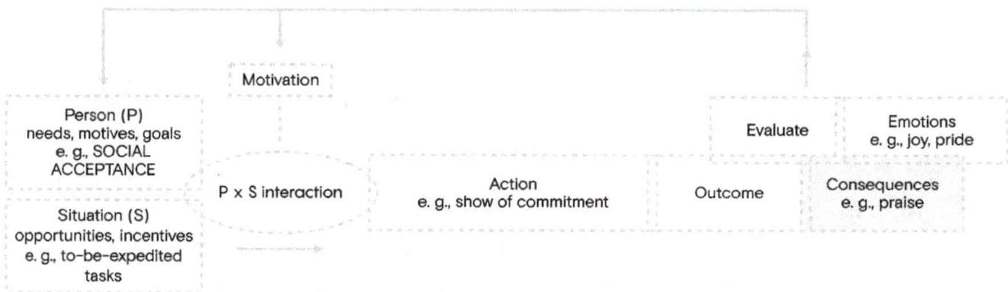

Fig. 2.2 The course of motivated action. (Adapted from Heckhausen and Heckhausen 2009)

2.2.1 Two Motivation Systems

Neuroscience distinguishes between the implicit and explicit motivation systems, each of which is independent of the other. These are also important in explaining motivation-driven action, because many processes unfold in the unconscious mind, and are not directly accessible.

- **Implicit motives are:**
  - unconscious;
  - not represented in language;
  - susceptible to certain stimuli that are acquired early in childhood;
  - affect-based and linked to physiological parameters (e.g., hormones); and
  - indirectly ascertainable, for example using projective measurement techniques.
- **Explicit motives are:**
  - conscious;
  - capable of verbalization;
  - learned in childhood in the process of dealing with one's social environment;
  - representative of the concept of the self; and
  - directly detectable, for example, through the use of questionnaires.

If implicit and explicit motives coincide in their expressions, this is called motive congruence. If the degree of expression of the implicit and explicit motives diverges, it is referred to as motive incongruence. This can reveal itself in a person's postponing of actions and a consequent dissatisfaction. Self-control and self-regulation can help in overcoming problems of motivation. If a person's implicit and explicit motives coincide, this leads to stronger intrinsic motivation (Brandstätter et al. 2013, p. 68 ff.).

Motives as Behavior-Relevant Personality Traits

- Motives are in part genetically conditioned and are relatively stable over time.
- Motives are an expression of needs.
- Motives are stimulated by incentives.
- Motives trigger behavior.
- Motives determine the direction and intensity of action.
- Motives are expressed with different strengths in different people.
- Motives exist on two independent levels – the implicit and the explicit.

A person's motivation depends on situational stimuli, personal preferences and the interactions between the two.

2.2.2 What Motives Are There?

Motivation psychology has distinguished motives by their thematic contents and combined them into motive groups. There is no consensus regarding how many motives are needed to describe the personality in a sufficiently nuanced way.

Researchers recognize three fundamental motives: power, affiliation and achievement (University of Luxembourg Manual 2018).

Power Motive

The power motive includes the need to exercise control and influence over other people, as well as the desire for status and prestige.

Affiliation Motive

The affiliation motive centers on the establishment and maintenance of satisfying interpersonal relations. The additional intimacy motive was later defined as being an independent but nonetheless related motive. While the affiliation motive primarily relates to contact with strangers, the intimacy motive centers on the establishment of connections with and affection for people who are comparatively close.

Achievement Motive

The achievement motive describes behaviors that are aimed at achieving a certain standard of quality.

Personality research often uses the five-factor model, also referred to as the Big Five. This was developed in the 1980s by psychologists Paul T. Costa and Robert R. McCrae on the basis of the previous work by German-British psychologist Hans-Jürgen Eysenck. The model describes the five basic factors of extraversion, agreeableness, conscientiousness, neuroticism and openness to experience. These express themselves in people with varying strengths, ranging between the extremes of "strong" and "weak." Numerous versions of the five-factor model have since emerged (Roth and Ryba 2016, p. 127 f.).

In 2017, the University of Luxembourg research team developed a new psychological model and test procedure, identifying 16 distinct motives that precisely distinguish the personality (Chap. 4). The 16 dimensions of ID37 enable a comprehensive description of personality at a level of detail that is not possible using other personality models such as the five-factor model (Big Five).

A Closer Look: Predecessors to the ID37 Personality Model

The process of research builds on existing knowledge and develops new knowledge along the way. In developing ID37, the University of Luxembourg research team relied on personality theories and concepts of motivation psychology that date back to the 1930s, and which continue to shape research today.

The illustration by Heckhausen and Heckhausen provides a view of the pioneers of personality-theoretic motivation research (Fig. 2.3).

Sigmund Freud (1856–1939), with his psychoanalytic model of motivation, is regarded as a pioneer in this strand of development. He was of the opinion that people are driven by the effort to avoid unpleasant experiences and obtain pleasure. The motivation-research developmental line split with the work of Kurt Lewin (1890–1947). He was probably the first to formulate behavior as an interaction between the person and the environment. The general behavioral equation, written as B = f(P, E), comes from this time. This equation was later given more precision by David McClelland and John

(continued)

William Atkinson, who added terms representing the subjective probability of achieving success and the incentive value of success, along with a disposition variable, the motive. German psychologist William Stern (1871–1938), who is viewed as the founder of differential psychology, explored the differences in traits between people with the help of psychometric procedures.

We offer here a short look at research by Murry, McClelland and Reiss as three representative examples of the motivation-psychology line of thought.

Henry Murray (1893–1988) taught and conducted research for more than 30 years at Harvard University. He was guided in his work by the basic ideas of Freud's psychoanalytic theory but developed these further. He was interested in the themes that reoccur throughout a person's life. For example, he explored the questions of how people emotionally experience their daily lives, and what they primarily strive for.

The American psychologist discovered that the type and strength of goal-oriented behavior are determined by needs and external environmental factors ("press"). In his theory of personality and needs, he postulated the existence of psychogenic basic needs, and from this explained specific behavioral patterns as well as the mechanisms of needs satisfaction and frustration.

In addition to his theoretical research, his empirical research was groundbreaking. Murray developed the Thematic Apperception Test (TAT) – a projective motive measurement technique that continues to shape motivation psychology today.

The theory later developed by American social and behavioral psychologist **David McClelland** (1917–1989), that human motivation comprises three dominant needs (the three fundamental motives), built on Murray's theory of personality and needs.

One of the more recent representatives of motivation research is **Steven Reiss** (1947–2016), who also developed the Reiss Motivation Profile personality test. His empirical research on needs, motivation and the sensitivity to anxiety has been incorporated into the ID37 personality model, as has other theoretical and methodological motivation-research work performed since Murray's time (see Brandstätter et al. 2013, p. 19 f.; Heckhausen and Heckhausen 2009, p. 28 ff.).

In 2017, the Computer-Based Assessment research team at the University of Luxembourg combined the existing motivation research conducted since Murray with current data and new methods of test development. The result is a test procedure that has been brought to market as **ID37** and the LUXXprofile. The development of the test was supported by an expert team with considerable practical know-how, whose more than 10 years of experience using the Reiss Motivation Profile was incorporated into the new test procedure (Sect. 4.2).

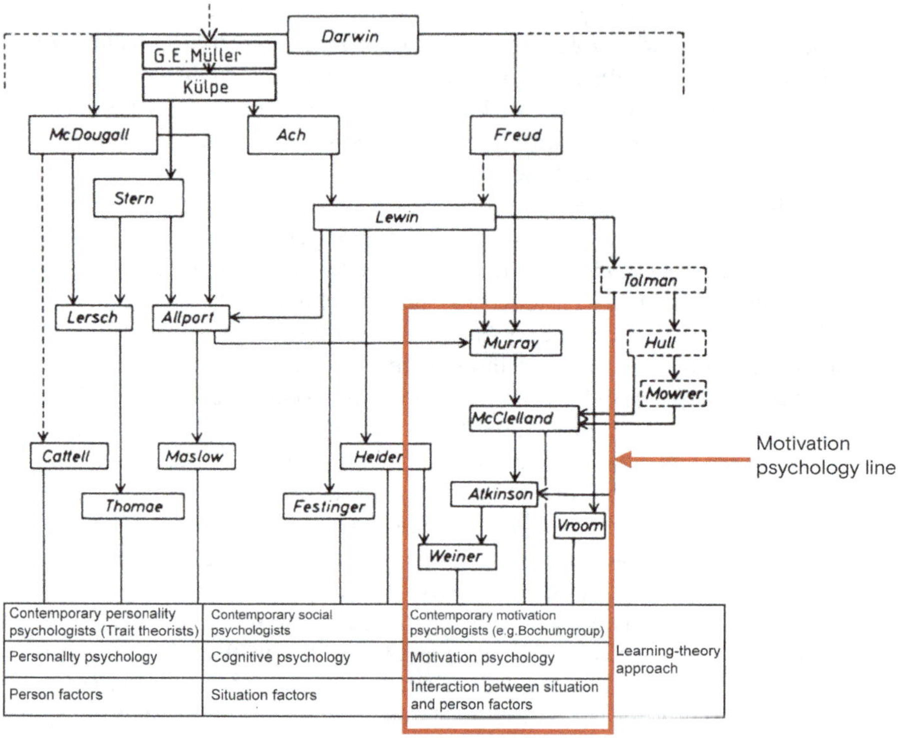

Fig. 2.3 Pioneers of personality-theory oriented motivation research. (Adapted from Heckhausen and Heckhausen 2009, p. 30)

2.2.3 How We Get from Wanting to Do Something to Taking Action

We all know the situation: One moment we feel motivated to do something but, in the end, it never takes place. Despite our best intentions, our motivation seems to vanish all at once. Why does this happen? Obviously, motive-based behavior is susceptible to disruption. We must overcome resistance and persevere instead of delaying in order to carry out an action. This is one of the key challenges when the goal is a lasting change in behavior. So how do we as coaches, consultants or ID37 experts support our clients in carrying out their new actions, and in helping them genuinely stay on course? One answer is as follows: New patterns of behavior take place unconsciously and automatically only if they have become ingrained and have taken on the status of a habit (Sect. 6.3).

Setting goals is the secret to success. Goals are the reasons why people decide at a certain point in time to initiate, carry out and terminate an action. Without goals, actions are unthinkable. Anyone who acts, for example out of the desire for personal development, needs a goal – an idea of what he wants to achieve.

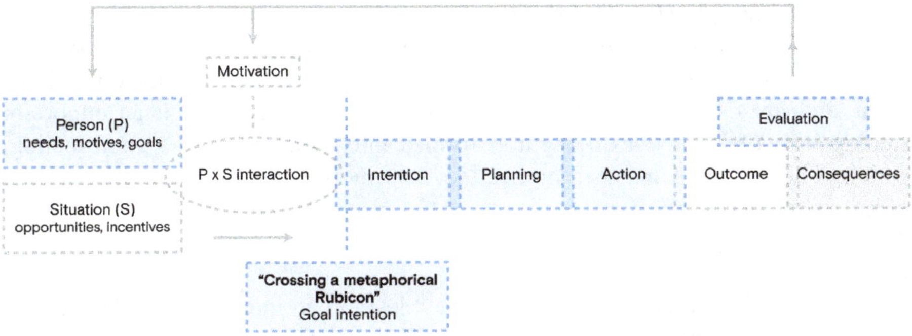

Fig. 2.4 The course of motivated action following the Rubicon model

One important aspect of personality and behavior is the distinction between goals and motives. Goals are what people consciously set for themselves, while motives are inherent in people, and thus already in place. Without goals, there is no motivation. The following sequence model of motive-driven action makes this clear.

Goals are the source of leverage in executing an action. Goals are what we consciously set out to do.

Rubicon Model of Action Phases

The Rubicon model of action phases, which draws on the work of motivation psychologists Heinz Heckhausen and Peter M. Gollwitzer, provides an overview of the various phases of action (Fig. 2.4).

According to the Rubicon model, motivated action involves the following phases:

Need

At the beginning of an action, there is a need and the desire to satisfy it. Basic needs are mostly unconscious. They register a state of lack with the wish to remedy this (a discrepancy between the actual state and the desired state; Heckhausen and Heckhausen 2009, p. 339). The need arises over and over again and is rooted so deeply in a person that it can only be temporarily satisfied. We distinguish between psychological needs, which give meaning to life when satisfied from those needs that must be satisfied in order to survive (e.g., sleep).

Motive

Once an incentive is involved, a need becomes a motive. Motives are thus indicators of needs. A strong need for acceptance, for example, must be satisfied because it is considered to be meaningful. Motives that derive from basic needs are fundamental motives that motivate us throughout the course of our lives.

Crossing a Metaphorical Rubicon/Goal Intention

In order for a motive to become an action, it must first transition through a phase of intention. This transition is referred to as "crossing a metaphorical Rubicon." At this point, a clear goal such as "exercising regularly" is targeted. This is an important step, as it involves motives being transformed into will. It creates a good feeling, which is an aspect of intrinsic motivation. The motive becomes binding, and the person is self-motivated.

Intention

Once a person's will has become clear, they develop an intention. In other words, they become determined to translate their goal into action and to remain persistent in the pursuit of that goal. This process of will formation is known as volition or, more commonly, as willpower. The more attractive the goal becomes and the sooner it can be realized through one's own actions, the stronger a person's will to achieve it will become.

Planning

Plans to take action are initiated. This means the person enters a planning phase as they prepare their behavior. This starts with questions regarding implementation, such as "What do I need to play sports?" or "Which type of sport should I choose?". The phase ends with an action plan, such as "I'm going to buy running shoes this weekend and, as of next week, will go running twice a week."

Action

These preconditions have created the optimal conditions for implementation. The action is carried out and, ideally, completed with success. The goal is achieved.

Evaluation

The last phase involves evaluating the process through affects, in other words, one's most basic emotional responses. These affects, or simple emotional responses, evaluate every situation, every object and every action in terms of the extent to which they satisfy our motives. They are either positive or negative, and they provide information as to whether something is good (resulting impulse signal: repeat) or not (resulting impulse signal: avoid). If a person's motives are satisfied, they will experience positive emotions.

In addition, they will compare what has been achieved with the goal. If the action was a success, for example, they might say: "My condition has improved noticeably." But if it proved a failure, they might say instead: "Unfortunately, I can no longer participate in weekly afterwork events due to running." If necessary, the alternatives to the action are re-assessed.

The model depicts a process reflective of an ideal type. We show how this can be translated into practice by means of the five-phase process of self-direction (Sect. 6.3).

2.2.4 Obstacles to Action

During the intention phase, a person considers their plan in the context of current conditions so that they may be able to react flexibly. This leads to an assessment of one's actions and efforts toward achieving the goal in question. This may result in a change in plans (e.g., postponing the decision to go jogging during a lunch break) or it may be that contextual factors (e.g., an unforeseen client issue) prevent a person from acting on their intention.

But it's also possible that the person fails to take action, as existing automatisms – such as the desire to watch one's favorite show – are activated. In other words, it's possible that the new intention has not yet anchored itself in the brain as an automatic process. Going for a jog in the evening on a regular basis has not yet become a habit. The inner conflict that takes place between continuing to pursue and letting go of a goal is also referred to as an action crisis (Krause and Stork 2014, p. 102). This kind of conflict is typical for those who do not act on their good intentions because their inner experience of them is unpleasant.

The motivation needed for attaining a goal arises during the intention phase. The experiential knowledge a person has gathered over the course of their life is also activated during this phase. Some of this is based on experiences they themselves have not had. The fear of elemental forces, for example, is inherited. German neurologist Dr. Gerhard Roth speaks of our emotional experiential memory (Roth and Ryba 2016, p. 445), which is located in the brain's limbic system. It evaluates and stores in one's memory everything the body does in terms of the positive and negative effects of such actions.

This emotional experiential memory, which is activated in the subconscious, helps a person orient themselves in a flash. It enables him to avoid a danger before he is even aware of it (e.g., hitting the brakes at the right time while in traffic) and provides him with an overview of – from his point of view – sound alternatives in actions to be taken. He develops a gut feeling that answers questions such as "Does it feel good? Should I continue with this?" At this point, so-called affect-logic patterns take over. These patterns attach an emotional value to various actions that can be taken and determine behavior. Formed over the years of a person's life, affect patterns become part of their automatic recall, which is why a person's response to conflict situations often follows a distinctive pattern. Automatisms can be implemented. In fact, we can apply this process to target behavioral change (Sect. 6.3).

> Deliberate behavior can be overwritten by affects. The person acts differently than planned. An action will be carried out smoothly only once automatisms have been formed.

Although it is a motivated process driven by internal forces, pursuing a goal often requires strategies in order to achieve it.

Self-Control

The strategy of self-control relies primarily on the intellect. It entails focusing on the most important goal at that moment, which is extremely demanding and consumes considerable energy. Since there are many things in everyday life that can get in the way of self-control (e.g., distraction, "having a lot on your plate"), it is effective only in the short term (e.g., studying for final exams instead of going to the lake with friends).

Self-Regulation

Making changes to action that are to be implemented with success in the long term takes place through self-regulation. A person sets and can achieve goals that are self-congruent by leveraging existing motivators and regulating emotions as they emerge. In self-regulation, regulatory processes are tailored to one's personality and synchronized with their targeted goal. With self-regulation, a person pursues their goal almost effortlessly (Krause and Stork 2014, p. 117 ff.). Emotion regulation plays an important role in self-regulation. This involves the ability to allow, attenuate or suppress one's own emotions. Those who know how to deal with their feelings can prevent these feelings from bringing about harm (e.g., an inappropriate outburst of anger) or can use them to do something useful (e.g., improve one's mood). This ability fosters goal-setting.

Self-control is effective only in the short term. Permanent behavioral change is achieved through self-regulation. Self-regulation works by synchronizing motives with goals that have been set consciously.

We see the concept of self-regulation as a key component of self-direction. In our view, self-direction involves the entire process of using self-determination to achieve life satisfaction and improved performance.

Rewards – Knowing How to Use Them!

The following e-mail from a client illustrates how self-regulation works:

Dear Thomas,

[...] By the way, I had a very interesting experience recently.

Since my motive for engaging in sports is not particularly strong, but I really do have to do something to combat my back pain, I managed the following coup, which fits right in with my motives profile:

I've become a member of co-ed fitness studio – where the mere sight of the trainer more than satisfies my motive EROS;-) and (!) I booked a personal trainer who has worked as a stuntman as well as a model. This combination has made me so motivated to get down on my knees in front of him and his six-pack that sport has become a real drug. Both STATUS (he's all mine for the half hour!) and EROS (what a man) are fully satisfied.

As you can see, the motives are bringing momentum and insight into my life!

Best regards,
Claudia L.

In the section addressing practical experience, we explain how this self-direction can be learned (Sect. 6.3).

2.2.5 Intuition-Driven Action

A person's decisions and actions are often guided by affects, stereotypes and heuristics (i.e., "rule of thumb"). This kind of intuition-driven action proves advantageous in everyday life because it saves us resources. But even if the much-praised gut feeling is useful, intuition-driven action runs the risk of being influenced by existing thought patterns. It can also be a disadvantage insofar as it results in hastily made conclusions that are subject to systematic distortions.

When Gut Feelings Are Deceptive
If a stout man and a petite woman sitting together in a restaurant order a large and small meal as well as a beer and mineral water, the waiter will most likely deliver the large meal and beer to the man. The waiter acts on his intuition because he has experienced this sort of thing countless times. He doesn't even think about it.

In this example, the waiter's premature conclusion has no significant consequences. However, in other, potentially more important or complex situations, such errors of judgment can have a broader impact.

Letting gut feelings determine decisions made in job interviews can have negative consequences. Say, for example, the issue of equestrian sports come up during an interview, and the interviewer has an aversion to the sport. In this situation, criteria that have little to do with the applicant's qualifications will suddenly matter. The interviewer is likely to be put off by the applicant. A similar thing can happen if the applicant happens to resemble an uncle whom the interviewer dislikes. Even though he may not be conscious of the similarity, the recruiter has an aversion to the applicant. And if we were to ask the recruiter to explain his aversion, he would most likely cite rational reasons.

Feelings and experience significantly impact behavior and decisions.

In addition to our feelings and experiences, our intellect, or capacity to reason, plays an important role in directing behavior. When reconsidering things, we rely on conscious reasoning. In doing so, we disregard the reservoir of experience that is elicited by intuition.

Our intellect is also engaged when the brain is confronted with a problem for which our emotional experiential memory has yet to provide any guidelines (Roth and Ryba 2016, p. 321). In situations with which we have no experience, we engage in conscious reasoning. A person lacking in expertise in a specific area can therefore not rely on his intuition. He must engage in conscious reasoning and gather information before taking action.

In situations defined by change, where new ways of thinking are required, we need training so that patterns can form within our minds and automatisms can be set in motion. This allows the brain to make the shift from thinking to taking action as part of a routine.

A Closer Look: Why a Person Is Usually Not Aware of His Behavior

Every person has a conscious and unconscious level of thinking that is derived from two systems within the brain. And while the idea of two separate physical systems within the brain does not really exist, they are associated with two different parts of the brain. The two systems differ significantly in how they operate and function. Whereas thinking at the conscious level – the intellect – involves a slower process of mental work in processing information sequentially that results in a right/wrong assessment (e.g., concentration, goal-setting), thinking at the unconscious level involves a rapid-fire and effortless processing of information that is done in parallel and results in a positive/negative judgment (affects). The unconscious thus automatically steers our thoughts and actions (Weber 2017, p. 13 f.).

Our actions therefore follow an inner script in which many things take place unconsciously. The ID37 personality assessment brings the motives behind our actions to light. Identifying these motives helps us understand our script and our behavior as it relates to our nature and unconscious. In this way, we can take conscious steps to direct our behavior.

2.2.6 The Role of Values

Values refer to a person's thoughts and attitudes toward important things in life with regard to oneself, one's friends or society and how one treats others (e.g., trust, honesty, politeness). Values are key factors in our identity and lives because they determine what we – as individuals and as groups – consider good, bad, important or unimportant. Unlike motives, values are not innate. They are formed during our socialization in systems such as our family of origin, schools, professional life, societies and cultural circles. They are also acquired through peer groups and later in our professional life, often unconsciously, through imitation and learning (Sauer 2018).

Going Vegetarian, with Pleasure

A young man has a very strong expression for the FOOD ENJOYMENT motive. Eating, including all kinds of dishes with meat, brings him considerable pleasure. Within the framework of his values, it's okay to eat animals. Then he gets to know a woman who is a committed vegetarian, as are most of her friends. Over time, his set of values undergoes some changes. Influenced by his new environment, he also reaches the conclusion that doing without meat is a good thing. However, his expression of the FOOD ENJOYMENT motive remains unchanged. He continues to think of food in terms of pleasure and reward.

Our values become the measure of how something should be. They are relatively constant but, unlike motives, they are easier to change, as they are more strongly influenced by external factors. Our set of values are influenced by a variety of factors. Motives, for example, also shape values. Behind every set of values, there are motives pushing the individual to lead a life in line with these values (Sauer 2018). Values and motives are to be distinguished from each other, but they are closely related.

Values are not innate; they are shaped by the environment. Strongly or weakly expressed motives provide us with clues about a person's values.

2.2.7 What Does this Mean for My Professional Work?

Consciously setting appropriate goals is a prerequisite for successfully implementing behavioral changes or plans. Appropriate goals are those that are tailored to a person's individual motives profile and their life situation. Since the personality diagnostics instrument ID37 provides a differentiated analysis of a person's motives, personal goals can be defined in precise terms.

Many of the problems often confronted in goal-achievement, such as reverting to behavioral patterns, can be solved by distinguishing between motives and goals: Setting goals such as engaging in regular exercise can be tailored to a person's motive expressions and their environment in ways that allow them to overcome obstacles. In this way, they can achieve their objectives sustainably and with success (Sect. 2.2.4, "Rewards – knowing how to use them!").

If a goal is supported by a motive or a combination of motives, it is achieved with a tailwind, so to speak, as the person is able to regulate himself. If, however, motives and goals are not in line with each other, realizing certain goals in the long term can be difficult or even a hopeless endeavor.

The better we understand our own goals, the more likely we are able to compare them with goals set by others and decide whether we want to accept them in the long term. Those who consciously deal with their inner and outer reality can steer themselves toward the things they like and find easy to do.

That's the good news! A precise personality assessment enables us to orient our goals in ways that allow us to achieve the greatest possible degree of well-being.

2.3 Emotions

Whether it's joy, fear, anger or sadness, our emotions find a way to express themselves. They are manifest in the reaction we have to our favorite team scoring the victory goal during injury time or in the beads of sweat we break into when the plane suddenly hits turbulence. We feel them when the bus drives away right in front of us when we're already running late or as a relationship once defined by passionate love comes to an end.

In most cases, emotions are clearly felt, though sometimes we experience them more vaguely as a mood. We cannot choose what or when we feel. This is because we often feel before we consciously think. However, it is possible to turn this around by engaging our intellect in a constant exchange with our feelings: We can influence our feelings with our thinking.

Emotion regulation – the ability to regulate feelings and moods – is an important skill. Key to developing this skill is being able to understand what feelings are, how they are triggered, and why we react emotionally.

Psychology distinguishes between feelings and emotions, but without offering a precise definition. A feeling is a pleasant or unpleasant state, and is a more complex form of affect. Feelings influence the organism in the sense that they trigger emotions. Whereas emotions are perceptible as physical signals, feelings are not or are only diffusely perceptible in this way. Moods arise when feelings persist over a long period of time (Stork et al. 2016, p. 10). For the purposes of this publication, we use the terms "feeling" and "emotion" synonymously.

2.3.1 Where Do Emotions Come from?

Everything starts with a stimulus, something that triggers a positive or negative feeling. This becomes an emotional experience, which initiates an action and results in an assessment that follows the execution. Emotional processes accompany all phases of an action:

> "Without emotion there is no motivation, and without motivation there is no emotion. "
> (Brandstätter et al. 2013, preface)

Emotions draw on the satisfaction of motives in guiding a person's actions. At the same time, they indicate whether the result is correct, that is, whether a specific motive has actually been satisfied. Emotions are very closely linked to a person's individual motives system. When describing emotions, we focus on a specific model. Deeper neuronal or physiological aspects of emotions are not taken into account.

We draw on the model for the development of emotions that was developed by the philosopher and psychologist Professor Dr. Albert Newen at the Ruhr Universität Bochum (◉ Table 2.1). According to this theory, emotions produce certain patterns that derive from our emotional experience, the physical expression of this experience, our behavior and mindset. A diffuse positive emotional state develops into a basic emotion such as joy, which can evolve and become cognitive emotions such as satisfaction or pride. Cultural environment and individual life experience play a role only at the last stage of development such as pride (Zinck and Newen 2008a).

At First, There Is Comfort or Distress

The first stage of emotions, the so-called pre-emotions, spontaneously express either comfort or distress. All aspects of emotions are already present in these pre-forms: physiological arousal, a rapid evaluation of the situation, physiognomic expression and its attendant feeling. But pre-emotions remain unfocused and are not

Table 2.1 How emotions develop

Phases	Emotions			
Pre-emotions	Comfort	Distress		
Basic emotions	Joy	Fear	Anger	Sadness
Primary cognitive emotions	Exhilaration, contentment	Menace, anxiety	Annoyance, frustration	Disappointment, dejectedness
Secondary cognitive emotions	Love, happiness, pride	Shame, jealousy, envy	Rage, contempt	Grief

Adapted from Zinck and Newen 2008a, with the permission of Springer Verlag

linked to an intention to act. A situation is only evaluated as either a positive or negative experience and is not subject to analysis.

It's the Same in All Cultures: Joy, Fear, Anger, Grief

At the next level, pre-emotions are delimited as one of the four basic emotions: Joy is registered with positive experiences, while fear, anger or sadness are registered with negative experiences. "These four emotions are universal in terms of developmental psychology," explains Prof. Newen. "They are betrayed by facial expressions – regardless of the cultural context" (Zinck and Newen 2008b). These emotions are basic affect programs that run independently of a conscious registration of stimuli and slower cognitive processes such as thoughts. They focus one's attention immediately on the situation at hand and elicit a rapid reaction. We experience fear before we know whether an object is a snake or a stick. This allows us to react immediately to something that we register as dangerous and which triggers the impulse to flee, that is, "fight or flight" behavior. At the same time, though slower, our conscious processing of a stimulus runs in parallel across the cerebral cortex, the so-called neocortex. As we take a conscious look at the snake (or stick), our impression is either confirmed or revealed to be mistaken. But we jump back, nonetheless. Behavioral reactions emerge from basic emotions through the conscious processing of stimuli: Danger triggers fear and "fight or flight" behavior. Sadness arises from our experience with separation and loss. Frustrations and obstacles result in anger. Achieving a goal through personal effort or experiencing social acceptance leads to feelings of joy.

Satisfied or Not – It's a Matter of Thoughts

In the next stage of primary cognitive emotions, the content of thoughts is added to a physical reaction. "If we continue with the example of fear, the basic emotion of fear results entirely from the fact that there is an unconscious evaluation of a situation as dangerous. However, primary cognitive emotion involves the conscious belief that a situation is dangerous. And that's when we speak of a threat," explains Professor Newen (Zinck and Newen 2008b). A situation is more carefully assessed with conscious belief. In the case of joy, satisfaction would be the primary cognitive emotion when a person finds themselves in a situation going just as they have expected and, to top it off, the sun is shining.

Pride and Shame Result from the Context

The secondary cognitive emotions that follow involve not only a belief but a mini-theory about social relationships. "Jealousy can be added to the dimension of fear as a secondary cognitive emotion – as the fear of losing one's partner," says Professor Newen (Zinck and Newen 2008b). This is where a mini-theory of social expectations and norms comes into play. In addition to one's expectations and hopes for the future, it includes a concept of one's self as well as opinions about social relations to specific individuals and general social norms. These complex emotions are therefore highly dependent on personal experience and cultural contexts. And this is why they differ considerably across individuals and cultures. There are, for example, with regard to shame and pride major differences between Western and Asian cultures in terms of the triggers and behaviors or evaluations of these emotions.

2.3.2 The Power of Emotions

As human beings, we rely on emotions to orient ourselves and make decisions. Emotions influence actions and also play a role in cognitive performance. The following scenario demonstrates how emotions are linked to thinking: If we see a person leaving a church with tears in their eyes, we think of the loss of a loved one and feel a certain sadness ourselves. If, in the next moment, we realize that a wedding has taken place in the church, our mood brightens. We unconsciously adapt our emotional reaction to the information we gather cognitively. Once emotions are triggered, they can keep us from thinking clearly.

A Red Card for the Referee

A referee flashes the captain of a soccer team the red card. Believing that he has been treated unfairly (context, motive, experience, etc.), the captain feels anger (emotional experience) as his pulse increases and his face turns red (physical aspect). With tightened lips and knitted brows (facial expression as observable behavior), he throws his captain's armband onto the pitch and disappears into the cabin (observable behavior). He is powerless against these emotions. Ten minutes later, he is no longer angry. He thinks things over and reaches the conclusion that he may have overreacted.

This scenario shows us how emotions switch off our thinking. Once emotions have been triggered, we have less room for solutions and options. In such situations, it is helpful to have the ability to regulate one's own emotions. If we manage to let emotions subside, we can consciously choose an alternative action that is suited to us and our goals.

Even if we are powerless against emotions, we can learn to regulate them. Becoming aware of emotions and their origins helps us achieve this.

2.3.3 What Does this Mean for My Professional Work?

Having knowledge about emotions and their processes is valuable for personal development.

The interesting question is the extent to which people can self-direct: How can we regulate emotions in a high-stress situation at work? How can we get a grip on nervousness before a presentation? How can we prevent an inappropriate outburst of anger or foster athletic performance with emotions? The goal of such conscious efforts to direct ourselves is to break out of the stimulus-response pattern in a structured manner and thereby achieve a better quality of life over time.

As Newen shows, feelings, physical processes and cognition work interact with each other and form shared patterns. When we quickly recognize such patterns, we become aware of emotions at an early stage of their formation. This is a prerequisite to regulating emotions.

As an ID37 Master, we analyze situations in which strong emotions have emerged and in which motives may have been triggered during our conversation with the client. We can clarify to what extent the client experiences his behavior as appropriate or inappropriate, positive or negative. Together with the client, we can then develop interventions for self-regulation (e.g., breathing exercises, stop signals) or initiate interventions for self-direction (e.g., priming, "if-then plans"; Sect. 6.3).

This helps clients learn how to access their positive and negative feelings and to remain flexible in dealing with them. Clients can then cope better with challenging situations and make better decisions.

References

Brandstätter, V., et al. (2013). *Motivation und emotion*. Berlin: Springer.

Csíkszentmihályi, M. (2005). *Flow* (12. Aufl.). Stuttgart: Klett-Cotta.

Eilles-Matthiessen, C., & Scherer, S. (2011). In B. Badura, et al. (Eds.), Fehlzeiten-Report 2011. *Bindung, Leistung, Kontrolle und Selbstwertschutz: Die Motive des Mitarbeiters als Perspektive sozial kompetenten Führungsverhaltens* (pp. 15–25). Berlin: Springer.

Heckhausen, J., & Heckhausen, H. (2009). *Motivation and action*. Cambridge: Cambridge University Press.

Krause, F., & Stork, M. (2014). *Selbstmanagement – Ressourcenorientiert* (5th ed.). Bern: Huber.

Martens, J. U., & Kuhl, J. (2004). *Die Kunst der Selbstmotivierung*. Stuttgart: Kohlhammer.

Rheinberg, F., & Vollmeyer, R. (2011). *Motivation* (8th ed.). Stuttgart: Kohlhammer.

Roth, G., & Ryba, A. (2016). *Coaching, Beratung und Gehirn*. Stuttgart: Klett-Cotta (E-Book).

Sauer, F. H. (2018). "Was sind Werte?" In *Akademie DA VINVI* (ed.), Enzyklopädie der Werte. https://www.wertesysteme.de/was-sind-werte/#ErsteDefinition. Accessed: March 13, 2018.

Stork, J., Morgenegg, C., et al. (2016). *Ich blicks*. Bern: Hogrefe.

University of Luxembourg Manual (2018).

Weber, J. (2017). *Ich fühle, was ich will*. Bern: Hogrefe.

Zinck, A., & Newen, A. (2008a). Classifying emotion: A developmental account. *Synthese, 161*(1), 1–25. https://doi.org/10.1007/s11229-006-9149-2.

Zinck, A., & Newen, A. (2008b). "Der Ursprung allen Ärgers – und aller Freude." [Classifying emotion: a development account. *Synthesis*, 161(1), 1-25.] Press release from March 10, 2008. http://www.pm.ruhr-uni-bochum.de/pm2008/msg00073.htm. Accessed: March 13, 2018.

Why It's Worth Taking a Closer Look at Your Personality

3

Those who pay close attention to their own personality can learn to understand and assess it, and are in a position begin changing behavior by addressing the sources of that behavior. These are core reasons for the use of a personality diagnostic tool in the professional environment. As previously shown, a person can step out of her own world only once he is conscious of it. He then is able to see more clearly where her reality ends and that of others begins.

In the following, we provide an overview of important reasons to examine and learn about one's own personality.

Self-Awareness and Self-Direction

A strong self-awareness involves knowledge about one's own person, and about how you process things. Self-awareness helps us identify what's truly important to us in life, along with the goals that best suit us. This allows each of us to make decisions that are in line with our personal goals. We can only be satisfied when we don't have to hide our true selves. Knowing yourself is the starting point for successful self-direction.

Learning to Understand Motivation and Behavior

Persistent patterns of behavior are a reflection of our personality. A person who reflects upon and understands their patterns has a grasp of what motivates him intrinsically and pushes him into action. This allows him to initiate processes of development and change with impact.

Learning to Differentiate and Regulate Emotions

Emotions have a strong impact on our actions and are generally a function of unconscious forces. However, a person who understands the pattern of their own affect logic can anticipate their feelings and thus train their capacity to regulate them. This provides the ability to break free of specific stimulus-response patterns and creates

T. Staller, C. Kirschke, *Personality Assessment with ID37*,
https://doi.org/10.1007/978-3-030-53921-4_3

the opportunity to find a better response to the situation. In this way, the frequency of stressful situations can be reduced, and life satisfaction can be increased.

Understanding Others
A person who understands himself also understands why other people are different. He can tolerate these differences at the rational level even if he can't understand them emotionally. Only by developing an understanding for other people, paired with the intention to assume the best of others, does it become possible to listen, learn empathy and ultimately speak a common language. This capability is particularly valuable for heterogeneous teams, and in developing relationships with other people.

Identifying, Avoiding and Solving Situations Involving Conflict
Given the differences among us in terms of personality, it's virtually impossible for us to truly understand each other. This becomes particularly evident in stressful situations. Under such conditions, we very often fail to remain rational and matter-of-fact in dealing with one another. Only by understanding our differences and the resulting emotional tensions can we avoid conflicts, get beyond them swiftly, or address them in a constructive manner. This is how we learn to bear the discomfort of difference or simply let unresolved conflicts stand, for example. In turn, this helps us get along better with one another.

Shaping Relationships
Relationships are relatively stable patterns of interactions. They inevitably lead to recurring situations, because they are based on the same stimulus-response patterns. Studies have shown that relationships between people with similar personalities tend to be more satisfying (Burgoon et al. 1995, p. 117 ff.). Similar partners even converge further in their corresponding traits (reciprocity), while unshared traits drift further apart. Opposites may attract for a short period of time, but people with similar profiles are happier in the long run. Relationships are easier when two individuals are similar and thus reinforce one another's patterns of motive expression, goals and life plans. Nothing helps maintain a relationship more than accepting the other for who he or she is. However, many relationship patterns are strongly regulated by social norms, and are accordingly ritualized (e.g., between employers and their employees, between business partners engaged in negotiations, or between strangers in a waiting room).

Reflective Self-Perception
We trust our own perceptions and experiences more than those of other people. We also tend to consider our personal values as being the best – not just for us, but for others as well. This motivational self-centeredness creates blind spots, or the natural tendency to perceive other people through the lens of our own interests, desires and motives. Rationally, we often know that people have different values and goals. But

we often fundamentally fail to grasp how it can be possible that they don't think, feel and act exactly like we do. Those who learn to understand their own personalities will be sensitized to the reality of others, but also to their own blind spots (Sect. 5.2).

Reflect on How Others Perceive You

We tend to assume that others see us in the way we see ourselves. Being aware of the fact that everyone creates their own reality and set of values is of great importance in everyday life. Through such awareness, we learn to assess reactions properly and recognize that our own behavior has no value for others. The conscious examination of the way we perceive ourselves and others produces many "aha" moments and is essential to ensuring successful collaborations and relationship-building. Instead of thinking in terms of "right vs. wrong," we learn to think in terms of "this as well as that." This means accepting that in cases of conflict and doubt, no one person is right, because there is no objective way of seeing things.

Selective Perception

What we perceive is directly related to our personality. We filter our environment through perception, focusing on stimuli that activate motives that are extremely strongly or weakly expressed. Other stimuli tend to fade into the background. Motives thus have a profound impact on our subjective reality. This influence is particularly strong for people's visual perception, meaning that our gaze is subject to unconscious direction. (Sect. 5.2).

Motivating Yourself Without Demotivating Others

It's virtually impossible to have a persistently positive influence on others' motivation by using external factors (for example, by offering material rewards). Instead of trying to provide externally driven motivation, it's much better to support others in motivating themselves. This form of motivation can lead to performance that is carried out happily and effortlessly over the long term (Sect. 2.1).

The ID37 personality assessment's multifaceted nature and grounding in current research makes it a highly effective instrument for initiating and accompanying processes of organizational or personal development (Sect. 4.2).

Reference

Burgoon, J. K., Stern, L. A., & Dillman, L. (1995). *Interpersonal adaption: Dyadic interaction patterns*. New York: Cambridge University Press.

The ID37 Personality Assessment 4

Our consulting activities using the ID37 psychological model and assessment procedures almost always evoke an "a-ha" experience. Discussing the assessment with a person whom we have never previously met elicits an amazed response when we can show them how they behave in certain situations. In this regard, our analysis is very accurate. In this chapter, we show why ID37 allows such precise statements about an individual personality to be made.

ID37 is a model and assessment procedure that describes a person on the basis of 16 clearly defined and explicit motives. Motives are understood here in the sense employed by motivation-research pioneers McClelland, Atkinson, Clark and Lowell – that is, as an expression of needs, or as a gap between conditions as they are and a set of desired circumstances. The underlying principle of action here is that people try to satisfy their strongly expressed needs (University of Luxembourg Manual 2018).

Empirical research carried out at the University of Luxembourg has shown that all 16 motives are present in every person. However, the intensity with which a person perceives each given motive fundamentally differs. Motives explain why a person behaves similarly across different situations, and why different people behave differently in similar situations.

The 16 motives measured with ID37 are: CURIOSITY, SOCIAL ACCEPTANCE, INFLUENCE, STATUS, RETENTION, AUTONOMY, SOCIAL PARTICIPATION, PRINCIPLES, SOCIAL ENGAGEMENT, STRUCTURE, SAFETY, REVENGE, PHYSICAL EXERCISE, FOOD ENJOYMENT, FAMILY and EROS.

T. Staller, C. Kirschke, *Personality Assessment with ID37*,
https://doi.org/10.1007/978-3-030-53921-4_4

Short Definitions of Motive Dimensions (University of Luxembourg)

- The **CURIOSITY** scale describes individual differences in the desire for knowledge, insight and intellectual challenges.
- The **SOCIAL ACCEPTANCE** scale describes individual differences in the desire for affirmation and acceptance.
- The **INFLUENCE** scale describes individual differences in the desire to influence people and processes and/or exercise control over them.
- The **STATUS** scale describes individual differences in the desire for prestige and a prominent position in society.
- The **RETENTION** scale describes individual differences in the desire to acquire and preserve material or financial possessions.
- The **AUTONOMY** scale describes individual differences in the desire for independence from the expectations of others.
- The **SOCIAL PARTICIPATION** scale describes individual differences in the desire for company and the degree of interest in other people.
- The **PRINCIPLES** scale describes individual differences in the desire for conformity with social norms that apply to certain social groups or society as a whole.
- The **SOCIAL ENGAGEMENT** scale describes individual differences in the commitment to the disadvantaged and those in need, and to a more equitable society.
- The **STRUCTURE** scale describes individual differences in the desire to structure one's surroundings in simple and consistent terms.
- The **SAFETY** scale describes individual differences in the desire for a quiet and secure life.
- The **REVENGE** scale describes individual differences in the desire for retribution when one has been subject to injustice.
- The **PHYSICAL EXERCISE** scale describes individual differences in the desire for movement and physical activity.
- The **FOOD ENJOYMENT** scale describes individual differences in the pursuit of an enjoyable experience in association with food intake. This goes significantly beyond the satisfaction of basic physiological needs.
- The **FAMILY** scale describes individual differences in the extent to which one cultivates a tight-knit familial network (e.g., with one's family of origin, or the family started with a partner).
- The **EROS** scale describes individual differences in the desire for sensual and erotic experiences as well as an active, fulfilled sexual life.

When It's All About Gaining Knowledge

A person who has a strongly expressed CURIOSITY motive, for example, typically spends considerable time engaged in mental and intellectual activity. Thus, he always strives to look for situations and create circumstances that enable him to pursue this inclination. This inclination is not at all limited to topics having to do with the field of professional activity. Rather, it is an inclination rooted deep within the personality itself. Since motives are understood as the driving forces behind behavior, this strongly expressed CURIOSITY motive allows us to recognize and predict that this person is likely to pursue an academic career or seek a position with strategic responsibility within a company, for example. Moreover, he is likely to spend more of his leisure time engaged in the acquisition of knowledge than would a person showing a weaker expression of this motive.

Of course, deciphering a personality is not entirely so simple. To make a reliable statement that does justice to a person's entire personality and overall uniqueness, it is necessary to be aware of all 16 motives, and to understand their interaction both with each other and in the context of the person's environment.

The ID37 Master training process teaches people to analyze the expression of individual motives and their interactions, and to translate these into action recommendations for the client. For example, one motive expression can strengthen or weaken another – with consequences for associated actions. ID37 Masters have a comprehensive understanding of what constitutes a person.

In this regard, the ID37 analysis holds a certain predictive power relative to a person's future behavior and can serve as a foundation for interventions dealing with motivation, self-direction and performance.

ID37 is a model and assessment procedure that describes a person on the basis of 16 clearly defined motives. The importance a person attaches to individual motives shapes their thought, feelings, behavior and individual reality.

4.1 How We Assess Personality: The ID37 Questionnaire

Readers who have not yet had the opportunity to draw up a personal ID37 personality assessment will have asked themselves what motives serve as their guiding forces: "Am I curious, sociable or conscientious? And if so, to what degree?"

Personality tests are the method of choice when it comes to investigating trait expressions – or, more colloquially, when "measuring the personality." The ID37 test ascertains the extent to which16 motives are expressed and makes it possible to identify patterns. It does not record performance, as might a language test, for example. Rather, it collects information about the self on the basis of a standardized, evidence-based test.

4.1.1 Taking the Test

The ID37 personality test is an online questionnaire consisting of 144 statements describing everyday behaviors, attitudes and habits. On average, it takes about 30 minutes to complete. The person taking the test evaluates each of the statements using a scale with six response options, ranging from "strongly disagree" to "strongly agree." An example of a scale describing an aspect of the self might be: "Being liked by others is very important to me."

To ensure that the test is used to its full potential, the following aspects should be taken into consideration:

- The test taker should be between 16 and 69 years old. Representative norms are available for this age range.
- Sufficient time should be provided for evaluation of the statements. Test takers should be able to take as much time as they need in order to finish at their own pace.
- The test should only be used if massive falsification of answers can be ruled out – for example, because the test taker skews responses with the goal of furthering his own interests. The social-desirability bias in test takers' evaluations of the statements can be minimized in the context of employee-hiring procedures if the candidate is made aware that the personality assessment is never used as the sole criterion for a staffing decision.
- Acceptance of the test can be improved when the test taker is transparently informed of the test's intended use and objective (e.g., to support team development) before the process begins.
- Use in a professional context should take place only if an ID37 Master is able to discuss the results with the test taker.
- In the case of very young people, consideration should be given as to whether the FAMILY motive should be a part of the self-reporting process. The test is constructed in such a way that this motive can be omitted.
- In a corporate context, we recommend omitting queries relating to the EROS motive, in order to exclude questions relating to sexuality. A version of the test adapted in this way is also available.
- The interpretation of results should be carried out by a certified ID37 Master, as should the in-person discussion of the test results. This can be done by experts from the fields of staff development, human resources (HR), consulting, psychology or related areas. They will have been extensively trained to bring the highest possible degree of expertise, quality and professionalism to the assessment session (Sect. 6.6).

In the ID37 test, each of the 16 motives is constructed on the basis of nine items or descriptive statements. The statements relating to the individual motive dispositions can be formulated so as to imply a strong motive expression (example item for the SOCIAL ACCEPTANCE motive: "Being liked by others is very important to me") or a weak motive expression (SOCIAL ACCEPTANCE example: "It doesn't bother me if someone rejects me").

The 16 motives are described in Sect. 4.4. That section additionally describes the behaviors associated with strong and weak motive expressions, along with how these expressions are experienced on an emotional level.

4.1.2 Scoring

ID37 test scoring is a computer-supported process carried out after the test taker has given a response to each statement. Before a person takes the test, the ID37 Master can specify whether an abridged version of the test is to be used, for example, if the FAMILY or EROS motives are to be omitted (Sect. 4.1.1).

The result is a motives profile that depicts the test taker's motive expressions both numerically and graphically (Fig. 4.1). In addition, a written summary is produced automatically. This describes the motive scales and the person's individual

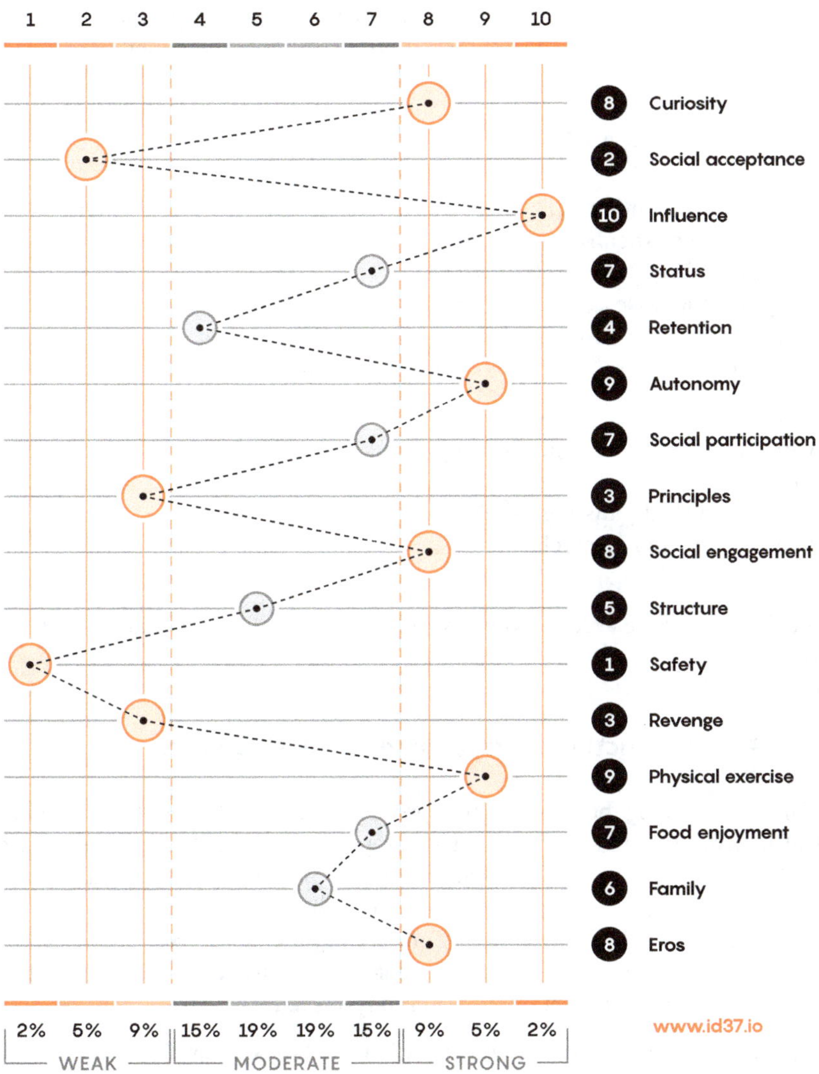

Fig. 4.1 Example of an ID37 personality profile

expressions, providing examples as illustrations. This summary is also referred to as the results report.

The assessment of personality traits is always carried out in relation to others. A statement such as "Person X has a strongly expressed SOCIAL PARTICIPATION motive" thus means "In comparison to the standard sample, the SOCIAL PARTICIPATION motive is strongly expressed in Person X."

The more precisely the personality is to be depicted, the higher are the requirements with regard to constructing the test. The computer-based-assessment scientific team around Samuel Greiff, Christoph Kemper and Jan Dörendahl developed the ID37 test at the University of Luxembourg with this in mind. This development process, which was led by Kemper, started with a review of existing personality diagnostics models. Here, existing motive concepts were put to the test, with the team subsequently employing state-of-the-art test-development methods (Fig. 4.2).

4.2 The Science of ID37

The goal in developing the ID37 test was to capture the personality from a dynamic perspective as holistically and precisely as possible. The focus was on answering the question, "Why does a person act?"

Every test that assesses personality traits must fulfill fundamental quality criteria, as well as specific criteria of psychometric quality.

According to Simon (2006, p. 44), a well-designed test must:

- Be able to be carried out routinely.
- Allow the test taker's positioning to be determined relative to other tested persons.
- Assess empirically distinguishable personality traits.
- Be based on valid research.

> Quality criteria are used to assess the quality and scientific validity of psychological tests.

4.2.1 An Introduction to Psychometric Testing Procedures

ID37 numbers among the psychometric procedures that helps people assess psychological motives through a process of self-reporting. Thus, it can investigate only those motives that survey respondents are aware of, and which they can verbalize. In the case of ID37, these are explicit motives. By contrast, implicit motives can only be investigated through the use of projective procedures (Sect. 2.2.1).

The idea of "measuring personality" means something somewhat different in the field of psychometrics than it does in everyday speech.

- In psychometrics, the verb "**to measure**" means "to compare." A subject's results are compared with a standardization sample and thus placed into a comparative relation with others' results.

- In everyday use, the word "**test**" is used synonymously with the word "examination," and is associated with a judgment of capabilities or even of a person. With a personality test, one can compare the personality with the requirements for a particular position or activity. However, the personality itself cannot be "tested."

ID37 test results are always value-free. There are neither right nor wrong answers; there are only different strengths of expression of personality traits.

In this book, the terms "personality assessment," "personality diagnostics instrument," "instrument" and "procedure" are all used as synonyms for "personality test."

In the interest of precision, we have been unable to avoid using some technical terms from the field of psychometrics. They thus appear in this book from time to time.

Technical Terms from the Field of Psychometrics

- **Item** or **test item** = a self-descriptive statement in a questionnaire paired with a set of potential responses (response scale) indicating a graduated level of agreement or disagreement. It serves as a means of investigating motive expressions. For the ID37 test, there are nine items associated with each motive. Example: "I often try to please others." (SOCIAL ACCEPTANCE)
- **Construct** = a state of affairs that can be deduced on the basis of observable data.
  Example: Motives can be deduced on the basis of behavior.
- **Trait** = an identifiable characteristic that distinguishes one person from another.
  Example: authoritarian
- **Motive dimension** = the theoretical construct that sits behind different but thematically related behaviors.
  Example: CURIOSITY.
- **Scale or test scale** = a set of items that can be consolidated according to statistical and theoretical analysis. ID37 has 16 self-description scales.

4.2.2 Development of the ID37 Test

The ID37 test was developed at the University of Luxembourg in a multi-stage process (Fig. 4.2). The first step was focused on determining what exactly the ID37 personality test should assess. The test is intended to capture the general population's intrinsic motives as broadly as possible.

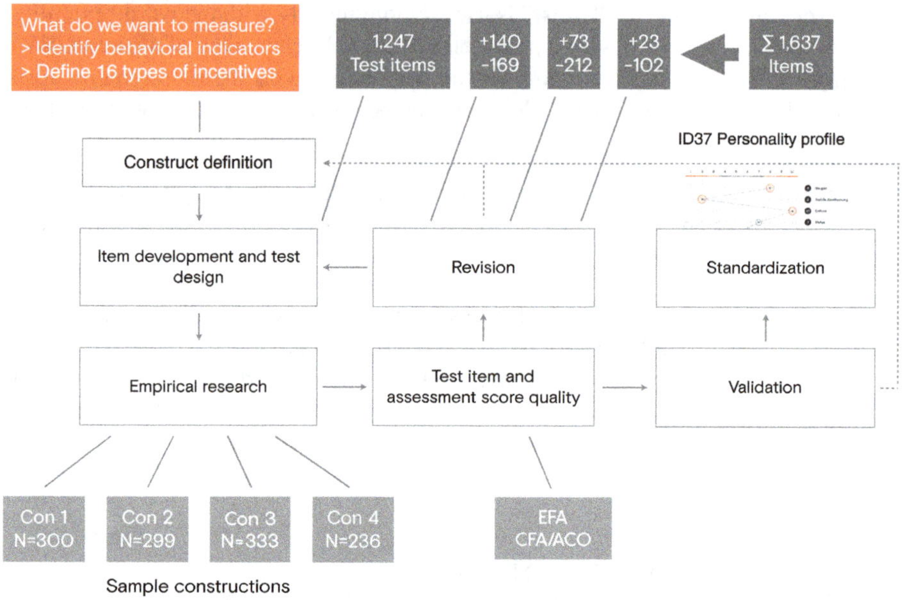

Fig. 4.2 Flow chart describing the development of the ID37 test. (Adapted from Kemper et al. (2015), with permission of the Huber Verlag). ACO Ant-Colony Optimization algorithm, CFA confirmatory factor analysis, EFA exploratory factor analysis, *Con* sample construction

The definition of the object to be assessed is the so-called construct description. In ID37, this draws on a variety of personality-psychology models (e.g., Murray 1938; Reiss 2004) and current motivation-research findings, while also integrating influences and lessons from the researchers' practical work.

After the University of Luxembourg-based research team of personality and motivation experts defined a pool of more than 1600 items, these were refined through a series of four preliminary studies with representative sample populations.

After each preliminary study, the items meeting the statistical and substantive criteria were identified. The final selection of items produced the previously mentioned set of 144 items. These are submitted to subjects in order to produce the individual ID37 personality profile. All preliminary studies were conducted using survey populations representative of the online population in Germany. The subjects evaluated the statements online. They were not informed of the objective of the process.

Out of the larger universe of possible motives, only those that were deemed universal and of psychological relevance were included in the model. These are motives that are satisfied only for their own sake.

During this process, factor analysis was used to validate these items, with the goal of identifying sets of items that assess the same dimension. Factor analysis (see Glossary) is a data-reduction procedure in which an unmanageable multiplicity of relationships is ordered and attributed to the underlying causes. Thus, after a subject in one of the preliminary studies had evaluated a large number of items, factor analysis was used to detect which statements on the questionnaire showed strong correlations. The ID37 development process employed exploratory factor analysis (EFA) and confirmatory factor analysis (CFA). The final pool of items was optimized using the Ant-Colony Optimization Algorithm (ACO; see Glossary). Factor analysis is also used as a method of deriving generally valid statements from observation material without allowing these statements to be influenced by preconceived opinions or scientific doctrines.

For example, the researchers were able to use factor analysis to identify the SOCIAL PARTICIPATION personality trait. People with high SOCIAL PARTICIPATION scores were more likely to say that they enjoyed spending time with other people. In comparison with people with lower scores in this area, they reported that they regarded social participation as an enrichment to their lives and were extremely pleased when they could be part of a group.

4.2.3 Objectivity, Reliability, Validity and Standardization in ID37

The most important quality criteria in the field of psychometrics are objectivity, reliability and validity. Each of these criteria must be fulfilled within a determined range in order for a test to achieve the desired results, and to be recognized by experts in the field. A scientifically valid test is distinguished from an unscientific one by the fact that the fulfillment of these quality criteria has been empirically supported (Fig. 4.3). This is true of ID37.

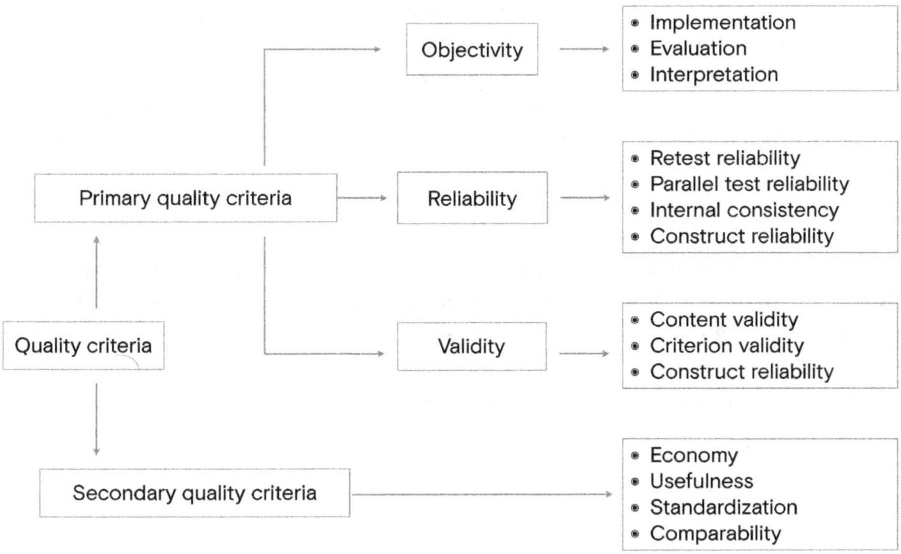

Fig. 4.3 Psychometric quality criteria (Adapted from Kemper et al. (2015), with permission of the Huber Verlag)

Objectivity

Objectivity in a test is intended to ensure that results are comparable between two people. Objectivity may be said to exist when the results of a test do not depend on whether test leader A or test leader B oversees, evaluates and interprets the testing process and results.

The ID37 test is completed solely by the test takers themselves. Each test taker receives written instructions in advance telling them how the process will unfold, along with an explanation of the objectives underlying the ID37 model. ID37 results scoring is done automatically once the test taker has completed the questionnaire. The standardized process and mathematical scoring process guarantee objectivity in the ID37 process.

To facilitate interpretation of the results, the ID37 Master receives an automatically generated motives profile and a results report. We recommend that the results be interpreted by trained ID37 Masters in order to ensure the highest possible level of quality during the assessment session.

Reliability

Reliability describes the degree of precision with which a test measures a particular trait. A measurement is precise if it is carried out without measurement errors to the greatest degree possible.

At the extremes, the description of reliability using a reliability coefficient expresses a test result entirely without measurement error (coefficient = 1.0) or a test result composed exclusively of measurement error (coefficient = 0).

In the case of ID37, verification of reliability entailed calculation of the so-called construct reliability, or the weighted omega, as described by Macdonald (1999). This parameter of reliability is more precise than the Cronbach's alpha parameter. However, due to the high prevalence of use of Cronbach's alpha, both coefficients are reported for ID37.

As a rule of thumb, reliability coefficients greater than 0.7 are deemed acceptable, while values from 0.8 to 0.9 are regarded as good. The values of ID37's reliability coefficients indicate that the motive dispositions detected are measured with great accuracy (Table 4.1).

Validity

Validity determines whether the test in fact measures what it is intended to measure. A high degree of validity is always dependent on a high degree of both objectivity and reliability. In the testing world, this is considered to be the most important test quality criterion. There are various avenues by which to determine validity, such as content validity, construct validity and criterion validity.

Table 4.1 Reliability coefficients for the 16 ID37 scales (Manual of the University of Luxembourg 2018)

Response scale	ΩW	α
CURIOSITY	.89	.88
SOCIAL ACCEPTANCE	.85	.82
INFLUENCE	.91	.87
STATUS	.87	.83
RETENTION	.85	.81
AUTONOMY	.65	.62
SOCIAL PARTICIPATION	.90	.88
PRINCIPLES	.80	.74
SOCIAL ENGAGEMENT	.91	.86
STRUCTURE	.92	.89
SAFETY	.85	.81
REVENGE	.91	.84
PHYSICAL EXERCISE	.96	.90
FOOD ENJOYMENT	.90	.84
FAMILY	.92	.89
EROS	.95	.90

Note: N = 1001

Means of Ascertaining Validity

- **Content validity**
  - Content validity refers to the representativeness of the items – thus, the degree to which the test's items constitute a representative sample of all possible test items. The assertion is whether the items are representative for the trait to be measured or not.
- **Construct validity (relationship between test content and constructs)**
  - Construct validity is used to determine whether the behavior shown in the test can be used to draw conclusions about underlying personality constructs.
- **Criterion validity (relationship between test content and external criteria)**
  - Criterion validity indicates the extent to which a measurement result can be transferred to other situations.
  - For ID37, this means that a motive scale possesses criterion validity if the answers provided by the test taker in the questionnaire can successfully be used to draw conclusions about behavior outside the test situation (criterion). The closer the relationship between the behavior within and outside the test situation, the greater is the criterion validity. The aspect of criterion validity is particularly important when using a test in practice, because a test should not only be able to precisely describe human experience and behavior, but also to predict it.

Using a comprehensive validity study, the University of Luxembourg team was able to show that all 16 motive scales are valid (University of Luxembourg Manual 2018). This rises to the level of predictive validity, meaning that the scales carry predictive power with regard to a person's future behavior.

Standardization (calibration)
Standardization is another quality criterion for scientific tests. Without standardization, tests produce numerical values which, on their own, have no meaning. Standardization, by contrast, delivers significance. Individual results obtain their significance only in comparison to other people and to a reference population: For instance, is the test taker's expression of a given motive of above- or below-average strength, or does it broadly correspond to the statistical norm?

The ID37 standardization process began with the collection of a comparative sample in Germany to be used as a reference framework for the individual results. The actual normative sample (calibration sample) was collected in 2017 and comprises 1001 participants (N = 1001). Given that ID37 is an online procedure, this sample is representative of internet users with regard to age and gender. ID37 is thus based on a modern and valid standardization process. According to DIN standard 33430, normative samples should be no more than eight years old (see Simon 2006, p. 44 ff.; Pospeschill 2010, p. 16 ff.; University of Luxembourg Manual 2018).

Recognized guidelines for proficiency assessment
In developing ID37, the University of Luxembourg also followed recognized guidelines for proficiency assessment. These include the quality standards included in DIN standard 33430, the so-called DIN screen (Kersting 2018). In particular, this serves as a benchmark enabling human-resources departments to assess the quality of a procedure. The test developers in Luxembourg also followed the Standards for Educational and Psychological Testing published by the American Educational Research Association (AERA), the American Psychological Association (APA) and the National Council on Measurement in Education (American Psychological Association 2014).

High level of scientific quality
The approach followed by the University of Luxembourg's scientific team with regard to test development and verification of the quality criteria corresponds to well-established standards for scientifically valid psychological tests.

The test procedure fulfills all of the psychometric quality criteria, thus certifying the ID37 personality assessment's high level of scientific quality. The test has been validated and standardized. The current standardization framework ensures that personal test scores have a high degree of relevance.

Further details can be found in the Manual for ID37 Masters (University of Luxembourg Manual 2018).

4.3 What the ID37 Personality Profile Tells You

We have already seen what motives mean with regard to "natural" behavior (Sect. 2.1). The ID37 personality profile reveals which motives people consider to be important and which drive avoidance-oriented behavior. It indicates which they seek to satisfy and which they try to avoid. In this regard, strongly and weakly expressed motives are particularly strong determinants of a person's personality, as they lead that person either to seek out or avoid certain situations in order to satisfy those motives. ID37 examines a person's largely unchanging essential features: the motives. It depicts a person's motive structure and explains his individuality.

People seek to satisfy their motives by developing behaviors and habits aimed at achieving this goal. Behaviors and emotions are observable. However, such observations are neither precise nor unambiguous. The ID37 personality assessment, by contrast, measures precisely which motives a person attaches a particular significance to, and the intensity of each.

The knowledge about a person's individual motive expressions and motive constellations gives the ID37 Master a statistically relevant factual basis to understand the person's patterns of behavior. This is the prerequisite for successful development and effective self-direction.

4.3.1 Prior to the Interpretation: How Motives Are Experienced

Motivation is the complex interplay of multiple drives to action within a given context. Whether a motive in fact triggers a certain behavior depends not only on the strength of the motive expression, but also on whether a stimulus or opportunity to act is present.

Motives fluctuate between states of deficiency and satiation. In the phase in which a person is not yet conscious of a need, we can speak of an unactivated motive. Needs become an activated motive only when a person is conscious of a state of deficiency, and when this has reached a certain level of intensity. The relevant threshold of intensity varies from individual to individual.

When the motive is activated, it motivates the person to engage in behavior that remedies the perceived state of deficiency.

Description of the Course of Motivated Behavior Associated with a Strongly Expressed PHYSICAL EXERCISE Motive

1. **Feeling of a state of deficiency**
   A person has been sitting at her desk for eight hours, for example, and notes a feeling of heavy legs and a cramped neck. He is very conscious of his lack of physical exercise.
2. **Expectation that the deficiency will be eliminated by specific behavior**
   The person expects that a brisk run through the forest will eliminate her sensation of deficiency.
3. **Behavior that leads to satisfaction**
   The person puts on her sports gear and leaves the house.
4. **Final action**
   The person runs through the forest for an hour.
5. **State of satisfaction or satiation**
   The lack of physical exercise has been eliminated. The person experiences a positive feeling. Satisfaction sets in.
6. **Following this satisfaction, the state of deficiency reoccurs.**

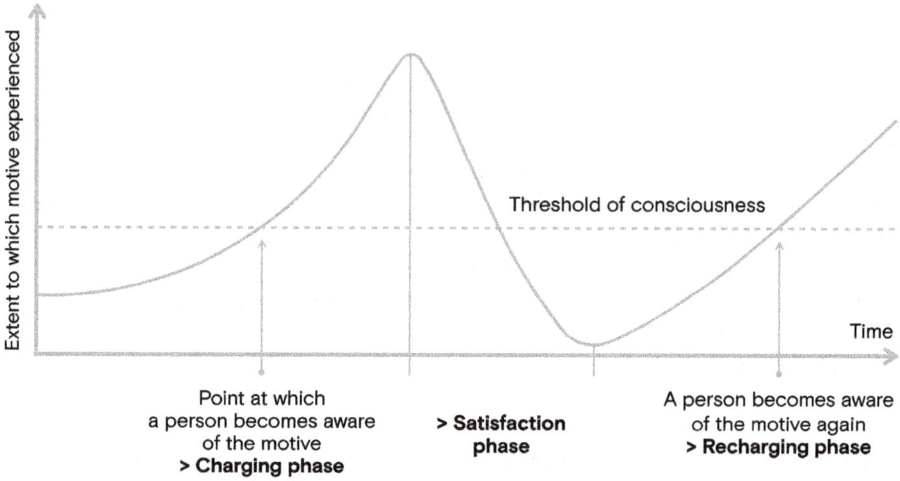

Fig. 4.4 Experienced intensity of a motive between a state of deficiency and satisfaction (Adapted from Rosenstiel 2010, p. 10); with the permission of Springer Nature)

Figure 4.4 illustrates the course of motive-driven behavior (Graumann 1996, cited in Rosenstiel 2010, p. 10).

Motives and their underlying needs can only be temporarily satisfied, and reliably make themselves known once again if they have not been satisfied after a certain amount of time. The more important the motive is for the person, the quicker the perceived state of deficiency returns.

Emotions are closely bound up with the process of motive satisfaction. Positive emotions are a signal that a motive has been temporarily satisfied, while negative emotions indicate that a motive is unsatisfied or must be satisfied.

The 16 motives can be regarded as intrinsic goals that are worthy of effort, and which are associated with positive emotions. These motives drive us from our youth (beginning around the age of 16) through the rest of our lives.

A perceived state of deficiency triggers behavior that satisfies this need. This process is a life-long cycle.

4.3.2 How to Read the Motives Profile

The characteristic ID37 motives profile is produced by the totality of the 16 motive expressions.

Motive scales are unipolar. Unlike their counterparts on a bipolar scale, values on a continuum of this nature are measured from “very weak” to “very strong.” The PHYSICAL EXERCISE motive, for example, measures whether a person has a very weak or very strong drive to engage in physical activity. This means that each successive value for the motive triggers different behavior.

The University of Luxembourg researchers recommend that the unipolar motives be represented using the STEN (standard tens) scale. ID37 follows this recommendation. Thus, motive expressions on each scale are assigned a score between 1 and 10 (standardized STEN scores). This differs from the LUXXprofile personality assessment. This related system is based on the same University of Luxembourg model and test procedure; however, it depicts motives on a z-scale with a mean value of 0. The z score of a LUXXprofile can be converted into a STEN score using the following formula (Kubinger 2009, p. 73):

Formula: STEN score = z score x SD + M
SD = standard deviation of the STEN standard scale = 2
M = Mean value of the STEN standard scale = 5.5

Example: Conversion of a z score of 1.5 into a STEN score
STEN score = 1.5 × 2 + 5.5 = 8.5
STEN scores are rounded to whole integers ⇒ STEN score = 9

Table 4.2 shows the assignment of z-scores to STEN scores.

The motive scores follow a normal distribution within the population, as depicted in Fig. 4.5.

A person with a **strongly expressed** PHYSICAL EXERCISE motive is intrinsically motivated to spend a considerable amount of time engaging in physical activity. This person has a score of ≥8 on the scale and demonstrates behavior similar to that of an athlete. Approximately 16% of the general population demonstrates this pattern.

A person with a **weakly expressed** PHYSICAL EXERCISE motive (score ≤ 3) develops behavioral patterns that serve to avoid physical strain, which is experienced as unpleasant. For this person, being comfortable and relaxed is a desirable state of being. This is true for approximately 16% of the general population.

Table 4.2 Assignment of z-scores to STEN scores

z score	STEN score
< −2.00	1
−2.00 ... −1.51	2
−1.50 ... −1.01	3
−1.00 ... −0.51	4
−0.50 ... 0.01	5
0.00 ... +0.49	6
+0.50 ... 0.99	7
+1.00 ... +1.49	8
+1.50 ... +1.99	9
≥ +2.00	10

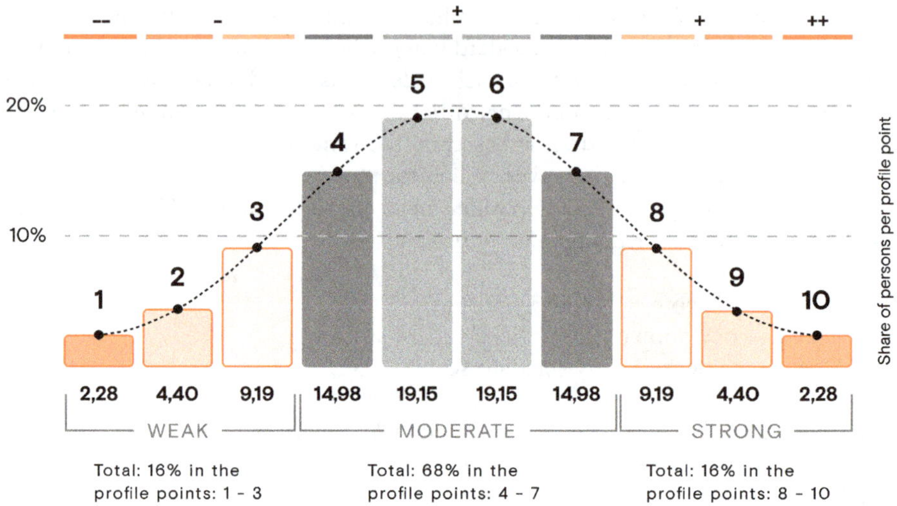

Fig. 4.5 Gaussian normal distribution of PHYSICAL EXERCISE motive scores

People with a motive expression of **average strength** (scores between 4 and 7, within one standard deviation) do not develop any particular preferences, and thus lack notable habits in this area. Everyday life presents them with enough situations to enable them to satisfy the demands of this motive's expression. In certain situations, these individuals will demonstrate behavior that may correspond with a strong or weak motive expression but lacks the same intensity or frequency. For example, the person might go to a gym once a week. But if, for whatever reason, they are prevented from doing so, they won't be too disappointed. This is true for approximately 68% of the general population.

A **very strong** or **very weak motive expression** (scores of 10 or 1, beyond the second standard deviation) occurs in only about 2% of all people.

The motives profile of a person with the PHYSICAL EXERCISE motive can be read on the STEN scale in the following way (Fig. 4.5):

- For the purposes of practical use, each motive scale is divided into 10 regions, corresponding to successively stronger motive expressions.
- Every score on the motive scale lies between 1 and 10 (in the following, these scores are also referred to as profile points); these values indicate how the strength of the person's motive expression compares to the norm. This score is derived from the answers provided by the test taker to the test items.
- Each motive follows a Gaussian normal distribution. That means that the majority of the population (about 68%) shows motive expressions of middling strength, ranging between 4 and 7.
- Each numerical score on an ID37 motives profile can be interpreted as a ranking:
- The higher the numerical score (to a maximum of 10), the more important is the satisfaction of this motive or the underlying need, and the faster a state of deficiency will occur.

- The lower the numerical score (lowest value 1), the less important is the satisfaction of the need, but the greater is the urge to avoid situations related to the motive's content.
- The more that the score deviates from the norm (≥8 or ≤3), the more extreme will be the person's experience of the motive. Similarly, the more intense will be the emotional response upon satisfaction or non-satisfaction. This has a direct effect on a person's daily behavior, decision-making and even perception.
- The more that the scores deviate from the norm, the stronger the motives will be prioritized in everyday life. This leads people to develop habits that satisfy these motives on a regular basis. These habits will often be perceived as personality traits.
- Motives with an average level of expression (scores ranging from 4 to 7) are those for which the person demonstrates no extreme behavior, and which do not produce extreme emotions. Thus, they are not significant from a scientific point of view. In our consulting practice, however, we have observed that some behavioral tendencies can be seen even with profile points at a level of 4 or 7. The mean value on the motive scale may arise in different ways – either by people regularly assigning medium-range evaluations to the items associated with the motive, or due to persistently high and low evaluations from which an average value is derived.

Taken together, the individual motives profile and the interpretation of the interactions between the motives produce a nuanced picture of the person. Knowledge of the person's life situation and circumstances also bring out a more nuanced and detailed image of their personality.

> Different motive expressions lead to different behaviors. The stronger the deviation from the norm, the more a person's behavior will differ from that of other people. The motives profile must always be considered within the individual context. In this way, the picture of the personality can be filled out.

4.4 The 16 Motives – What They Are and Their Impact

The following description of the 16 motives of the ID37 personality model attempts a balancing act. The aim is to describe the motives as universally as possible, while still doing justice to the complexity of the human personality.

Notes on the text:

- This book defines the 16 motives, as well as the interactions that result from their combination, in simplified form. That means that we generally use just one or two motives in our example explanations of behavior, and in indicating the breadth and depth of the insights derivable through the analysis of the personality. In real life, the entire set of motives, as well as a variety of other non-motive-based factors, will always influence both the personality and the behavior deriving from it.

- Weak and strong motive expressions have a particularly strong effect on personal experience and observable behavior. Therefore, we prefer to use these in the book's selected examples so as to illustrate the motives' impact as clearly as possible.
- Use of signs:
  - Very strong expressions (profile point 10) are identified using two plus signs (++).
  - Strong expressions (profile point 8 or 9) are indicated with a single plus sign (+).
  - Expressions of middling strength (profile points between 4 and 7) are indicated with a plus-minus sign (±).
  - Weak expressions (profile point 2 or 3) are depicted using a minus sign (−).
  - Very weak expressions (profile point 1) are identified using two minus signs (−−).
- We consistently use all-uppercase text for the motive names (e.g., CURIOSITY). In some cases, we instead use a short version of the name, which will also be written using capital letters (e.g., CUR).

In the following, each motive is described with reference to both its strong and weak expression. The descriptions correspond to the texts produced by the University of Luxembourg and are highlighted as such for recognizability. We see the provision of these texts as an important service to our readers, allowing them to refer to the original source materials.

In addition to these descriptions, we offer example explanations of behaviors and emotional experiences associated with each of the various motives. These explanations are derived from our many years of practical experience with personality assessment.

4.4.1 The CURIOSITY Motive (CUR)

University of Luxembourg Text

The **CURIOSITY** scale describes individual differences in the desire for knowledge, insight and intellectual challenges.

People with **high scores** on this scale attach particular importance to knowledge and insight. They enjoy immersing themselves in intellectual activities. They prefer activities that challenge their minds, such as learning, analyzing, reflecting, questioning or brain teasers. They are inquisitive and enjoy acquiring new skills and capabilities. They do not shy away from familiarizing themselves with complex issues and usually do so until they have fully understood them. They like to set themselves goals that they can achieve with mental effort.

(continued)

For people with **low scores** on this scale, knowledge and insight play only a minor role in their lives. They don't derive pleasure from engaging in intellectual activities such as learning, analyzing, reflecting, questioning or brain teasers. They generally do not enjoy taking an intellectual or abstract approach to issues and problems. They tend to avoid tasks that require intensive intellectual effort, such as acquiring new skills and capabilities or wrapping their heads around complex issues.

Self-descriptive statements (items) – Excerpt from the ID37 questionnaire
- I very much enjoy thinking about how specific incidents could be related to each other.
- Mastering new skills and capabilities is one of my favorite activities.
- I like to carry on working on complex issues until I have fully understood them.

4.4.1.1 How Does a Strongly Expressed CURIOSITY Motive Manifest Itself in Behavior and Associated Emotions?

Quote: "As a theorist, it's important to pursue one's curiosity and to attempt to understand things, even when you have no idea what the value of that understanding could be." (Hänsch, quoted in Gräff 2005)

Behavior: Behavioral indicators and attribute descriptors
abstract, analytical, reasoned, research-oriented, cerebral, intellectual, speculative, theoretical, knowledgeable

Emotions
Well-being, if the strongly expressed motive is satisfied
- A sense of fulfillment at having worked through a problem intellectually
- Satisfaction at quenching one's thirst for knowledge, regardless of its use
- Fascination for new insights
- Pleasure at intellectual clarity
- Pride at being an intellectual
- Enthusiasm over an article in the science section of the newspaper

Anxiety, if the strongly expressed motive cannot be satisfied
- A sense of boredom and mental emptiness when carrying out practical tasks
- A feeling of dread at routine work
- Joylessness when carrying out rote tasks
- Frustration by "mindless" activities
- Contempt for simple-mindedness and superficiality

4.4.1.2 How Does a Weakly Expressed CURIOSITY Motive Manifest Itself in Behavior and Associated Emotions?

Quote: "I'm not going to fill my head with junk." (Client)

Behavior: Behavioral indicators and attribute descriptors
action-oriented, concrete, useful, pragmatic, practical, relevant, purpose-driven

Emotions
Well-being, if the weakly expressed motive is satisfied
- Satisfaction with taking direct action
- A good feeling when applying knowledge
- A feeling of dedication to making things
- Pleasure in the clarity of practical solutions
- Gratitude at having a complicated subject be presented simply
- Pride at having built something genuinely useful

Anxiety, if the weakly expressed motive cannot be satisfied
- Irritated by endless theoretical discussions
- Frustration by having to grasp details
- A feeling of being put upon by having to engage in mental effort
- Anxiety at the sight of a stack of technical literature that still has to be read

The CURIOSITY motive is about knowledge for its own sake.

4.4.2 The SOCIAL ACCEPTANCE Motive (SAC)

University of Luxembourg Text
The **SOCIAL ACCEPTANCE** scale describes individual differences in the desire for affirmation and acceptance. This desire is associated with behavior aimed at receiving praise and recognition from others (e.g., partners, family members, employers, friends and even complete strangers), as well as behavior directed at avoiding criticism, refusal or rejection.

For people with **high scores** on this scale, being liked or disliked by others plays a particularly important role in their lives. They care about what others think of them. They therefore tend to calibrate their behavior to the views and perception of others. For example, before taking action, they will consider the potential impact of their actions on others. They want to please others and are therefore uncomfortable with contradicting others or refusing their requests.

(continued)

People with high scores on this scale fear being rejected and therefore try to avoid situations in which they might be subject to rejection. For example, they try to ensure that their work and tasks are completed with as few errors as possible, particularly if they are subject to evaluation by others.

People with **low scores** on this scale generally act independently of the opinions of others. They attach little importance to the positive views and perceptions of others, basing their behavior instead on alternative standards. They are rarely concerned with how other people might react to them. Being liked by others plays a minor role in their life. They usually have little or no problem with contradicting others or refusing their requests. This means they do not generally seek to avoid situations in which they could be judged or rejected. In addition, when carrying out tasks and activities, they are not afraid of making mistakes for which they could be criticized later.

Self-descriptive statements (items) – Excerpt from the ID37 questionnaire

- Before I do anything, I think about whether it could lead to others rejecting me.
- I have to prevent others from having a false impression of me.
- I constantly strive not to make any mistakes.

4.4.2.1 How Does a Strongly Expressed SOCIAL ACCEPTANCE Motive Manifest Itself in Behavior and Associated Emotions?

Quote: "Pleasing others is very important to me." (Client)

Behavior: Behavioral indicators and attribute descriptors
extroverted, invested, affirmative, friendly, pleasing, appreciated, eager to give praise, commendable, perfectionist, agreeable, acquiescent

Emotions

Well-being, if the strongly expressed motive is satisfied

- Happiness when receiving honest praise
- Euphoria when receiving affirmation by another person
- Taking pride in one's performance when receiving positive feedback
- Joy in pleasing everybody
- Triumph at having finally lived up to your own standards for once

Anxiety, if the strongly expressed motive cannot be satisfied

- Feelings of self-doubt when criticized
- Feeling uncertain when others do not provide feedback
- Feeling dissatisfied at the end of a day lacking in affirmation by others

- Fears of not being enough
- Fear of failure
- Feeling despair over not having lived up to your own standards
- Fear that the lecture will be poorly received
- Fear that one's contribution to the discussion is misunderstood
- Fear of embarrassment
- Fear of saying the wrong thing
- Shame over not having an answer to a simple question
- Angry at – once again – having been too shy
- Constant dissatisfaction with one's own performance

4.4.2.2 How Does a Weakly Expressed SOCIAL ACCEPTANCE Motive Manifest Itself in Behavior and Associated Emotions?

Quote: "I take note of praise that has been offered. But it doesn't matter to me." (Client)

Behavior: Behavioral indicators and attribute descriptors
unyielding, hard-headed, direct, headstrong, determined, uncompromising, self-confident, self-satisfied, stubborn, abrasive

Emotions
Well-being, if the weakly expressed motive is satisfied
- Pleasure at being presented with new and challenging tasks
- A feeling of self-confidence in the face of criticism directed at oneself or one's work
- Defiance when criticism is coming from all sides
- Equanimity when saying no
- Confidence to focus on doing a good job, without needing to be a perfectionist
- A feeling of superiority in doing one's own thing
- Triumph in admitting to one's own feeling of superiority
- Satisfaction at having driven a hard bargain
- A relaxed approach to one's own mistakes

Anxiety, if the weakly expressed motive cannot be satisfied
- A feeling of listlessness when underchallenged
- A feeling of irritation at failure
- A feeling of impatience when excessive sensitivity is demonstrated toward others
- Astonishment at negative feedback on one's own performance
- Distrust of people who constantly offer praise
- Consternation at one's own lack of certainty

> The SOCIAL ACCEPTANCE motive is about avoiding criticism and rejection.

4.4.3 The INFLUENCE Motive (INF)

University of Luxembourg Text

The **INFLUENCE** scale describes individual differences in the desire to influence people and processes and/or exercise control over them.

For people with **high scores** on this scale, it is very important to be able to control the environment they live in. They enjoy exerting their influence, for example, by being able to convince others of their opinion and to steer them toward their own goals. They strive for positions in which they can take responsibility and make decisions for others. This can be seen in their private and professional lives, for example, in a strong preference for taking the lead in a group or acting as the head of a project team. People with high scores on the INFLUENCE scale like to assume a leadership role.

People with **low scores** on this scale attach little value to being able to influence people and processes in their environment. They pursue other goals in life. It's not important to them that other people listen to what they have to say or be convinced by their opinions. They are rather uncomfortable with having to take responsibility for the actions of others and making decisions for others. They therefore avoid positions that are associated with influence and responsibility. For example, they like to leave the leadership of groups to others.

Self-descriptive statements (items) – Excerpt from the ID37 questionnaire:

- I like feeling I am in control.
- I like to take on the role of leader.
- I like it very much when others do what I say.

4.4.3.1 How Does a Strongly Expressed INFLUENCE Motive Manifest Itself in Behavior and Associated Emotions?

Quote: "I love it when people do what I say." (Client)

Behavior: Behavioral indicators and attribute descriptors
authoritarian, effectual, determined, dominant, influential, decisive, controlling, trend-setting, leading

Emotions

Well-being, if the strongly expressed motive is satisfied

- Taking pleasure in being able to influence processes and people
- A sense of fulfillment through having sole authority
- Satisfaction at having everything under control
- Pride in one's own ambition
- A sense of triumph at having made a clear statement that shows who's in charge

Anxiety, if the strongly expressed motive cannot be satisfied

- A sense of helplessness and powerlessness at the loss of control
- Vulnerability
- Frustration over not having asserted oneself enough during a meeting
- Anger toward that person who prevailed
- Despair at not being able to intervene
- Bitterness over being a mere figurehead
- Contempt toward those who do not try hard enough

4.4.3.2 How Does a Weakly Expressed INFLUENCE Motive Manifest Itself in Behavior and Associated Emotions?

Quote: "My leadership style? Empowering colleagues." (Client)

Behavior: Behavioral indicators and attribute descriptors
validating, approving, empowering, laissez faire, informal, supporting, accountable, responsible, casual

Emotions
Well-being, if the weakly expressed motive is satisfied

- A sense of equanimity with regard to influence
- Joy at being able to give other people free rein

Anxiety, if the weakly expressed motive cannot be satisfied

- A sense of burden at having sole authority
- Aversion to taking responsibility for other people
- Discomfort with bearing decision-making responsibility
- Annoyance, as a manager or executive, with having to always bear responsibility for everything

The INFLUENCE motive is about being an alpha type.

4.4.4 The STATUS Motive (STA)

University of Luxembourg Text
The **STATUS** scale describes individual differences in the desire for prestige and a prominent position in society.

For people with **high scores** on this scale, their reputation and social standing play a particularly important role in their lives. They attach great importance to distinguishing themselves from other people and having this publicly

(continued)

acknowledged. They like it when people demonstrate their respect for them. They try to render their position in society apparent by, for example, surrounding themselves with others who enjoy prominence or respect, or by buying things to impress others. People with high scores on this scale often take care to maintain and improve their social standing.

For people with **low scores** on this scale, social standing plays only a minor role in their lives. They do not attach any particular importance to distinguishing themselves from their fellow human beings and do not strive for social standing and significance. Status symbols, such as possessions or titles, are of little use to them. As a rule, they rarely worry about their reputation or think about how they can improve their social standing. They pursue other goals in life.

Self-descriptive statements (items) – Excerpt from the ID37 questionnaire:

- I enjoy it when people show me their respect.
- I like to surround myself with people of good standing.
- My social standing is very important to me.

4.4.4.1 How Does a Strongly Expressed STATUS Motive Manifest Itself in Behavior and Associated Emotions?

Quote: "I adore my Hermès scarf – it feels sublime to wear it." (Client)

Behavior: Behavioral indicators and attribute descriptors
striking, exceptional, elitist, exquisite, hierarchically-minded, superior, luxurious

Emotions

Well-being, if the strongly expressed motive is satisfied

- Feeling a sense of superiority by belonging to a selected circle of people
- Joy at having a higher status in society
- Joy at having prerogatives and privileges
- Hope of achieving global fame
- A sense of satisfaction with having the respect of others

Anxiety, if the strongly expressed motive cannot be satisfied

- Anger at equality-oriented treatment
- Angered by losing Lufthansa Senator status
- Envy for the elite
- Bitterness about the lack of Facebook-Likes for the photo from the VIP lounge
- Fear of being irrelevant

4.4.4.2 How Does a Weakly Expressed STATUS Motive Manifest Itself in Behavior and Associated Emotions?

Quote: "I know how to control the universe. Why would I run to get a million, tell me?"
(G. Perelman, mathematician, quoted in Spiegel online 2016)

Behavior: Behavioral indicators and attribute descriptors
of equal worth, equal, equitable, impartial, modest, natural, parity, inconspicuous, co-essential

Emotions
Well-being, if the weakly expressed motive is satisfied
- A sense of satisfaction when everyone engages at eye level
- Humility in the idea that all creatures are equal
- Taking pleasure in the fact that the signs reserving specific parking spaces for the company's Executive Board have been removed

Anxiety, if the weakly expressed motive cannot be satisfied
- A sense of discomfort toward privileges
- Feeling embarrassed when one is subject to preferential treatment
- Outrage at the preferential treatment afforded VIPs and celebrities

The STATUS motive is about standing out as an individual.

4.4.5 The RETENTION Motive (RET)

University of Luxembourg Text
The **RETENTION** scale describes individual differences in the desire to acquire and preserve material or financial possessions.

For people with **high scores** on this scale, material possession plays a particularly important role in their lives. It is of central importance to them to accumulate and save possessions, to care for them and keep them together. They find themselves continually driven to amass resources and avoid waste. They would rather save money than use it to pay for something, even if they can afford it. Before every expenditure, they give careful consideration to their resources. For example, before any purchase, they think carefully about whether they should transact the business, or whether they should instead save the money.

For people with **low scores** on this scale, material possession plays only a minor role in their lives. Possessions are not particularly important to them. They have little interest in amassing, caring for or keeping them together. They tend to consume rather than accumulate their resources. They enjoy spending money. They may also be wasteful at times.

(continued)

Self-descriptive statements (items) – Excerpt from the ID37 questionnaire:
- I prefer saving money to spending it.
- I take care of my possessions.
- The main aim in my life is to keep my belongings together.

4.4.5.1 How Does a Strongly Expressed RETENTION Motive Manifest Itself in Behavior and Associated Emotions?

Quote: "I hate waste, and I hate when people are careless with my things." (Client)

Behavior: Behavioral indicators and attribute descriptors
acquisitive, possessive, protective, retentive, economical, stockpiler, frugal, collector

Emotions
Well-being, if the strongly expressed motive is satisfied
- A sense of contentment when surrounded by one's own possessions
- Relief at knowing that one's personal items are nearby
- Triumph at being able to get things for a slightly lower price or – even better – for free
- Joy at being able to repair a beloved item that has been broken

Anxiety, if the strongly expressed motive cannot be satisfied
- Fear at the prospect of losing one's belongings
- Pain when having to part with things
- Outrage at waste
- Angry at losing an umbrella
- Regret over the broken mug with your logo

4.4.5.2 How Does a Weakly Expressed RETENTION Motive Manifest Itself in Behavior and Associated Emotions?

Quote: "I go through the apartment and look around to see what I can throw out." (Client)

Behavior: Behavioral indicators and attribute descriptors
giving, generous, altruistic, open-handed

Emotions
Well-being, if the weakly expressed motive is satisfied

- A sense of liberation from financial and ownership-related obligations
- Pleasant anticipation when thinking of clearing things away
- Relief after tidying up

Anxiety, if the weakly expressed motive cannot be satisfied
- A sense of being constrained by ownership-related obligations
- Irritation at having to calculate to the penny when splitting a meal bill

The RETENTION motive is about hoarding material things and not wanting to let go of them.

4.4.6 The AUTONOMY Motive (AUT)

University of Luxembourg Text
The **AUTONOMY** scale describes individual differences in the desire for independence from the expectations and influence of others.

For people with **high scores** on this scale, independence plays a central role in their lives. They prefer to live their life independently. They attach considerable importance to orienting themselves toward standards they have chosen themselves and to following their own path. For them, the influence of others is often experienced as a form of restriction, meddling with or constraint on their actions; they will try to avoid or limit such influence as much as possible. For example, they reject offers of help from others, do not want to be pitied and/or owe others something. They prefer to work alone. They prefer to rely on themselves rather than on others.

For people with **low scores** on this scale, independence plays only a minor role in their lives. They attach little importance to autonomy and accept the influence of others. For example, they may look to or rely on others in managing tasks and problems or in making decisions. They generally do not experience these forms of influence as interference, meddling or as a constraint on their actions. They are open to emotional ties in their social relations and are willing to deal with the expectations and obligations that this entails.

Self-descriptive statements (items) – Excerpt from the ID37 questionnaire:
- It is extremely important to me that I am able to decide for myself how close someone gets to me.
- I prefer to solve personal problems by myself.
- I prefer to rely on myself rather than on other people.

4.4.6.1 How Does a Strongly Expressed AUTONOMY Motive Manifest Itself in Behavior and Associated Emotions?

Quote: "Being too close to a person diminishes the flattering view I might have of them." (Turrini, quoted by Schurian 2012)

Behavior: Behavioral indicators and attribute descriptors
self-sufficient, autonomous, distant, reserved, independent, unobtrusive, inapproachable, standoffish, inaccessible, restrained, closed, withdrawn

Emotions
Well-being, if the strongly expressed motive is satisfied
- A sense of freedom associated with not having to be emotionally committed to anyone
- Satisfaction with not owing anyone anything
- A sense of euphoria associated with being able to "do your own thing"

Anxiety, if the strongly expressed motive cannot be satisfied
- A sense of being constrained by emotional ties
- Anxiety when somebody takes responsibility for you
- Startled when hugged by a stranger
- Aversion to physical contact in the midst of a heated debate
- Annoyance with oneself when having to ask somebody for help

4.4.6.2 How Does a Weakly Expressed AUTONOMY Motive Manifest Itself in Behavior and Associated Emotions?

Quote: "The most important thing is that we're together." (Client)

Behavior: Behavioral indicators and attribute descriptors
belonging, fraternal, communal, intimate, collective, cooperative, with each other, team-oriented, connected, united, familiar, solidarity, cohesive

Emotions
Well-being, if the weakly expressed motive is satisfied
- Happiness with a sense of belonging and inner solidarity
- Security when others are there for you
- High spirits when friends demonstrate happiness without envy for you
- Enthusiasm for intimate exchange

Anxiety, if the weakly expressed motive cannot be satisfied
- Hurt by exclusion
- Fear of an inner void
- Sadness at not having a close circle of friends
- Resentment at not being invited
- Disappointment at not having been included

> The AUTONOMY motive is about maintaining a self-determined emotional "buffer zone."

4.4.7 The SOCIAL PARTICIPATION Motive (SPA)

University of Luxembourg Text
The **SOCIAL PARTICIPATION** scale describes individual differences in the desire for company and the degree of interest in other people.

People who have **high scores** on this scale enjoy spending time with other people and see social participation as enriching their lives. They typically cultivate a large circle of friends with whom they regularly spend time. They strongly appreciate being able to be a part of a group such as a club, a clique or a project group at work. They take advantage of a wide variety of opportunities to make new contacts. They make frequent efforts to expand their circle of friends, for instance by attending celebrations, parties, receptions or other social events. Others perceive these people as being sociable and outgoing.

People who have **low scores** on this scale have modest requirements with regard to social contact. Social participation plays only a minor role in their lives. They rarely feel a need to spend time with other people. They don't need the presence of others in order to be happy. They typically have a rather small circle of friends and acquaintances with whom they occasionally spend time. They have little interest in new friendships or in making new contacts. They often avoid social events such as celebrations, parties and receptions, and instead engage in alternative pursuits.

Self-descriptive statements (items) – Excerpt from the ID37 questionnaire:
- Establishing new contacts is very important to me.
- I need the company of other people in order to be happy.
- I enjoy going to parties and festivities.

4.4.7.1 How Does a Strongly Expressed SOCIAL PARTICIPATION Motive Manifest Itself in Behavior and Associated Emotions?

Quote: "I'm happy to meet anyone." (Client)

Behavior: Behavioral indicators and attribute descriptors
extroverted, hospitable, sociable, talkative, outgoing, fun-loving, gregarious, entertaining, approachable

Emotions
Well-being, if the strongly expressed motive is satisfied
- High spirits when with other people
- A sense of fun when spending time with people

- Happiness at having made new friends
- Delight at an unexpected visit by friends
- Joy at not having to eat lunch at work alone

Anxiety, if the strongly expressed motive cannot be satisfied
- Fear of loneliness
- Bitterness at having to spend a Sunday alone
- Envy of the little group of friends at the next table who are having a good time together

4.4.7.2 How Does a Weakly Expressed SOCIAL PARTICIPATION Motive Manifest Itself in Behavior and Associated Emotions?

Quote: "When I do go out, it's just to convince myself that I'm not actually missing anything." (Mateschitz, quoted by Michlits 2012)

Behavior: Behavioral indicators and attribute descriptors
reclusive, withdrawn, introverted, shy, reserved, unsociable, closed, taciturn, retiring

Emotions
Well-being, if the weakly expressed motive is satisfied
- Relief about being able to withdraw from company
- Joy at having time to oneself
- A comfortable feeling when alone
- Relief when the party's canceled
- Satisfaction at having peace and quiet in the bathroom
- Elation at having the weekend all to oneself

Anxiety, if the weakly expressed motive cannot be satisfied
- Frustration at losing time to small talk
- A sense that being among people involves effort
- A feeling of powerlessness when forced to play the icebreaker games at weddings
- Longing to vanish into thin air at a party
- Anger at the group of travelers celebrating in the train
- Annoyance at all the people in the narrow pedestrian zone
- Fear of meeting the neighbors in the stairwell
- Uncomfortable with sitting with other people at a table in the restaurant

> The SOCIAL PARTICIPATION motive is about enjoying your time with others.

4.4.8 The PRINCIPLES Motive (PRI)

University of Luxembourg Text

The **PRINCIPLES** scale describes individual differences in the desire for conformity with social norms that apply to certain social groups or society as a whole. Social norms involve expectations regarding individual behavior, and express themselves in the forms of traditions, conventions, prohibitions and laws, generally speaking in the form of rules and principles.

People who have **high scores** on this scale ascribe great value to rules and principles. They take great pains to comply with these rules and principles, trying not to deviate from them even if such behavior entails disadvantages or restrictions, or makes it more difficult to attain their personal goals. Specifically, this can mean that agreements, appointments, laws, regulations and family traditions represent strong behavioral points of reference and are usually observed. People with high scores orient their actions toward moral standards. They describe themselves as conscientious and loyal. They find it difficult to tolerate deviations from norms, whether in themselves or in others.

People with **low scores** on this scale base their behavior on other standards. Social expectations play a minor role for these people. They are often driven by cost-benefit calculations. They tend not to attribute much importance to moral concepts, rules or family traditions, particularly when these are incompatible with personal goals. They experience rules and precepts as being constraining, and they find it easy to interpret them flexibly or even ignore them. Moreover, they have no problems tolerating similar behavior in others.

Self-descriptive statements (items) – Excerpt from the ID37 questionnaire:

- Acting in a conscientious way is of the greatest importance to me.
- I think it's terrible when someone disregards rules or regulations.
- I always keep my promises, even if doing so puts me at a disadvantage.

4.4.8.1 How Does a Strongly Expressed PRINCIPLES Motive Manifest Itself in Behavior and Associated Emotions?

Quote: "Even at night, I wait for the red light at the crosswalk to turn green before crossing." (Client)

Behavior: Behavioral indicators and attribute descriptors
honorable, scrupulous, upright, loyal, moral, conscientious, principled, compliant, virtuous, incorruptible

Emotions
Well-being, if the strongly expressed motive is satisfied

- A sense of satisfaction at following the rules

- Pride at having been with a company for 20 years
- Panicky about being late for an appointment
- A sense of acting honorably when making good on a lost bet

Anxiety, if the strongly expressed motive cannot be satisfied

- Bitterness at the unexpected termination of a longtime colleague's contract
- Bitterness about the fact that a colleague broke his promise
- Frustration that other people are breaking the rules
- Anxiety at not being able to admit to having told a white lie
- Shame at being caught out, even for something small

4.4.8.2 How Does a Weakly Expressed PRINCIPLES Motive Manifest Itself in Behavior and Associated Emotions?

Quote: "Who cares what I said yesterday?" (Author unknown, although often attributed to Konrad Adenauer)

Behavior: Behavioral indicators and attribute descriptors
self-serving, nonconforming, opportunistic, situation-oriented, skeptical, purpose-driven, utilitarian

Emotions
Well-being, if the weakly expressed motive is satisfied

- A sense of freedom when not hemmed in by rules
- Delight in a really good excuse
- Relief that a small insurance fraud hasn't been exposed

Anxiety, if the weakly expressed motive cannot be satisfied

- An oppressive feeling of being trapped by principles and rules
- Anger at a colleague who keeps saying, "We can't do that as a matter of principle."

> The PRINCIPLE motive is about living in abidance with one's morals and acting with integrity.

4.4.9 The SOCIAL ENGAGEMENT Motive (SEN)

> **University of Luxembourg Text**
> The **SOCIAL ENGAGEMENT** scale describes individual differences in the commitment to the disadvantaged and those in need, and to a more equitable society.
>
> For people with **high scores** on this scale, social justice plays a particularly important role in their lives. When they see need and disadvantage, they feel

(continued)

compassion for those affected. Social injustice is difficult for them to accept. They care about the welfare of other people and are often actively involved in helping the needy and disadvantaged. They support others, for example by donating money to charitable causes or by engaging in volunteer activities. Through their engagement, they are trying to help make the world more just.

For people with **low scores** on this scale, social justice plays only a minor role in their lives. They pursue other goals in life, and do not see social engagement, including activities such as charity donations or voluntary work, as their personal obligation. It may be, for example, that they prefer to support people who they are close to rather than those whom they hardly know or have never met. They rarely occupy themselves with issues such as poverty, hunger or oppression.

Self-descriptive statements (items) – Excerpt from the ID37 questionnaire:
- I can hardly bear social injustice.
- I have a strong desire to involve myself in helping others.
- One of the main aims I have in life is to support those who need help.

4.4.9.1 How Does a Strongly Expressed SOCIAL ENGAGEMENT Motive Manifest Itself in Behavior and Associated Emotions?

Quote: "I fight on a daily basis for a more just world." (Client)

Behavior: Behavioral indicators and attribute descriptors
altruistic, compassionate, kindhearted, willing to volunteer, charitable, humanitarian-minded, idealistic, empathetic, selfless, social, philanthropic

Emotions
Well-being, if the strongly expressed motive is satisfied

- Compassion for the disadvantaged
- Fulfillment at having helped someone
- Satisfaction at having helped addressed the community's education crisis

Anxiety, if the strongly expressed motive cannot be satisfied

- Frustration at the suffering experienced by others
- Despair at the sight of starving children who one wants to help, but can't

4.4.9.2 How Does a Weakly Expressed SOCIAL ENGAGEMENT Motive Manifest Itself in Behavior and Associated Emotions?

Quote: "If everyone were to attend to themselves, everyone would be taken care of." (Client)

Behavior: Behavioral indicators and attribute descriptors
selfish, self-serving, rational, realistic, self-centered

Emotions
Well-being, if the weakly expressed motive is satisfied
- Satisfaction with one's own realism
- No feeling of obligation to help relieve other peoples' hardship
- Equanimity with regard to one's own indifference to the current refugee problem

Anxiety, if the weakly expressed motive cannot be satisfied
- A lack of understanding toward claims that interfere with one's own

The SOCIAL ENGAGEMENT motive is about the altruistic pursuit of making the world a better place.

4.4.10 The STRUCTURE Motive (STR)

University of Luxembourg Text
The **STRUCTURE** scale describes individual differences in the desire to structure one's surroundings in simple and consistent terms.

People with **high scores** on this scale attach particular importance to order and cleanliness. They enjoy introducing structure into their daily lives in a variety of ways. For example, they tend to plan their daily routines in advance. They feel comfortable when their daily lives unfold in an accustomed way. They appreciate routines and rituals. In addition to this ordered daily routine, they also like their surroundings to be well-arranged. They create this order by regularly tidying up things at home and keeping it clean, for example. More generally, they enjoy activities that produce structure and order both in their thinking and in their surroundings.

For people with **low scores** on this scale, order and tidiness play only a minor role. Their well-being does not depend on whether they are successfully able to structure and order their thoughts or their surroundings. They generally do not enjoy activities aimed at such goals, such as planning their daily routines in advance, or sorting through and tidying things up. They place little value on habits, routines or rituals. They find it easy to tolerate a certain amount of disorder in their surroundings, even at home, for example. Tidying up and cleaning things at home may be something they do only infrequently.

Self-descriptive statements (items) – Excerpt from the ID37 questionnaire:
- I need my daily routines in order to be happy.
- I can only feel good if my surroundings are neat and tidy.
- I like sorting my things and putting them in order.

4.4.10.1 How Does a Strongly Expressed STRUCTURE Motive Manifest Itself in Behavior and Associated Emotions?

Quote: “A tidy house, a tidy mind.” (idiom)

Behavior: Behavioral indicators and attribute descriptors
proper, collected, detailed, exact, neat, thorough, hygienic, tidy, orderly, pedantic, precise, careful, structured, systematic

Emotions
Well-being, if the strongly expressed motive is satisfied
- Delight at having an exact plan
- Pride in one’s own fastidiousness
- Joy at being able to plan a vacation down to the exact details
- Joy at having a tidy e-mail inbox

Anxiety, if the strongly expressed motive cannot be satisfied
- Annoyance at the lint on a favorite coat
- Anger at the sight of a bed full of crumbs
- Stunned by a colleague’s carelessness
- Astonishment that a project has turned out to be a success despite chaotic planning
- Disgust that a colleague has used a coffee mug for several days without washing it

4.4.10.2 How Does a Weakly Expressed STRUCTURE Motive Manifest Itself in Behavior and Associated Emotions?

Quote: “Whatever wants to grow in my garden is free to do so.” (Client)

Behavior: Behavioral indicators and attribute descriptors
agile, adaptable, chaotic, flexible, improvisational, colorful, spontaneous, unruly disorganized, multifaceted, follower of the 80/20 rule

Emotions
Well-being, if the weakly expressed motive is satisfied
- A feeling of freedom when not constrained by structures or plans
- A feeling of happiness when traveling without a watch
- Looking forward to living moment-to-moment while on vacation

Anxiety, if the weakly expressed motive cannot be satisfied
- Frustration at getting trapped in the details

> The STRUCTURE motive is about the joy experienced by planning.

4.4.11 The SAFETY Motive (SAF)

University of Luxembourg Text

The **SAFETY** scale describes individual differences in the desire for a quiet and secure life.

For people with **high scores** on this scale, safety plays a particularly important role in their lives. Their behavior is characterized by a strong sense for potential danger. They tend to be very cautious and avoid risks, particularly in unfamiliar situations. They avoid risky activities of any kind. For them, the physical experience of things like inner tension that are associated with thrilling or stressful situations are unpleasant. Other people often perceive them as being risk averse. People with high scores on this scale need a safe and predictable environment in order to feel good.

For people with **low scores** on this scale, safety plays only a minor role in their lives. They tend to take risks and, if necessary, take on situations that may entail hazards. When assessing new and unknown situations in particular, they do not focus on the risks. When they find themselves in thrilling, risky or stressful situations, they do not experience the inner tension associated with such situations as unpleasant. They may enjoy the thrill these situations bring and actively seek them out, for example, by engaging in extreme sports. They describe themselves as risk-seekers and adventurers.

Self-descriptive statements (items) – Excerpt from the ID37 questionnaire:

- I avoid dangerous situations.
- I hate to feel inwardly tense.
- I try to be extremely careful in situations that are unfamiliar to me.

4.4.11.1 How Does a Strongly Expressed SAFETY Motive Manifest Itself in Behavior and Associated Emotions?

Quote: "I always have a Plan B in my pocket." (Client)

Behavior: Behavioral indicators and attribute descriptors
attentive, anxious, risk-conscious, prudent, foresighted, anticipatory, cautious, precautionary, observant

Emotions

Well-being, if the strongly expressed motive is satisfied

- A sense of equanimity when looking at the year ahead
- Satisfaction with a stable way of life
- Satisfaction with leading a quiet life
- Happiness when achieving inner peace

Anxiety, if the strongly expressed motive cannot be satisfied

- Fear of an unfamiliar body of water in which small insects that can lay their eggs under your skin might be living
- Anxiety that something's not right
- Fear of the black hole that the CERN facility near Geneva could generate
- Fear of being singled out at customs
- Fear of poverty in one's old age
- Fear of a major life change
- Worrying about whether or not the stove has been turned off
- Fear of having assessed a project's risk as too low

4.4.11.2 How Does a Weakly Expressed SAFETY Motive Manifest Itself in Behavior and Associated Emotions?

Quote: "Inspiration is a product of pressure." (Client)

Behavior: Behavioral indicators and attribute descriptors
adventurous, fearless, calm, daring, bold, risk-seeker, carefree, heedless, reckless, intrepid

Emotions
Well-being, if the weakly expressed motive is satisfied

- Feeling a sense of triumph when making it at the last second
- A sense of thrill at not knowing what's coming
- Excited to find out how things turn out
- Taking pleasure in abiding by the motto "no risk, no fun"
- Happiness at being seduced by adventure

Anxiety, if the weakly expressed motive cannot be satisfied

- Fear of being bored by everyday life
- Feeling fatigued when getting stuck in a routine

> The SAFETY motive is a about the desire for a quiet and secure life.

4.4.12 The REVENGE Motive (REV)

> **University of Luxembourg Text**
> The **REVENGE** scale describes individual differences in the desire for retribution when one has been subject to injustice.
>
> People with **high scores** on this scale tend to get back at those who have betrayed, insulted or deceived them. They generally find it difficult to ignore it when somebody has offended them or hurt their feelings. They tend to let one know if one has hurt their feelings. Responding in this way can be accompanied by positive feelings.

(continued)

People with **low scores** on this scale do not tend to get back at those who have treated them unfairly or have offended or deceived them. They are generally able to ignore it when somebody has offended them or hurt their feelings. Feelings of revenge are alien to them. They usually don't attach much importance to retaliation.

Self-descriptive statements (items) – Excerpt from the ID37 questionnaire:
- I pay someone back if they insult me.
- I find it difficult to forgive anyone who has offended me.
- I make sure that others do not put me at a disadvantage.

4.4.12.1 How Does a Strongly Expressed REVENGE Motive Manifest Itself in Behavior and Associated Emotions?

Quote: "After the director humiliated me in the nude scene, I peed in his thermos flask during break." (Kate Beckinsale, quoted by Michaelsen 2017)

Behavior: Behavioral indicators and attribute descriptors
aggressive, feisty, assertive, vindictive, quarrelsome, impetuous, uninhibited

Emotions
Well-being, if the strongly expressed motive is satisfied
- Taking pleasure in a fit of rage
- A sense of triumph at having broken the heart of the person who was unfaithful to you
- Satisfaction after having screamed in rage
- Feeling gratification at expressing this rage to the person one feels is responsible
- Hoping for a short burst of anger instead of a long and tortuous harmony-driven discussion
- Gloating over another person's defeat
- Joy when entertaining revenge fantasies

Anxiety, if the strongly expressed motive cannot be satisfied
- Anger that one's interlocutor can remain so calm during a confrontation
- Anxiety over making up prematurely
- Wanting to seek revenge against a colleague who has sold one's own idea as theirs

4.4.12.2 How Does a Weakly Expressed REVENGE Motive Manifest Itself in Behavior and Associated Emotions?

Quote: "An eye for an eye makes the whole world blind." (Gandhi, quoted by Oernng 2003)

Behavior: Behavioral indicators and attribute descriptors
equanimous, composed, level-headed, defensive, tolerant, peaceful, kind, harmonious, consensual, yielding

Emotions

Well-being, if the weakly expressed motive is satisfied

- A sense of satisfaction with one's equanimous friends
- Satisfaction with a consensus-oriented meeting
- Joy about the kind new colleague
- Happiness at the happy end of a Rosamunde Pilcher romance novel or film
- A sense of devotion while performing a Zen ritual

Anxiety, if the weakly expressed motive cannot be satisfied

- Anxiety, if a quarrel is started
- Discomfort in situations involving an aggressive atmosphere
- Frustration with the quarrelsome colleagues in the morning meeting
- Feeling surprised about other people's outbursts of anger and violence

The REVENGE motive is about the sense of satisfaction involved with getting even with someone.

4.4.13 The PHYSICAL EXERCISE Motive (PEX)

University of Luxembourg Text

The **PHYSICAL EXERCISE** scale describes individual differences in the desire for movement and physical activity.

For people with **high scores** on this scale, physical exercise plays a particularly important role in their lives. Staying physically fit is one of their most important goals in life. They take great pleasure in being physically active. They enjoy, for example, playing sports intensively and on a regular basis. They also don't mind doing physically demanding work. They are always striving to achieve and maintain physical fitness. They would feel uncomfortable without a certain amount of exercise and physical exertion in their daily life. Physical exercise is an important factor in their sense of life satisfaction.

For people with **low scores** on this scale, physical exercise plays only a minor role in their lives. For them, there are more important things than doing sports and being physically active. They have little or no drive to exercise and usually do not enjoy physical activity. For example, they would be reluctant to engage in heavy fitness training or physically strenuous work. Most likely, they will try to avoid such activities.

Self-descriptive statements (items) – Excerpt from the ID37 questionnaire:

- Being physically fit is one of the main aims I have in life.
- I need to be physically active on a regular basis in order to feel good in everyday life.
- I enjoy exercising very much.

4.4.13.1 How Does a Strongly Expressed PHYSICAL EXERCISE Motive Manifest Itself in Behavior and Associated Emotions?

Quote: "I don't know why I run. It's just what I do. My body has always wanted to run. I feel light, powerful." (Client)

Behavior: Behavioral indicators and attribute descriptors
athletic, physically fit, body-conscious, strong, sporty, trained

Emotions
Well-being, if the strongly expressed motive is satisfied

- Taking pleasure in having sore muscles after a hard training session
- Satisfaction after physical exhaustion

Anxiety, if the strongly expressed motive cannot be satisfied

- Feeling angry with oneself if another day goes by without any sport activity
- Disdain for physical weakness
- Bitterness about the wear and tear one's own body is subject to
- Disgusted with one's imaginary fat

4.4.13.2 How Does a Weakly Expressed PHYSICAL EXERCISE Motive Manifest Itself in Behavior and Associated Emotions?

Quote: "Going to the bakery involves enough sport." (Client)

Behavior: Behavioral indicators and attribute descriptors
complacent, easygoing, laid-back, calm, relaxed, unathletic, wimpy

Emotions
Well-being, if the weakly expressed motive is satisfied

- Taking pleasure in a leisurely after-dinner walk
- Contentment at the end of a day with little exercise

Anxiety, if the weakly expressed motive cannot be satisfied

- Anger about the "little bike tour" organized by a friend that turns out to be a strenuous full-day trip

> The PHYSICAL EXERCISE motive is about wanting to experience and strengthen your body.

4.4.14 The FOOD ENJOYMENT Motive (FEN)

University of Luxembourg Text

The **FOOD ENJOYMENT** scale describes individual differences in the desire for an enjoyable experience in association with food intake. This goes beyond the satisfaction associated with fulfilling basic physiological needs.

For people with **high scores** on this scale, food enjoyment plays a particularly important role in their lives. They often describe themselves as gourmets. They enjoy eating and have an active interest in the topic of food. For example, they also think about food or like to talk about it when they are not hungry. They take advantage of various occasions to enjoy a good meal including, for example, at a restaurant. In addition to their interest in the act of eating, they might also have a strong interest in planning and preparing a meal. People with high scores on this scale often like to cook. But even if they cannot cook, they will take time to eat and enjoy their daily meals.

For people with **low scores** on this scale, food plays only a minor role in their lives. They don't take particular pleasure in eating. For them, food has little significance beyond satisfying hunger. They may regard food as a biological necessity (food intake). It is often the case that they can only appreciate the smell of food or a conversation about food when they themselves are hungry. They usually spend little time planning and preparing food or meals. They may eat irregularly and occasionally skip meals.

Self-descriptive statements (items) – Excerpt from the ID37 questionnaire:

- I like talking about food, even when I am already full.
- I love eating my daily meals.
- When I think about delicious food, my mouth starts watering immediately.

4.4.14.1 How Does a Strongly Expressed FOOD ENJOYMENT Motive Manifest Itself in Behavior and Associated Emotions?

Quote: "You haven't lived if you've never eaten Nutella with a spoon." (Client)

Behavior: Behavioral indicators and attribute descriptors
indulgent, pleasure-oriented, culinarily-minded, opulent, feast-oriented

Emotions

Well-being, if the strongly expressed motive is satisfied

- Delight over thoughts of a sticky cinnamon with one's favorite coffee
- Joy when looking at the shopping list
- Looking forward to the first ice cream sundae of the year
- Happy when full
- Mouth starts to water when leafing through a cookbook

Anxiety, if the strongly expressed motive cannot be satisfied

- Despair at having taken too little food on the hike
- Fear of being hungry

4.4.14.2 How Does a Weakly Expressed FOOD ENJOYMENT Motive Manifest Itself in Behavior and Associated Emotions?

Quote: "If there was a way I could not eat so I could work more, I would not eat. I wish there was a way to get nutrients without sitting down for a meal." (E. Musk, quoted in Vance 2015, p. 51)

Behavior: Behavioral indicators and attribute descriptors
lack of appetite, austere, spartan

Emotions
Well-being, if the weakly expressed motive is satisfied

- A sense of satisfaction if a meal can be eaten while doing something else
- Joy at feeling "light"

Anxiety, if the weakly expressed motive cannot be satisfied

- Fear of "having to" eat
- A feeling that meals are a nuisance

> The FOOD ENJOYMENT motive is about taking pleasure in satisfying hunger and not just being full.

4.4.15 The FAMILY Motive (FAM)

> **University of Luxembourg Text**
> The **FAMILY** scale describes individual differences in the extent to which one cultivates a tight-knit familial network (e.g., with one's family of origin, partner and/or children).
>
> For people with **high scores** on this scale, the family is an important reference point with regard to intimacy, trust and security. A harmonious family life, characterized by the feeling of close familial ties, is of great importance to them, and contributes to their life satisfaction. They are willing to make the necessary sacrifices for their families at any time, putting aside their own interests and desires. They enjoy spending time with their families. It is often hard for them to be separated from their families, for instance due to their work or other circumstances. For example, it would be very difficult for them to imagine living apart from their families. If they do happen to be separated from their families, they typically feel concern for the well-being of their family members.

(continued)

For people with **low scores** on this scale, family plays only a minor role in their lives. Family life is of little importance to them. Their feelings of life satisfaction are derived from other sources. They are rarely willing to put aside their own interests and desires and make sacrifices for the family. Joint activities that bring the family together, such as family parties, are sometimes perceived as being tedious. Their thinking is rarely shaped by concerns for the well-being of family members. They typically find it easy to be separated from their families, for instance by work or other circumstances.

Self-descriptive statements (items) – Excerpt from the ID37 questionnaire:

- Being able to spend time with my family is very important to me.
- My family life absolutely has to be harmonious if I am to be happy.
- I very much like feeling connected to my family.

4.4.15.1 How Does a Strongly Expressed FAMILY Motive Manifest Itself in Behavior and Associated Emotions?

Quote: "My family is the most important thing in my life." (Client)

Behavior: Behavioral indicators and attribute descriptors
concerned, caring, fond of children, maternal, selfless, paternal

Emotions
Well-being, if the strongly expressed motive is satisfied

- Fulfillment through love of the family
- Happiness at being able to horse around with one's own children, and at being able to spend plenty of time with them
- Looking forward to the family's return from vacation
- Proud of one's own home

Anxiety, if the strongly expressed motive cannot be satisfied

- Sadness at a family life that is not intact
- Concern that something might happen to the kids on their way to school
- Fear of not doing enough to care for the family
- Envy of people with an intact family life

4.4.15.2 How Does a Weakly Expressed FAMILY Motive Manifest Itself in Behavior and Associated Emotions?

Quote: "You can't choose your family – but you can avoid them as often as possible." (Client)

Behavior: Behavioral indicators and attribute descriptors
bound by family ties, companionable, partnership-focused

Emotions
Well-being, if the weakly expressed motive is satisfied
- Joy at being free from obligations to care for others
- Relief at being able to go home after a two-day family celebration

Anxiety, if the weakly expressed motive cannot be satisfied
- A feeling of being pressured to take care of the family
- A feeling of constraint and a lack of freedom due to family obligations

The FAMILY motive is about taking care of and maintaining one's own clan.

4.4.16 The EROS Motive (ERO)

University of Luxembourg Text
The **EROS** scale describes individual differences in the desire for sensual and erotic experiences as well as an active, fulfilled sexual life.

For people with **high scores** on this scale, eroticism, sensuality and passion play a particularly important role in their lives. They attach particular importance to being able to actualize their sexuality and do so regularly within and/or outside a partnership. They enjoy being sexually active and seek out situations in which they can live out their sexuality. For example, they may actively seek out potential sexual partners. They often feel the urge to develop intimacy, for example, by flirting. Having a fulfilled sex life contributes significantly to their quality of life.

For people with **low scores** on this scale, eroticism, sensuality and passion play a minor role. A fulfilling sex life is not integral to their happiness in life. Their desire for eroticism and intimacy is usually rather weak. They therefore rarely seek out situations in which they can be sexually active. They may not be particularly comfortable with physical intimacy and may be more likely to avoid situations where sexual contact is possible.

Self-descriptive statements (items) – Excerpt from the ID37 questionnaire:
- I am happiest when I have a satisfying sex life.
- I enjoy being sexually active.
- Having a satisfying sex life is very important to me.

4.4.16.1 How Does a Strongly Expressed EROS Motive Manifest Itself in Behavior and Associated Emotions?

Quote: "I'm always thinking about sex." (Client)

Behavior: Behavioral indicators and attribute descriptors
animalistic, desirous, erotic, love-crazed, lustful, sexual, instinct-driven, uninhibited, sensual, unbridled

Emotions
Well-being, if the strongly expressed motive is satisfied
- Feeling a constant yearning for ecstasy
- Desire for sex. Right now. Just like that.
- Desire to have sex with the total stranger across the street, right now
- Proud to wake up next to a complete stranger in bed

Anxiety, if the strongly expressed motive cannot be satisfied
- Fear that one's desire will remain unfulfilled

4.4.16.2 How Does a Weakly Expressed EROS Motive Manifest Itself in Behavior and Associated Emotions?

Quote: "An intense sex life would only get in the way of my sleep." (Client)

Behavior: Behavioral indicators and attribute descriptors
abstinent, ascetic, self-abnegating, abjuring, chaste, platonic, modest, virtuous

Emotions
Well-being, if the weakly expressed motive is satisfied
- Joy at being in a partnership

Anxiety, if the weakly expressed motive cannot be satisfied
- Fear of having to have sex
- A sense of shame when talking about sex

The EROS motive is about wanting to experience sexuality.

4.5 Motive Constellations

The interplay of motives plays a critical role in the explanation of individual behavior. The impact of motives can be reinforced or weakened through their interaction with each other. A single motive and/or a particular combination of various motives, for example, may result in a disposition, or tendency to act in a certain way, becoming a notable trait or, alternatively, render it so subtle it is not recognized as such.

Motives that have a reinforcing effect

A person who, for example, has a very strongly expressed INFLUENCE (INF ++) motive, is usually authoritarian and determined. If this person also features a weakly expressed SOCIAL ACCEPTANCE (SAC –) motive and a strong expression of the AUTONOMY motive (AUT +), his behavior is underscored by a strong sense of self-confidence and a tendency to distance himself from others. Overall, this person is likely to be perceived as being very dominant (Fig. 4.6a).

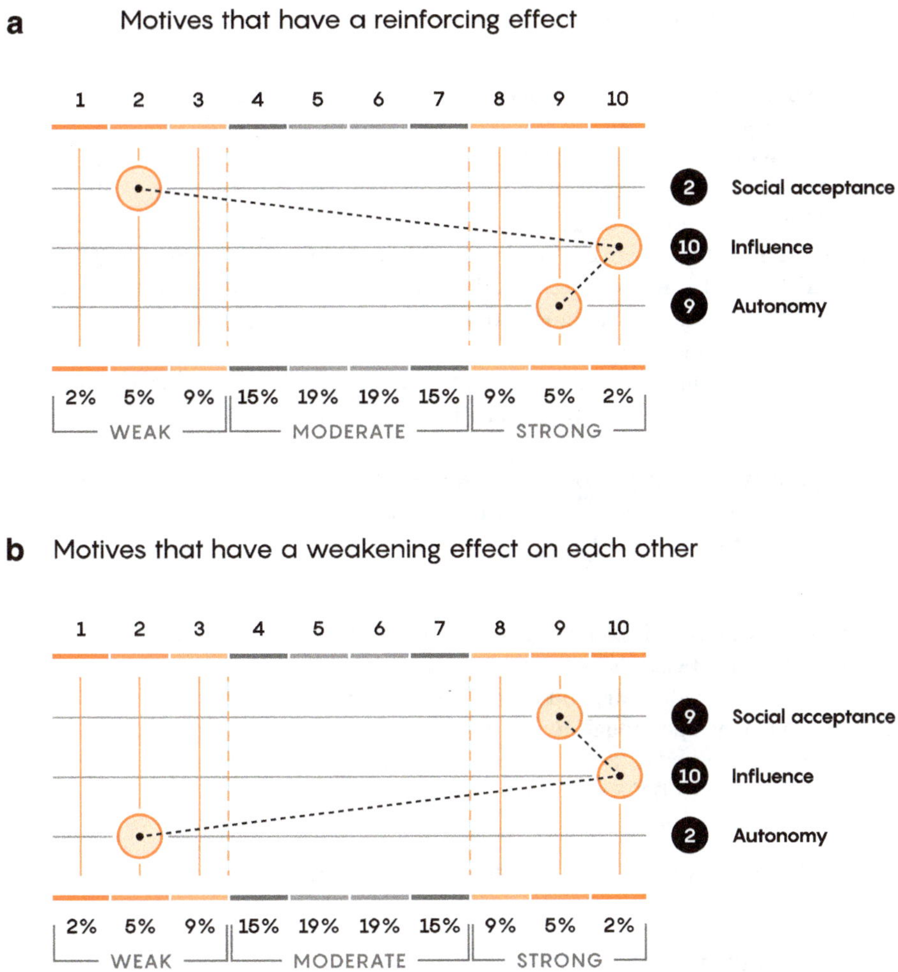

Fig. 4.6 Motive constellations. (**a**) Motives that have a reinforcing effect, (**b**) Motives that have a weakening effect on each other

Motives that have a weakening effect on each other

A person who, for example, has a very strongly expressed INFLUENCE (INF ++) motive, is usually authoritarian and determined. If this person also has a strongly expressed SOCIAL ACCEPTANCE motive (SAC +) and a weakly expressed AUTONOMY motive (AUT –), he will be perceived as being more amiable and team-oriented. Overall, this person is likely to be perceived as being people-oriented and cooperative. Others will most likely experience him as being dominant only in certain situations (Fig. 4.6b).

The following example demonstrates how difficult it is to suppress strongly or weakly expressed motives in stressful situations.

When Under Stress, We Experience the Expression of Our Motives in Their Purest Form

Let's take the example of a team leader who is under extreme pressure to succeed. Because this team leader has a very strong expression of the AUTONOMY motive (AUT ++), a very weak expression of the SOCIAL PARTICIPATION motive (SPA ––) and a strongly expressed SOCIAL ACCEPTANCE motive (SAN +), he becomes completely absorbed in his work, skips meetings and stops communicating with his team. His motives intensify as he increasingly distances himself from his team. This can lead to a situation in which the team becomes unsettled and begins to focus entirely on the question of what's going on and thereby unnecessarily wastes time and energy that could be spent on relevant tasks. Some team members (SAC +) will probably even begin to ask themselves what they might have done wrong that would compel the team leader to cancel meetings and stop communicating with them.

An ID37 Master will pay special attention to motive constellations in order to explain a person's behavior with greater precision and to suggest appropriate interventions. Understanding the complexity of interaction between motives while taking into account individual life circumstances is most meaningful when the assessment session takes place in person. In professional contexts, this service is provided by certified ID37 Masters.

Each ID37 motive is distinct. But they can reinforce or weaken each other.

4.5.1 Difficult Motive Constellations

Motive constellations can lead to behavior that may seem contradictory to other people, but which seems entirely normal to the person concerned.

"Why Does He Even Bother to Ask Me That?"
A manager has a weakly expressed AUTONOMY motive (AUT –) and a very strong expression for the INFLUENCE motive (INF ++). In terms of his behavior, this combination can mean that, on the one hand, he involves his team in projects and strives to build a consensus with them. On the other hand, it's important to him to be the one making decisions. This can go so far as to him interfering in employee decisions. His participatory approach, coupled with his authoritarian behavior, can lead to team members becoming annoyed or even demotivated. "Why does he bother to ask me if he's going to do it his way anyway?"

Knowing what effect such a combination of motives can have makes it possible to avoid such situations or anticipate and effectively counteract them early on with confidence. Having an ID37 personality assessment is the first step toward self-awareness. It creates transparency and broadens one's scope of potential actions that can be taken. For example, the manager can train himself to rein in his impulse to wield power when delegating tasks. Alternatively, he can develop together with the team a clear set of rules for making decisions.

The maximum benefit for the team as a whole is achieved when the personality profiles of all participants are taken into account.

Motive conflicts are conflicts that people experience themselves. Intrapersonal conflicts arise when the satisfaction of one's own motives seems contradictory. Motive conflicts are perceived, for example, as stressors, paradoxes or dilemmas and often lead to decisional conflicts.

Kurt Lewin, one of the most influential psychologists in motivational, social, organizational and educational psychology, has identified a number of decision-making situations (Lewin 1931, quoted by Heckhausen and Heckhausen 2010, p. 8-f.). These include:

- **Approach-approach conflict** (appetence-appetence conflict)
  - This involves having to make a decision between two seemingly equally important goals that cannot be achieved at the same time.
  - An example: A manager with a strong expression for both the INFLUENCE motive (INF +) and the FAMILY motive (FAM +) will have to choose between either taking part in strategy meetings held in the evening or putting his small children to bed at night.
- **Avoidance conflict** (aversion-aversion conflict)
  - This involves having to choose between, two seemingly disadvantageous situations.
  - An example: A team member with a strong expression for both the SOCIAL ACCEPTANCE (SAC +) and REVENGE (REV +) motives has a colleague who has been negligent in managing a deadline. The team member must either confront his colleague, which he dreads (SAC +) or carry out the task himself over the weekend, a prospect which he considers extremely unfair (REV +).

- **Approach-avoidance conflict** (appetence-aversion conflict)
  - This involves having to choose between two options that both contain positive as well as negative effects that render each goal appealing and unappealing at the same time. This conflict is also often referred to as an ambivalence conflict.
  - An example: A consultant with a strong expression of the PRINCIPLES motive (PRI +) can take on an assignment with a well-known company, which would satisfy his STATUS motive (STA +). However, given that the client is a weapons manufacturer, for the consultant, signing a contract with them would involve violating his own set of moral principles.

When a person experiences a motive conflict, his targeted goal and/or options for action are not in keeping with his motives.

A first step toward solving all three conflict situations involves knowing one's own motives profile. Using their profile, a person can bring their intellect, or rational thinking, into synch with their emotions through an inner dialogue.

- **Intellect**: Drawing on the high and/or low scores on their ID37 motives profile, a person can create an individualized list of priorities ("What do I want to draw my attention to?").
- **Emotion**: A person can then reflect on the affects or feelings associated with a specific decision ("Does this evoke a positive or negative feeling?").

For example, if the manager with the approach-approach conflict outlined above has motives profile with a higher score for the FAMILY than the INFLUENCE motive (e.g., FAMILY 10 and INFLUENCE 8), one can assume that family matters are given the highest priority in his life. If leaving the workplace behind induces a positive feeling in the manager and this is aligned with his personal goals (career is obviously not the primary objective in this scenario), then prioritizing family in this situation is certainly the right decision. Unless there are other factors to consider in the broader view of the manager's personality structure, one can conclude that the FAMILY motive has a higher priority than does the INFLUENCE motive.

Being aware of this enables a person to make a "good" decision. The more frequently one manages to come out of a decision with a positive feeling, the greater their sense of satisfaction.

In other words, making decisions can lead to emotional tension if a person's motives are not compatible with the goals set and/or the alternatives with regard to actions to be taken. If these tensions are felt intensively, one can speak of motivational conflicts. These kinds of conflicts can be resolved by dealing with one's own motives profile. If no tension is experienced in association with the decision, one can assume that the person lives in harmony with his motives and is satisfied.

Conflicts cannot be inferred from the motives profile alone. A one-on-one personal conversation is required in order to determine whether the client is experiencing a conflict in motives. If a client does not perceive himself to be experiencing such a conflict, he lives in harmony with his motives and is satisfied.

4.5.2 Specific Personality Traits

"Can the combination of motives explain specific traits within a personality?" This question is often raised in our Masters' courses and during assessment sessions. The answer is yes – and no. When we define "specific traits," the ID37 personality assessment usually offers clues regarding an individual's personality and patterns of behavior. However, attributing this to one or more motives is not always a straightforward matter.

A person's specific traits can never be explained entirely by motives. They are always derived from the combined effect of personality traits, abilities, skills as well as social and cultural influences.

Motives are something we have. Abilities and skills are things we can learn or develop. And whereas abilities can be based in a talent or a gift, skills are what we acquire by subjecting our abilities to practice (see Häcker 2018; Heuer 2018). Certain combinations of motives can prove helpful in learning certain skills.

> Motives are innate. Abilities and skills can be learned. We can improve our understanding of specific traits by taking a closer look at the combination of motives that underlie them.

Can I Infer Pragmatism from an Individual Motives Profile?

Let's assume that a consulting firm is looking for a very pragmatic project manager among its pool of consultants for an assignment with a client. We would recommend that the company choose the consultant who scores very low on the ID37 motives of CURIOSITY (CUR --) and PRINCIPLES (PRI --) – provided that the consultant's professional qualifications, availability etc. match the project requirements. What's behind this recommendation? For starters, we would define in advance with the customer what "very pragmatic" means to them. For the purposes of this example, we use here the definition of pragmatism as provided by Wikipedia (2018):

"The term pragmatism [...] is used colloquially to describe a behavior that is based on known practical circumstances and which places practical action above theoretical reason. In pragmatism, the truth of a theory is measured by its practical success, which is why pragmatic action is not tied to unchangeable principles."

The characteristics of placing "practical action above theoretical reason" and not being "tied to unchangeable principles" are clear indicators of the combined CURIOSITY (CUR --) and PRINCIPLES (PRI --) motives.

How might we explain why somebody is exceptionally creative? Are there particular motive constellations that facilitate courage? And what about those people who are as steady as a rock no matter what comes their way? In the following, we offer examples of how to use the ID37 motives to better understand the qualities of being creative, courageous, resilient, socially competent and extroverted.

4.5.3 Creativity

First, we clarify what creativity is. Creativity is understood as the ability to think and act with imagination. It brings forth new questions, surprising insights and original ideas for solving problems. Creativity is related to being open to new experiences and non-conformist (Asendorpf 2015, p. 83).

Following this definition, we can associate being "non-conformist" with a weak expression of the ID37 PRINCIPLES (PRI –) motive. Being "open to new experiences" points in the direction of the CURIOSITY motive. It remains unclear, however, whether the person's openness is more a factor of their theoretical gain in knowledge or whether new experiences are simply a matter of practicality. We therefore cannot specify a specific point on the CURIOSITY motive scale for creativity, as it could be found anywhere across the scale. Ultimately, this definition merely suggests that the PRINCIPLE motive will be weakly expressed in creative people. If we look a different description of creativity, we arrive at a different conclusion.

The Institute for Personality Assessment (IPAR) at the University of Berkeley, for example, conducted extensive studies on creativity in the early 1960s. According to their studies, creative people rely more on their own resources than on the support of others (Little 2015, p. 199 f.). This suggests that such individuals will show a strong expression of the AUTONOMY motive (AUT +).

The IPAR studies also describe creative people as follows:

> "Although creatives have many admirable qualities, it can be excruciating to work with them. They can be egocentric and irascible, treat more mundane tasks with scorn and demonstrate no interest whatsoever in the social exchange that breeds a mutually supportive and collegial workplace environment." (Little 2015, p. 228)

This also suggests that creatives will have low scores for the SOCIAL ACCEPTANCE (SAC –), STRUCTURE (STR –) and SOCIAL PARTICIPATION (SPA –) motives.

But if we look at another description of creativity, we arrive at yet another different conclusion:

> "Creativity is not a personality trait. Creativity is [a] process and can be learned and applied." (SlidesShare 2015)

This is the result of many years of research conducted by Dr. Min Basadur, former professor of innovation and the driving force behind many now-innovative companies, such as Procter & Gamble and Coca-Cola (SlideShare 2015).

From our point of view, creativity is not a psychological construct; it is something that anyone – who wants to and is allowed to – can learn and practice.

Creativity can be understood as a skill that can be learned and developed.

4.5.4 Courage

According to Merriam-Webster, courage is defined as "the mental or moral strength to venture, persevere and withstand danger, fear or difficulty." (Merriam-Webster 2020).

Having courage therefore does not involve the absence of fear. It refers rather to being able to act in spite of fear. It's not the case that brave people have no fear. In fact, fear is a basic human emotion that helps us react quickly in dangerous situations and warns us in the face of recklessness.

In our Master training courses, we find that being courageous is often attributed to those in whom the SAFETY motive (SAF −) is weakly expressed. People featuring this kind of motive expression are often in search of a "kick" and are willing to take risks in order to avoid what they consider to be a cautious and boring life. They are likely to be more capable of taking action in dangerous situations than are other people. Examples of people with a weakly expressed SAFETY motive (SAF −) could be BASE jumpers who parachute down from skyscrapers or similar objects, or figures such as the British entrepreneur and adventurer Sir Richard Branson. They know what it means to experience fear, and they usually do not consider their actions to be courageous. They simply operate within the bounds of their emotional comfort zone. Our experience has shown that it is usually people who themselves have a strong need for security and are generally unwilling to take incalculable risks (SAF +) that attribute the quality of courage to those on the opposite end of the scale.

The following examples show that being courageous can be tied to different motives:

- A person who is afraid of negative feedback, but who nevertheless speaks out in a public debate in order to defend his position against that taken by the well-known speaker, shows courage in this situation. He liberates himself from the judgment of others at that moment. In this example, courage is correlated with the SOCIAL ACCEPTANCE motive (SAC +).
- A person who speaks out publicly in favor of human rights in the context of a dictatorial regime can be considered to be courageous. This is likely to be the view among those who do not feel strongly about making the world a better place, that is, those in whom the SOCIAL ENGAGEMENT motive (SEN −) is weakly expressed. If the human rights activist has a strongly expressed SOCIAL ENGAGEMENT motive (SEN +), he will probably not see himself as courageous, but will take his commitment for granted.
- In the 90th minute of a soccer match, the courageous player who decides to shoot the penalty kick is not the one with a weakly expressed SAFETY motive (SAF -), but the one with a strong desire for security (SAF +). The likelihood of remaining cool in such situations of high stress is much lower for the latter individual. Daring to place oneself in a situation of uncertainty and remain effective takes courage.
- In terms of our approach, a manager is courageous when he recognizes that he must, in certain situations, act in ways that run counter to his motives if doing so helps a company meet its goals. This might involve, for example, a CEO who is

empathetic, shows moral responsibility and is sensitive to criticism (i.e., shows strong expressions for the SOCIAL ENGAGEMENT and SOCIAL ACCEPTANCE motives), but who decides, on the basis of strategic considerations, to get rid of an entire division within the company and dismiss its employees. Making this move marks a courageous decision on the part of the CEO because he has to act against his motives.

Bold action can be associated with any motive. Whenever a person experiences fear in a situation and nonetheless takes action, they are showing courage.

4.5.5 Resilience

Some people are calm and cool-headed, while others are sensitive and prone to self-criticism. Some will therefore find it easier to deal with stress, while others will languish under the same distressing conditions.

Neurologist Gerhard Roth explains:

> "People differ in how quickly and effectively they recognize potentially negative and threatening things, how quickly the stress axis activates the body and brain, and how quickly it can downregulate this excitation. This is called stress resilience." (Roth and Ryba 2016, p. 147)

Resilience
Derived from the Latin "resilire" (to leap or spring back, recoil), resilience describes the ability to master crises in a life cycle by drawing on the personal and social resources at hand and to use such crises as an opportunity for development (Stangl 2006).

A person shows resilience when they remain healthy despite being exposed to psychological stress. Those who are resilient have access to their own cognitive resources, are able to regulate themselves and their emotions, and can develop strategies to maneuver their way out of the stressful situation. Current research shows that building and maintaining a solid social network is another important component of resilience (Storch et al. 2017).

The following motive constellation can facilitate stress resilience: a very weak expression of both the SAFETY (SAF --) and SOCIAL ACCEPTANCE (SAC --) motives. This is because those who do not require much security in life and can handle their mistakes with confidence have the motivational prerequisites to remain calm when facing uncertainty and danger and are not easily defeated by crises. In addition, the combination of a weakly expressed AUTONOMY motive (AUT –) with a strongly expressed SOCIAL PARTICIPATION motive (SPA +) can prove facilitative of resilience. People with this constellation of motives find it easy to build up a sustainable social network that they can fall back when facing difficult situations in life.

What remained for many years unclear has now been confirmed by scientific evidence: Resilience can also be successfully developed in adulthood. We can, as adults, learn to self-regulate and build resilience in facing challenges. This is a long process, but it's clear that participating in training sessions has a positive effect on our mental health and can help us learn to manage personal resources effectively (Ayan 2017).

Particular constellations of motives are conducive to building resilience. But even people with a different motive constellation can learn resilience.

Vulnerability, or mental fragility, is often cited as marking the opposite of resilience (Fichte 2017, p. 11). A person who lets negative experiences, criticism or crises get to himself and has difficulty processing such events is, in psychological terms, more vulnerable. Their basic motivational framework is the inverse of resilience. Vulnerable people therefore feature particularly strong expressions of both the SAFETY (SAF ++) and SOCIAL ACCEPTANCE motives (SAC ++). If they also have a strongly expressed AUTONOMY motive (AUT +) and a weakly expressed SOCIAL PARTICIPATION motive (SPA –), they probably also lack a social network that could provide them with support.

Vulnerable people can also learn resilience by acquiring skills such as self-efficacy and self-regulation. This will probably take longer for them than it would for those whose motivational framework is more conducive to building resilience.

4.5.6 Social Competence

According to the psychologist Professor Dr. Jens B. Asendorpf, social competence describes the ability to be assertive and form relationships:

- **Assertiveness** is the ability to protect one's own interests in relation to others.
- **Interpersonal competence** refers to the ability to establish and maintain positive relationships with others.

> "A person who is socially competent has both of these abilities and is thus able to establish a balanced relationship between his own interests and the interests of others. The ruthless pursuit of one's own goals undermines the prospect of having positive relationships with others in the long run and is therefore a marker of social incompetence. Conversely, the tendency or desire to always please others is not an indication of social competence because, in the long run, it leads to self-abandonment." (Asendorpf 2015, p. 85)

Social competence therefore involves much more than just getting along well with other people.

Assertiveness

If we look at the quality of social competence in terms of motivations, the aspect of assertiveness can be traced to a high level of self-confidence in terms of SOCIAL ACCEPTANCE (−) and a strong willingness to make decisions INFLUENCE (+).

Interpersonal competence

The aspect of interpersonal competence is facilitated by the combination of a high score for the SOCIAL PARTICIPATION motive (+) and a low score for the AUTONOMY motive (−). Both of these motives provide clues as to how relationships with other people are formed. A person in whom the SOCIAL PARTICIPATION motive is strongly expressed is very open with regard to other people and is inclined to establish contact with many people. A weak expression of the AUTONOMY motive suggests that a person seeks closeness with others and close relationships. People in whom these motives are expressed in their aforementioned form are people-oriented and place importance in their relationships to others. These motives reinforce each other in this particular constellation. At the same time, it is important to note that both motives are distinct from each other and therefore suggest different things. People with this kind of motive constellation find it easier to solve social conflicts conscientiously and carefully.

Being socially competent requires a combination of assertiveness and interpersonal competence. There are particular motives conducive to building such skills, which can be learned.

Demonstrating social competence usually also requires demonstrating empathy (Asendorpf 2015, p. 86). Empathy is the ability to put yourself in another's shoes, that is, to be able to understand what they think and feel, and to feel how they feel (Brandstätter et al. 2013, p. 193). Empathy can be facilitated by a motives profile featuring predominantly medium-strength expressions. For example, people in whom the SOCIAL PARTICIPATION motive is moderately expressed may perceive being alone as well as with others in society as equally important. They can therefore more easily identify with the emotions, thoughts and actions associated with both solitude and fellowship. Empathy can also be learned.

Leading the Boss

A socially competent employee manages to persuade his boss – who normally refuses input from employees – to change his mind with regard to a particular decision. The employee does so by signaling to his boss that he respects his authority as a superior while clearly communicating that he largely understands the reasons behind the decision the boss has made. He then convincingly presents the team's counter-arguments and shows how they contribute to achieving the goal at hand.

4.5.7 Extraversion

Linkages between the traits of extraversion and introversion and their suitability for particular types of jobs are often made in the professional world. The idea that extraversion makes for good salesperson is a persistent assumption (Little 2015, p. 57).

Extraversion is one of the five personality traits identified by the Five Factor model (Big Five). There are six facets of extraversion: activity level, excitement seeking, cheerfulness, friendliness, gregariousness and assertiveness.

In terms of behavior, people with high extraversion scores tend to be lively, risk-seeking, good-humored, friendly, outgoing and dominant. They are receptive to stimuli from their surroundings (Asendorpf 2015, p. 69).

> "Introversion should not be understood as the opposite of extraversion, but rather as the absence of extraversion. Introverts often prefer to do things on their own and seem rather closed off. This is due not to a lack of social skills or anxieties, but simply because they often prefer to be alone and independent. They are not necessarily unhappy; they simply lack the extrovert's need for conviviality and affectionate warmth. (Asendorpf 2015, p. 69)

The validity study carried out by the University of Luxembourg in developing the ID37 also analyzed correlations between the ID37 motive dimensions and the personality dimensions of the Five Factor model. The researchers were able to show convergent and discriminatory validity for the 16 motivational scales and the personality dimensions of the Five Factor model (University of Luxembourg Manual 2018).

The study confirmed the greatest positive correlation between gregariousness as a facet of extraversion and the SOCIAL PARTICIPATION motive. A moderate correlation between assertiveness and the INFLUENCE motive was also confirmed. In addition, the study found a negative correlation between the facet of excitement seeking in the Big Five and the SAFETY motive scale (University of Luxembourg Manual 2018). These findings show that extroverted people usually feature strong expressions of the SOCIAL PARTICIPATION and INFLUENCE motives, as well as a weakly expressed SAFETY motive.

Despite the widespread belief that extroverts are the most productive salespeople, research by corporate psychologist Adam Grant, for example, has shown weak and contradictory correlations between extraversion and sales performance. According to these studies, more ambivalent individuals, that is those with both extra- and introverted qualities, perform better in this respect (Grant 2013, quoted by Little 2015, p. 57 f.).

4.5.8 How Can I Identify an individual's Motives Without Using ID37?

Conducting a personality assessment may not always be a readily available option. However, when equipped with the knowledge of how human drives work, anyone can develop a good sense for the personalities they are dealing with. It is true that our motives and behavioral dispositions are rarely present in their pure form. But when we can observe people over a longer period of time, their behavior, language and environment provide clues to the overall picture.

Behavior

When observing behavior, we should bear in mind that while everyone has their own personal preferences, people are also capable of displaying different types of behavior. For example, a person who enjoys socializing and enjoying a beer with colleagues after work will typically – but not always – enjoy taking part in this kind of activity. Even people who prefer solitude, will not always enjoy being alone. It's therefore important to not hold on too tightly to one's first impression. Situations involving stress and pressure elicit the most natural behavior in people because, in such contexts, the brain has no time to intervene cognitively and regulate.

Language

People usually express their personality unconsciously through language. A person's choice of words, and in particular how they express something, reveals a lot about their personality. Tone, pitch and timbre give important clues as to the person behind the voice. The more similar people's personalities are, the more similar their speech patterns will be. As a result, language that is characterized by a strong influence motive can seem dominant: "Get out of the way!" (Nöllke 2016, p. 45). This demand places direct pressure on the addressee to act. Addressees with similar motives will speak the same language. However, this kind of dominance-driven language can repel or even discourage an addressee with a different motivational expression. The person making the statement is perceived to be disagreeable, and it really doesn't matter – to the addressee – what was actually said.

Environment

Looking at a person's desk or apartment can offer some indication of their STRUCTURE motive. Clutter and a used coffee cup left standing on the counter from the day before can be markers of a weak expression of this motive. Finding a hanger with a clean shirt for an emergency in the car of a person with this personality would be unusual. But in this case as well, what matters is the overall impression, and this can be based on several parameters. A person who, for example, receives guests in a sparkling clean apartment could be motivated by a strong desire for either STRUCTURE or SOCIAL ACCEPTANCE, for example.

Our observations of people can help us deduce specific motives. We must, however, always take the possibility of error into account since motivational expressions can be masked by language and behavior patterns that are not distinct or which overlap. And since it is part of human nature to "pigeonhole" others, being able to draw on our understanding of motives and their effects provides us far more solid ground upon which to make an assessment. Drawing simplistic comparisons along the lines of "so and so is just like a bureaucrat" are not helpful. We should accept the fact that people are unique, and that each person is an individual.

4.6 What Distinguishes ID37 from Other Tools

The high degree of differentiation between each of the 16 distinct ID37 motives and the instrument's assessment accuracy are its unique selling point. The analysis generated by the instrument provides access to a person's individual behavior and experience.

As one of only a few diagnostic instruments in use today, ID37 offers a standardized, objective test with highly reliable results that are derived from current data.

The ID37 personality assessment provides sound information that helps people bring their lives in harmony with their motives and thereby manage them more effectively so that they can achieve their goals.

The underlying model of the ID37 assessment tool has been reconceptualized by a team of researchers at the University of Luxembourg. This process involved subjecting existing models of motives to critical analysis and empirical testing. The outcome is a superior personality assessment that is grounded in state-of-the-art research.

Unlike other models, the ID37 instrument emphasizes the importance of transparency. It openly discloses the quality criteria used and makes them available to ID37 Masters.

For most laypersons, the instrument's scientific quality and assessment accuracy is a given. In fact, however, these are its proven strengths. Understanding and predicting individual behavior and experience require a scientific basis and exacting results. Experience with the ID37 personality assessment shows that the informative and predictive power of the instrument is so precise that it can be used effectively in practical coaching contexts, in the field of human resources, in leadership contexts, in teams and in competitive sports.

And while there are other personality tests that can deliver a precise personality assessment, they are too complicated for use in consulting and business environments. There are still other more easily implemented procedures, but these are based on the primacy of face validity (i.e., based on common sense) or are insufficiently anchored in theory. The Myers-Briggs Type Indicator (MBTI) developed in the 1960s is one such example. Based on C. G. Jung's personality typology, the test remains popular even though it is considered to be obsolete. The main criticism directed at the MBTI is that it is neither scientifically tenable nor up-to-date with modern society (Little 2015, p. 3-f.). Given the constant development of science, research and business, tests with strong applicability must be able to take into account the most recent findings delivered by each realm.

ID37 is an easy-to-use instrument that meets this requirement. It's based not only on the latest scientific methods in test development, but also on more than 10 years of practical experience with the Reiss Motivation Profile personality test. The ID37 personality assessment is available at www.ID37.io

Key Features of the ID37 Personality Assessment

- New conceptualization of 16 motives based on current findings from research on motivation
- Verifiable psychometric data
- Precise coverage of motive dimensions through:
  - 9 items per motive
  - Positive and (occasionally) negative-poled items
  - 6-step response format
- No typified classification of people
- Standardization process: up-to-date, transparent, extensive (N = 1001), German, random selection
- Draws on DIN standard 33430 for suitability assessment
- Incorporates standards issued by the American Educational Research Association (AERA), American Psychological Association and the National Council on Measurement in Education

Consultants, coaches, human resource managers, executives or teams can use the ID37 personality test to get a precise picture of a person – quickly and easily. Instead of either investing painstaking effort to determine what makes a person tick or simply relying on one's gut instincts, they can use the ID37 assessment to move with confidence straight to the consultation process (Sect. 6.4).

References

American Psychological Association. (2014). The standards for educational and psychological testing. http://www.apa.org/science/programs/testing/standards.aspx. Accessed 20 March 2018.

Asendorpf, J. B. (2015). *Persönlichkeitspsychologie für Bachelor* (3rd ed.). Berlin: Springer.

Ayan, S. (2017). Resilienz lässt sich trainieren. Interview with Klaus Lieb, Deputy Director at the German Resilience Center Mainz and Director of the Clinic for Psychiatry and Psychotherapy at the University of Mainz. *Gehirn and Geist, 11*, 18–19.

Brandstätter, V., et al. (2013). *Motivation und emotion*. Berlin: Springer.

Fichte, J. (2017). *Resilienz und emotionale Stabilität von Managern*. Wiesbaden: Springer.

Gräff, F. (2005). Ist man als Nobelpreisträger noch neugierig?. http://www.zeit.de/2005/52/Interview_2fNobelpreis. Accessed 23 April 2018.

Heckhausen, J., & Heckhausen, H. (2010). *Motivation and action*. Berlin: Springer.

Häcker, H. O. (2018). Fähigkeit. In M. A. Wirtz (Ed.), *Dorsch – Lexikon der Psychologie*. https://m.portal.hogrefe.com/dorsch/faehigkeit/. Accessed 20 March 2018.

Heuer, H. (2018). Fertigkeit. In M. A. Wirtz (Ed.), *Dorsch – Lexikon der Psychologie*. https://m.portal.hogrefe.com/dorsch/faehigkeit/. Accessed 18 March 2018.

Kemper, C., Ziegler, M., Krumm, S., Heene, M., & Bühner, M. (2015). Testkonstruktion. In G. Stemmler & J. Markraf-Stiksrud (Eds.), *Lehrbuch Psychologische Diagnostik* (pp. 157–221). Bern: Huber.

Kersting, M. (2018). Einführung in die DIN 33430 – Anforderungen an berufsbezogene Eignungsdiagnostik. http://kersting-internet.de/qualitaetssicherung/din-33430-folien/. Accessed 16 April 2018.

Kubinger, K. D. (2009). *Psychologische Diagnostik* (2nd expanded ed.). Göttingen: Hogrefe.

Little, B. (2015). *Mein Ich, die anderen und wir*. Berlin: Springer.
University of Luxembourg Manual 2018.
McDonald, R. P. (1999). *Test theory: A unified treatment*. Mahwah: Erlbaum.
Merriam-Webster. (2020). Courage. https://www.merriam-webster.com/dictionary/courage. Accessed 10 April 2020.
Michaelsen, S. (2017). "Meine Mutter sagte: streng dich mehr an!" Interview with Diane Kruger. *DB mobil, 12*, 25–28.
Michlits, C. (2012). Die Welt des Didi Mateschitz. https://kurier.at/stars/die-welt-des-didi-mateschitz/1.045.290. Accessed 23 April 2018.
Murray, H. A. (1938). *Explorations in personality*. Oxford: Oxford University Press.
Nöllke, M. (2016). *Die Sprache der Macht* (2nd ed.). Freiburg: Haufe.
Oerning, M. (2003). Auge um Auge, Zahn um Zahn. http://www.uni-heidelberg.de/presse/ruca/ruca03-3/auge.html. Accessed 23 April 2018.
Pospeschill, M. (2010). *Testtheorie, Testkonstruktion, Testevaluation*. München: Reinhardt.
Reiss, S. (2004). Multifaceted nature of intrinsic motivation: The theory of 16 basic desires. *Review of General Psychology, 8*(3), 179–193. https://doi.org/10.1037/1089-2680.8.3.179. Accessed 21 April 2018.
Rosenstiel, V. L. (2010). *Motivation im Betrieb* (11th ed.). Leonberg: Rosenberger Fachverlag.
Roth, G., & Ryba, A. (2016). *Coaching, Beratung und Gehirn*. Stuttgart: Klett Cotta (e-book.
Shurian, A. (2012). "Piraten sind eine feige Bande." https://derstandard.at/1334796780331/Josefstadt-Premiere-Piraten-sind-eine-feige-Bande. Accessed 23 April 2018.
Simon, W. (Ed.). (2006). *Persönlichkeitsmodelle und Persönlichkeitstests*. Offenbach: Gabal.
SlideShare. (2015). "What is creativity?" https://de.slideshare.net/strategicplay/what-is-creativity-53932926. Accessed 20 March 2018.
Spiegel online. (2016). "Das scheue Mathe-Genie wird 50." http://www.spiegel.de/wissenschaft/mensch/grigorij-perelman-russisches-mathe-genie-wird-50-a-1096281.html. Accessed 23 April 2018.
Stangl, W. (2006). Keyword: Resilienz. Online Lexikon für Psychologie und Pädagogik. http://lexikon.stangl.eu/593/resilienz/#EPIMvei8wde1mRlj.99. Accessed 20 March 2018.
Storch, M., et al. (2017). Werkzeugkiste (53): Das Zürcher Ressourcen Modell. *Organisations Entwicklung, 4*, 91–97.
Vance, A. (2015). *Elon Musk: Tesla, SpaceX, and the quest for a fantastic future*. New York: Ecco/Harper Collins.
Wikipedia. (2018). Keyword: Pragmatismus. https://de.wikipedia.org/wiki/Pragmatismus. Accessed March 18 2018.

Life Satisfaction and Success

5

"Wouldn't it be really cool to be satisfied?" asks Wolf Lotter in the German-language *brand eins* business magazine, evidently under the impression that only superlatives and emotional high points matter, and that everyone is searching for happiness (Lotter 2016). In this chapter, we show why satisfaction is in fact the "true happiness," and what we can do to help people achieve personal success.

5.1 What is Satisfaction?

Pleasure, satisfaction, happiness – in the course of everyday use, these concepts are generally used as synonyms, signifying a notion of the good, successful life. The concepts are closely related, and describe subjectively experienced emotional states of well-being. Subjective well-being is dependent on numerous factors such as personal memories, social norms and time. Empirical studies show that aspects of a person's objective living conditions, such as material wealth, can also play a role. However, their influence on well-being is relatively minimal in comparison to emotional and cognitive factors (Brandstädter 2015, p. 41 f.). Psychologist Todd B. Kashdan defines happiness in the following way:

> A happy person is one who is acquainted with the feeling of satisfaction (Kashdan 2013, cited in Reinhardt 2014).

T. Staller, C. Kirschke, *Personality Assessment with ID37*,
https://doi.org/10.1007/978-3-030-53921-4_5

A Closer Look: Flow

Psychologist Mihály Csíkszentmihályi explored how people can achieve happiness by establishing control over their own inner lives. "Flow," which he named and made the subject of his research, refers to a state in which people are able to carry out a difficult task over a long period without having to expend willpower. Csíkszentmihályi himself referred to flow as an "optimal experience" (Csíkszentmihályi 2005, p. 11) and as "pleasure, creativity and the process of being completely at one with life" (Csíkszentmihályi 2005, p. 15). A person is able to attain the flow state when he is intrinsically motivated. In Chap. 2, we described self-motivation as a state in which one is completely intrinsically motivated to carry out an activity for its own sake. In the flow state, there is a very high degree of alignment between the requirement and the activity. In this state, a person carries out a task without effort. The person is satisfied and efficient, thus freeing up considerable energy and resources that can be used for other tasks. In the working world, a person can reach a self-motivated state when he combines an appealing goal with a task whose degree of difficulty matches her abilities – thus, when the task is neither too easy nor too difficult. With immediate feedback on their own actions, the person corrects herself, expanding her capabilities without feeling overwhelmed (for example, a musician when making music). The ID37 personality assessment reveals which individual motives lead to this rewarding and productive state (Sect. 4.3).

When we refer to satisfaction in this book, we do not mean the situational, short-term experience of happiness. Rather, we mean a fundamental life satisfaction that persists over a long period of time, and which is closely associated with the personality. We have already become familiar with three key aspects of satisfaction as they relate to motives:

1. Every person strives to ensure that he attains a maximum amount of well-being under the given circumstances. At the same time, he tries to avoid sadness, anxiety and pain. In this regard, motives are the drivers, and the positive emotion is the goal (Sect. 2.1).
2. Satisfaction is a positive, complex emotional state that is achievable only when thought (cognition) comes into play, for example in the form of evaluation, comparison or a toting up of positives and negatives. Happiness is the maximum stage of development for positive emotions conditioned by the culture and personal experience (Sect. 2.3).

3. What makes a person satisfied differs from individual to individual. Because each person has different preferences in life (which can be seen quite clearly in his motive profile), everyone also has highly individual life goals (Sect. 2.1).

Satisfaction
Psychology describes satisfaction quite generally as the result of a comparison between expectation and the actual occurrence of what has been expected. The smaller the experienced discrepancy, the more satisfied a person is. Even the impression of being well on the way to achieving the goal can be satisfying (Stangl 2017a).

Life satisfaction is a person's own assessment of his or her general situation in life. It is an individual phenomenon that consists of a complex of sensations and conscious and unconscious components, including genetically conditioned components such as motives (Roth and Ryba 2016, p. 219). This means that everything that is intrinsically motivating and thus personally meaningful for a person, and which is or can be achieved, raises his level of satisfaction (Brandstädter 2015, p. 46, 84). Examples of key characteristics and associated behaviors that are demonstrably satisfying include:

Not Too Self-Critical

Studies by psychologist Todd B. Kashdan show that satisfied people refrain from constant self-scrutiny, judge their performance less severely, and are less perfectionistic than less satisfied people (Kashdan 2013). Transferred to the ID37 model, this refers to the SOCIAL ACCEPTANCE motive. The finding from the study is that people with a weak expression of this motive (SAC –) have a positive self-image, and are comparatively less sensitive to criticism. This makes them more easy to satisfy than people in whom this motive is more strongly expressed (SAC +).

Capable of Relationships

Social connection can be another basis for a high level of satisfaction (Brandstädter 2015, p. 59 f.). As a rule, people make better life decisions when they are accompanied in their thinking and emotional responses by another person. For example, when they have someone with whom they can discuss their problems, they tend to be healthier, and slip less often into addictive behaviors when faced with problems. People with a weakly expressed AUTONOMY (AUT –) motive and a strongly expressed SOCIAL PARTICIPATION motive (SPA +) find it easy to build a variety of relationships. However, having a sustainable social network means having strong relationships, not necessarily a large number of connections. Maintaining relationships with just few people is also possible for people with a strongly expressed AUTONOMY (AUT +) motive and a weakly expressed SOCIAL PARTICIPATION (SPA –) motive.

Socially Engaged

Altruism can also contribute to satisfaction (Brandstädter 2015, p. 85). A person who has a strongly expressed SOCIAL ENGAGEMENT (SEN +) motive, and is able to act on it, will be accordingly satisfied. A good example might be doctors who use their yearly vacation time to provide medical services in needy areas.

All 16 motives contained in the ID37 system provide the basis for life satisfaction. This is because the satisfaction of our motives, as expressed, is what gives our lives meaning. If we are acquainted with our motive profile and can live according to our pattern of expression, this produces satisfaction.

5.1.1 Satisfaction Can Be Achieved

As brain researcher Gerhard Roth has pointed out, most people are either slightly positive and happy in their general attitude toward life, or slightly negative and unhappy. While a majority of people have a relatively stable sense of satisfaction, a minority shows significant fluctuations. For example, evidence shows that lottery winners are no happier over the long term than those who have never won a large sum of money, and physically disabled people are not on average unhappier than those without such issues (Roth and Ryba 2016, p. 217).

There are well-founded concepts that lead to higher levels of satisfaction and performance, such as:

Synchronization of Motives and Goals

Using the ID37 personality assessment, it swiftly becomes clear what is important and meaningful for a person, and what he needs in order to feel comfortable in her life. Is this social participation, or instead the freedom to be alone? By comparing these results with the realities of life, the discrepancy between what is and what is desired becomes clear. This enables the development of personally tailored goals that the person can achieve on their own. Bringing motives into harmony with personal goals is an essential step for long-lasting satisfaction and the ability to perform one's best. This self-congruence is understandable: It is easier to identify with one's goals when they are in harmony with one's real self. If a person does something that does not correspond with his motive profile, this is a motive-goal mismatch, which typically leads to dissatisfaction. If goals are not suited to one's own personality, it makes it more difficult to achieve these goals, reducing performance levels and efficiency. Over time, such a situation can even make a person sick (Roth and Ryba 2016, p. 228).

The Experience of Self-Efficacy – Setting and Reaching Realistic Goals

A person who sets and achieves self-determined goals rewards himself for this success, gaining the experience of self-efficacy (Roth 2007, p. 255). Self-efficacy is the subjective assessment that the realization of goals can be influenced by one's own actions, or the conviction that one can overcome future challenges on one's own. Self-efficacious people are those who persistently pursue realistic but challenging goals, and are able to take pleasure in their own success. They show perseverance, persistence and flexibility in seeking to attain their goals. They are also able to make realistic assessments with regard to how long the pursuit of the goal remains reasonable, and when the goal should be adjusted. In this regard, it is important to understand how much progress is being made toward the goal (Roth and Ryba 2016, p. 228). The expectation of self-efficacy can provide the impetus for an intrinsic increase in motivation, and a positive experience of self-efficacy can raise ambition levels for the next task. A number of studies show that the experience of self-efficacy has a positive effect with regard to reducing stress and improving the sense of well-being (Brandstädter 2015, p. 252).

Individual Stress Management

People who consciously engage with and are able to manage problems in life are more satisfied, because they feel less stress (Roth and Ryba 2016, p. 219 f.). How easy it is for a person to cope with stress depends on their personality (Sect. 4.5). Stress management is a skill that can be learned and trained. Most people even become calmer as they get older. This is partially related to the increasing wealth of experience, but the brain also plays a role. The areas of the brain that process negative feelings are less active in old age (Brandstädter 2015, p. 65).

Control Over One's Own Life

One key aspect of satisfaction is the degree to which a person can create the freedom for individual action. Subjective feelings of well-being are strongly influenced by the degree to which the person has the opportunity to make changes in his life, as well as his general sense of freedom. This correlates strongly with the feeling of personal control over one's own life (Asendorpf 2015, p. 117 f.).

Individual circumstances are also critical in determining when a person is satisfied, or when he experiences actions as being satisfactory. Therefore, the context for one's own goal-achievement and stress-management strategies must be taken into account. For example, simply going for walk can sometimes make a person feel quite satisfied. This may be true, for example, if this person has long lacked the opportunity to engage in any kind of fitness-related activity, perhaps because an illness has kept her in bed. If this person has a strongly expressed PHYSICAL EXERCISE motive, walks will take on an even greater importance.

> The more fully that motives and goals are synchronized, the more the achievement of those goals will contribute to satisfaction. Everything we find meaningful enhances our satisfaction.

However, approaches such as the following are less helpful, even if they are intended to produce satisfaction.

- **General or vague advice:** "Be happy and satisfied." Such admonitions are vague, and have no connection to the specifics of the individual situation. Thus, they are ineffective.
- **Exclusively positive thinking:** "Focus on what you want to achieve, hold this positive state of affairs in your mind, and then everything will work out." While it is very important to be able to imagine a state in which you are satisfied, negative emotions too must be allowed to make an appearance. They have a warning and activation function that ensures we remain attentive. This attentiveness makes it possible for us to find our way out of an unpleasant situation, for example (Wilhelm 2014).
- **Holding tight to an attitude:** Thoughts like "That's just how I am," or the constant repetition of a goal ("If I only had another job") will lead to no positive effect if no action follows from them. In some cases, people who think this way get stuck in their habitual patterns of thought. As a consequence, they are no longer able to recognize positive opportunities, and don't consider alternative options. They can't let go, can't accept new thoughts, and are no longer able to break out of their cycle of dissatisfaction (Sauerland 2015, p. 11).

5.1.2 What Does this Mean for My Professional Work?

Everyone can contribute to improving their own life satisfaction if they know themselves well. For example, a person can take on projects in which he finds meaning and define goals that are meaningful and motivating for him. The will to develop personally, the confidence to choose the direction of your own life, and the feeling of control are fundamental elements determining the quality of life. With their ID37 personality profile, we can show clients the way forward in this regard and accompany them through this process.

The aim is to empower people to control their own lives, and thus improve their life satisfaction. Life satisfaction is anything but fleeting. It is a goal worth working toward.

5.2 Obstacles to Achieving Satisfaction

Humans have a natural tendency toward self-centeredness that gets in the way of their satisfaction.

5.2.1 Natural Self-Centeredness

Self-centeredness refers to people's natural inclination to think that their own set of values are correct. One's own set of standards becomes a standard for all values and actions. However, self-centeredness is not to be confused with egoism, in which a person is exclusively concerned with his or her own welfare.

Self-centeredness is particularly noticeable in the case of strong and weak motive expressions. In the case of strong expressions, efforts to satisfy the motive are vigorous, and can take up considerable space in the person's thoughts, feelings and actions. This narrows the perception. A weak motive expression can also place limits on perception, due to the strong need for avoidance. This often leads to conflicts, complicating efforts to live and work with others and reducing life satisfaction.

Typical natural tendencies include:

- blind spots
- value tyranny
- confirmation bias

5.2.1.1 Blind Spots

Blind spots refer to characteristics that people are unable to perceive in themselves. Such individuals are effectively blind to one or more traits within their own personalities. This can lead to misjudgments regarding others' perceptions of them. Blind spots also carry the risk that a person will misjudge a situation and react incorrectly. For example, a person with a strongly expressed CURIOSITY motive (CUR +) may fail to consider that his listeners might not share her thirst for knowledge. This could lead her to give a highly intellectual and detailed presentation in which he overwhelms and loses her audience or the participants in a meeting with the depth of her information. Consequently, his message would then reach only those people in the audience with a similar motive expression.

People tend to have a positive self-perception. Everyone lives in his own reality, convinced primarily by his own ideas, and with faith in his own feelings. If a person encounters someone with similar motive expressions, he thinks he knows him. This can produce spontaneous trust and sympathy. The perception of people with significantly different motive expressions tends to be negative, because their behavior and values seem alien. This can cause mistrust and antipathy, along with repeated misunderstanding.

Examples of the Possible Effects of Unrecognized Blind Spots

- **Conflicts within teams**

  A team leader is very organized, detail-oriented, and holds himself to an exacting standard of work. His ID37 personality profile reveals a strongly expressed STRUCTURE motive (STR +). He himself does not see this, because a highly structured life and plan-based approach is entirely normal for him. This team leader is regularly annoyed by a team member he considers to be lacking in discipline, chaotic and careless. The person in question has a weakly expressed STRUCTURE motive (STR –). He sees himself as flexible, spontaneous, open and quick to respond, and feels unfairly treated by the leader's criticisms of his working style. For his part, he considers his team leader to be a pedant who is overly precise, and who can't get the hang of the agile, often unpredictable working world. The potential for conflict lies in the discrepancy between the team leader's self-assessment and the team member's perception. If this blind spot remains unresolved, it could result in emotionally explosive situations over time. What applies between two people also applies within teams. For successful work in teams, it is critical that team members understand how others perceive them. Mutual understanding and continuous work on dealing with diversity leads to more effective collaboration in an open work atmosphere.

- **Misjudgment by managers**
  Within companies, especially those that have reduced or even eliminated hierarchies, individual responsibility is demanded from all employees. People who require considerable freedom and few guidelines due to their constellation of motives – for example, those who have weakly expressed STRUCTURE (STR –) and PRINCIPLES (PRI –) motives – can adapt well to this new organizational structure, and can work in a self-motivated way. Unreflective managers with a motive profile of this type may have a blind spot here. They assume that everyone on the team will be able to handle the new organizational structure as well as they can. If such a manager remains aware of this misjudgment and fails to take measures tailored to the individuals involved, there is a strong likelihood of losing team members. Self-reflection, as well as the willingness to listen and understand others, are essential requirements for successful leadership.
- **Delusion**
  Another example of the dangers of blind spots was displayed at the "elephants' roundtable" (Elefantenrunde) on Germany's national election night in 2005, which featured the leaders of all the major political parties discussing the outcome of the elections. Gerhard Schröder, still chancellor at that point in time, appeared unable to admit his defeat. Even further, viewers took away the impression that he hadn't yet understood the election results. He radiated a self-confidence that bordered on hubris. In the live TV discussion with successor Angela Merkel and the heads of the parties then represented in the Bundestag, he appeared to be still convinced of his claim to power. We can assume that Schröder has a strongly expressed need for INFLUENCE (INF +) and a weakly expressed SOCIAL ACCEPTANCE (SAC –), which is why he continued to press his claim to power, unfazed by the reality of the night's results. He may even have wondered to himself about people's reactions, and the verbal attacks that in his view would have been inappropriate.

5.2.1.2 Value Tyranny

By value tyranny, we refer to the tendency to make one's own motives the measure of all things. We judge or condemn others on the basis of our values, which are based on our personal motives.

For example, if one person repeatedly seeks to convince another that he cannot be happy in life without STRUCTURE, even though he values flexibility, we call this value tyranny. In such a situation, the first individual very often wants the best for the other, because from his point of view, his conception of value is the only correct point of reference. Contrary to what the term implies, value tyranny is not necessarily driven by bad intent, but instead by the desire to win another person over to a deeply held conviction.

People acting in this way may lack the ability to look at themselves from the outside. They fail to recognize or accept that other people have other priorities and standards. They may confuse individuality with anomaly, saying, "But that's just weird," or "There's something off about him."

Typical Examples of Everyday Value Tyranny

- **Parent-child relationships**
  Reasoning from his own strongly expressed INFLUENCE (INF +) and STATUS (STA +) motives, a father may want to convince his son of the importance of doing well in school. "This B grade isn't good enough," he says. "You have to do better next time, or you'll amount to nothing." In so doing, he fails to recognize and accept that his son is in fact satisfied with his school grade, has a weakly expressed STATUS motive (STA –), and regards his SOCIAL ENGAGEMENT with Greenpeace (SEN +) as being much more important.
- **Couple relationships**
  Value tyranny can take place in relationships too. For example, one partner with a strongly expressed SOCIAL PARTICIPATION motive (SPA +) may want to convince the other of how rewarding it is to go out every weekend or invite people to their home. The partner in whom this motive is weakly expressed (SPA –) has trouble understanding how superficial contacts and conversations can provide pleasure. Similarly, the first partner can't understand how someone can reject something from which he himself draws so much energy.

If the couple's motive expressions are very different, they lack a certain amount of fit at the personality level. Recurring disputes are likely. Of course, this does not mean that people cannot have a good relationship as a result. However, it will require more mutual consideration, appreciation and attention.

But even if we know and respect the fact that everyone has their individual ideas of value, it is difficult to understand how others really think, feel and act. The actual emotional significance remains inaccessible to us, because we never or rarely experience it as fulfilling. Cognitively, we can learn to understand what is happening on the "other side." But the associated emotions remain foreign to us.

If the value tyranny manifests within a context of professional or private dependence, this lack of understanding can become frustration. A person forced to suppress his own motives can adapt for a period of time, and work to understand what is so important to the other. Over the long term, however, a compromise of this kind can lead to dissatisfaction at the very least. As a result, demotivation, aggression, and ultimately even psychological and physical impairments can emerge. The adaptive behavior will do nothing to transform inner convictions, because the motive-based personality traits are virtually unchangeable.

5.2.1.3 Confirmation Bias

A confirmation bias is the tendency for people to look primarily for information or primarily perceive things that confirm them in their preconceived opinions. In this regard, people prefer to affirm their (pre-)judgments rather than questioning them. Due to this confirmation bias, people assess new information as being less accurate if the information does not fit with their worldview. They tend to believe only what they want to believe (Stangl 2017b).

If the team leader from the above-described example (Sect. 5.2.1, "Examples of the possible effects of unrecognized blind spots"), who has a strongly expressed STRUCTURE motive (STR +), is convinced that the other team member (STR −) acts chaotically, he will probably primarily perceive this person's undisciplined behavior – such as regularly arriving late to work. In so doing, the team leader will probably unconsciously disregard all information that fails to confirm his expectations, such as the fact that the team member just as often appears on time.

A Closer Look: Confirmation Bias – An Internet Boom

The phenomenon of confirmation bias shows itself in the way people use the internet. Especially within social networks, people tend to search for and consume information that aligns with their own convictions. This creates "echo chambers" in which people primarily encounter mutually confirming opinions. The effect is reinforced by the algorithms that search engines, Facebook and other services use to personalize their results. In these "filter bubbles," users are supplied only with messages that correspond to their already-existing preferences (Holzer 2016). An echo chamber of this kind is not negative per se as long as the user is conscious of it. With the awareness that he may be getting only one side of the story, closing himself off to other informational perspectives, he can ultimately himself make the decision to stay in the filter bubble or leave it.

The consequences of confirmation bias can include self-fulfilling prophecies and selective perception.

Self-Fulfilling Prophecy

If a person expects a behavior or an event, and additionally contributes unconsciously to the realization of this expectation, this is a self-fulfilling prophecy. A self-referential perspective creates the preconditions for the occurrence of the expected results. The self-fulfilling prophecy can function either optimistically (e.g., having faith in one's own ultimate success) or pessimistically (e.g., stigmatization) (Asendorpf 2015, p. 101). The experiment in this area conducted by American psychologists Robert Rosenthal and Lenore F. Jacobson, who researched U.S. elementary schools, has become quite well known (Rosenthal and Jacobson 1968, among other sources). The researchers conducted an intelligence test with each participating student, and then selected a small number of the students at random. However, they told the teachers that the members of this group of children were particularly intelligent. After one year, tests showed that the subsequent "increase in intelligence" was greatest precisely among these randomly selected students. The reason? Teachers' expectations had influenced their behavior toward their supposedly most intelligent students. They had given these children special support and praise, so that the researchers' prophecy ultimately came true. Let's return once again to the example of the team leader (STR +) from above (Sect. 5.2.1, "Examples of the possible effects of unrecognized blind spots"). He is probably trapped in his own mindset and does not trust that the team member (STR −) who is in his view hopelessly chaotic will be able to work responsibly. Such an outcome does not fit into his own constellation of values, and thus violates his expectations. In his mind, there is no success without structure. To a great degree, he will probably unconsciously ignore and even bypass this team member, refusing to assign him any tasks that require responsibility. The predicted lack of success will then occur, making the team leader feel justified.

Selective Perception

Even what we perceive visually is unconsciously influenced by our personality. We perceive only certain aspects of our surroundings, while disregarding others – essentially filtering our environment. This selective perception is always guided by a person's unconscious or conscious motives, goals, convictions and expectations, and oriented toward stimuli that are in harmony with these factors. On the one hand, this is practical and efficient, as it enables swift reactions and decisions. On the other, opinions and judgments can in this way become stubbornly ingrained. The actions of people we are sympathetic to, for example, will be viewed much more positively than the actions of those toward whom we are less sympathetic. Emotions too are one of the key factors influencing the process of perception. Strong feelings such as fear, for instance, can have the effect of intensifying perceptions. Thus, every person perceives the world in a subjective and individual way (Stangl 2017c).

A Closer Look: Misunderstandings Are the Rule in Communication

Conflicts are caused when people don't understand each other. The one person can't understand what is important to the other, or what emotions may be triggered in him by an event, situation or person. When people communicate with one another, they exchange signals. The sender sends a signal, while the receiver decodes it, in so doing activating his entire highly personal network of experiences and associations. It quickly becomes clear that it is difficult for the sender and receiver to interpret the meaning in the same way. Gerhard Roth clearly illustrates this difficulty with the simple word (serving in this case as a signal) "horse." "The word 'horse' may engender a sense of pleasure for one person, for example, because he previously felt this pleasure while riding in a competition. For another person, the term might evoke an unpleasant, anxious memory, because he was bitten by an aggressive pony in the past. The significance of the experience thus arises from the relationship between the individual elements; that is, it is context-dependent" (Roth and Ryba 2016, p. 309).

Moreover, many people are not aware of the difficulties associated with this lack of understanding. They take leave of one another with the feeling that they have understood each other. This is intensified in situations in which people share emotions. Feelings are "infectious." In such moments, we think that we understand one another magnificently. In most cases, conflict occurs only when one person realizes that another is not acting as expected (e.g., an employee who does not follow his manager's instructions, or a child who does not do what her parents want). This can happen because the receiver has interpreted the communication differently in his understanding, or because he has been disrupted in his intention to act.

5.2.2 What Does this Mean for My Professional Work?

People exhibit inclinations that lead to a narrowing of perception and the potential for conflict. With their ID37 personality profile, we can sensitize them to perception traps. Based on his motive profile, for example, we can show a client where his blind spots may be. This helps him understand that he himself may often be the cause of a problem.

With the help of the individual motive profile, we can think ourselves into the client's reality. From within this reality – looking out through the lens of his motives – we can support him in expanding his field of perception, Especially where he has particular motives that are particularly strongly or weakly expressed.

In doing so, we want to initiate a process that promotes self-awareness and the willingness to engage in self-reflection, while also encouraging people to step beyond habitual modes of thought, expand their narrowed fields of perception and understand differences as being enriching. These reflexive processes of self-examination will help reduce future stress and avert conflict.

Even as a coach, manager or ID37 Master, we can be subject to a tendency toward self-centeredness or confirmation bias. It is thus advisable to keep our own personality profile always in mind, in order to avoid and correct false judgments.

5.3 What Is Success?

The question of what success is has a simple answer: the achievement of personal goals.

5.3.1 Success: Achieving Personal Goals

Success is something highly individual – it is simply what each person individually defines as success for themselves. This could certainly be a position with power and influence, but could also be a happy family, a good relationship, or the ability to contribute to a better society. In any case, success is associated with a positive feeling.

If we know what satisfies us emotionally, we have a set of bearings around which we can orient our life. If we accomplish that much, we are satisfied, and success will follow. Musician and Nobel Prize in Literature winner Bob Dylan defines success in the following way:

> “A man is a success if he gets up in the morning and goes to bed at night and in between does what he wants to do (Dylan 1967, quoted in Lachetta 1967).

5.3.2 Failure Is Part of Success

Anyone who has set personal goals may ultimately be unable to realize them. What failure means for each individual differs. For one person, there may be no such thing as defeat. Another may believe that he is constantly failing – even a client presentation that doesn’t go perfectly might be regarded by him as a failure.

The motive profile offers us clues regarding how people deal with failure. Consider, for example, the SOCIAL ACCEPTANCE motive:

- **SOCIAL ACCEPTANCE strongly expressed**
  - For such people, the spontaneous impulse is one of self-doubt and a fear of failure. They fear failure more than they look forward to success. Individuals with this pattern of motive expression want to avoid possible consequences of failure such as contempt or condemnation. Therefore, they avoid acting, or act only tentatively. They are likely to miss out on possible opportunities. The fear of failure can be paralyzing.
  - However, the fear of failure can also prompt the person to make a special effort. Fear is in this case a driver that actually reduces the probability of failure. One can learn to deal with the fear of failure.

- **SOCIAL ACCEPTANCE weakly expressed**
  - The spontaneous impulse felt by such people is to analyze failure comparatively soberly, in order to learn from it and check it off as an experience. They are more confident of success. However, if their analysis of the failure is inaccurate or altogether lacking, this can have fatal consequences. In such a case, people with this expression may be prone to overestimating themselves. They may not see relevant warning signs, either ignoring them or simply making the same failure again. This can lead to a downward spiral.

Learning from Failure

For extreme mountain climber Reinhold Messner, failure is an essential prerequisite for success. "I learn more from my failures than from my successes," he says. "If I've been successful, I generally can't tell afterwards why I had that success. Then it doesn't matter anymore. What remains is only a feeling of success, without any process of learning. But if I fail, then I know that I must have done something wrong. I then think back through my expedition, in order to find the crucial point: Maybe I had the wrong partner" (Walther 2008).

5.3.3 Paying Attention to Both Success and Failure

In order to pave the way for successful experiences over the long term, it is critical to know how you deal with both success and defeats. Sometimes a successful action is noticed only if it was associated with effort (for example, at the end of a difficult project), or when another person points out the success.

Achieving a goal easily is often not perceived as success at all. In such a case, you lose the opportunity to associate this process with the experience of success. The conscious evaluation of actions that have resulted in the achievement of goals is important for two reasons: First, for the experience of self-efficacy, and second, for the longer-term experience of success, which must develop in the brain as a schema.

> Each confirmatory response reinforces the existing synaptic connection weights of the neuronal excitation pattern underlying the schema, so that in the future this schema can be more easily activated (Grawe 1998, quoted in Krause and Storch 2014, p. 185 f.).

Personal success requires repeated attention. But failure too requires attention. In this case, the focus should be on analyzing the events experienced. For example, this may involve a reappraisal of the stimulus-response pattern: What influenced a decision or triggered an action that led to the defeat? On the basis of this analysis, strategies can be developed that will help things go better the next time (for example, by preparing for reactions when the stimulus appears again).

Over the course of a long lifespan, the achievement of personal goals generally entails an alternation between success and failure. Those who learn to deal with this flexibly develop the capacity for autonomy and satisfaction.

5.3.4 What Does this Mean for My Professional Work?

Though it might seem simple to say: The road to success is a challenging one.

Goals are the key to satisfaction and success, because we choose them ourselves. Unlike our partially genetically determined personality traits or the changing environment around us, our own goals are subject to our personal influence. Goals can at any time be flexibly adjusted and recalibrated in the direction of a happy life.

The ID37 motive profile allows you to set self-congruent goals. People are more successful in accomplishing goals if these are aligned with their motives. Once people understand their motives, they gain access to inner resources that support them in achieving their goals.

In everyday life, however, there are many factors that may also affect the realization of goals, such as a relapse into old patterns of behavior due to stress. We can successfully counteract this through the use of individualized strategies. To this end, we work with the client to determine how he can regulate his emotions on his own, and how he can remain in control in difficult situations. We can't always behave according to our personality, but we can work to step out of ourselves when necessary. In addition, once you understand yourself, you can learn to deal constructively with failure.

Drive, satisfaction and success are a natural trio. While one can philosophize about the relative order of satisfaction and success, drive is the beginning of everything. If we know what drives us, we can find goals that suit us and the motivation to pursue them. It is drive that inspires us and paves the way to satisfaction and success (Fig. 5.1).

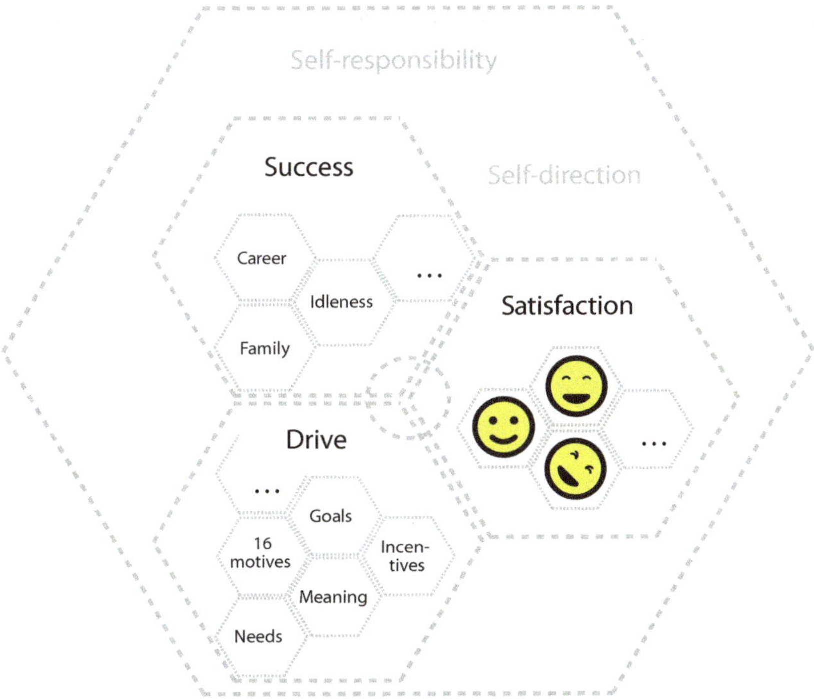

Fig. 5.1 Relationship between drive, satisfaction and success

References

Asendorpf, J. B. (2015). *Persönlichkeitspsychologie für Bachelor* (3rd ed.). Berlin: Springer.

Brandstädter, J. (2015). *Positive Entwicklung* (2nd ed.). Berlin: Springer (e-Book).

Csíkszentmihályi, M. (2005). *Flow* (12th ed.). Stuttgart: Klett-Cotta.

Holzer, B. (2016). "Gefangen in der Filterblase?" http://www.faz.net/aktuell/wissen/ins-netz-gegangen/internetnutzer-befinden-sich-in-einer-filterblase-14503725.html. Accessed: March 21, 2018.

Kashdan, T. B. (2013). *Mindfulness, acceptance and positive psychology*. Oakland: Context Press.

Krause, F., & Storch, M. (2014). *Selbstmanagement – ressourcenorientiert* (5th ed.). Bern: Huber.

Lachetta, M. (May 8, 1967). *New York Daily News*.

Lotter, W. (2016). Das Lustprinzip. *brand eins, 8*, 38–45.

Reinhardt, S. (2014). Zufriedenheit: Das wahre Glück. *Psychologie Heute, 1*, 20–27.

Rosenthal, R., & Jacobson, L. (1968). Pygmalion in the classroom. *The Urban Review, 3*(1), 16–20.

Roth, G. (2007). *Persönlichkeit, Entscheidung und Verhalten*. Stuttgart: Klett-Cotta.

Roth, G., & Ryba, A. (2016). *Coaching, Beratung und Gehirn*. Stuttgart: Klett-Cotta (e-Book).

Sauerland, M. (2015). *Design your mind – Denkfallen entlarven und überwinden*. Wiesbaden: Springer.

Stangl, W. (2017a). Keyword: Zufriedenheit. Online Lexikon für Psychologie und Pädagogik. http://lexikon.stangl.eu/6737/zufriedenheit/. Accessed: March 21, 2018.

Stangl, W. (2017b). Keyword: Bestätigungstendenz. Online Lexikon für Psychologie und Pädagogik. http://lexikon.stangl.eu/3159/bestaetigungstendenz-bestaetigungsfehler/. Accessed: March 21, 2018.

Stangl, W. (2017c). Keyword: selektive Wahrnehmung. Online Lexikon für Psychologie und Pädagogik. http://lexikon.stangl.eu/1708/selektive-wahrnehmung/. Accessed: March 21, 2018.

Walther, P. (2008). Der Mensch lernt nur durch Versuch und Irrtum. Interview with Reinhold Messner (in German). *managerSeminare, 122*, 30.

Wilhelm, K. (2014). Glück kann unaufmerksam und verführbar machen. *Psychologie Heute, 1*, 28–30.

Applying ID37 in Practice

6

Particularly in today's working world, we find ourselves in a perpetual learning process. We learn new technologies, cope with the growing flood of information, work in heterogeneous and often culturally diverse teams, and continually develop new means of cooperation. Nor do the processes of change stop at the borders of our private lives. For some this is a blessing, while for others it means great uncertainty, stress or even anxiety. So how can we cope with these challenges, and even use them for our own benefit?

The self-direction needed for this task can be learned. To this end, it has proven useful in our experience to identify and activate one's own individual resources – for example, one's own motives. The ID37 personality assessment is an effective instrument for doing so.

It also serves as the basis for improved cooperation and communication – between coaches and clients, between managers and employees, within teams, and even in everyday interactions.

6.1 Fields of Application

Anybody can take the evidence-based ID37 test (Sect. 4.1). The opportunities for use of this instrument are wide-ranging. The following overview offers just a brief selection of such applications.

- **Coaching**
  In the coaching process, ID37 helps define a person's current life situation and their feelings about it, and it helps give people the ability to act in changing circumstances. It serves as a starting point with regard to helping people lead a self-determined, more satisfied life.
- **Business coaching**
  ID37 is often used in a business-coaching context when the focus is on achieving professional satisfaction, as this is a requirement for high-level performance over

T. Staller, C. Kirschke, *Personality Assessment with ID37*,
https://doi.org/10.1007/978-3-030-53921-4_6

the long term. In such an application, the analysis of motives helps to reveal possible discrepancies between personal goals and the requirements of a given role.

- **Businesses and organizations**
  In the human-resources-management context, the ID37 personality diagnostics instrument is used for a number of tasks, ranging from staff selection and development to executive and team development. Companies need holistic personnel strategies along with networked and customizable concepts in order to attract suitable applicants, help their employees reach their potential, and keep them within the company. ID37 helps companies take a systematic approach to these tasks. A sound talent-management process enables companies to help their employees develop in the best possible way and is a success factor in the competition for high-skilled workers (McKinsey Deutschland et al. 2011).
  - **Staff selection and development**
    Personality plays a significant role in hiring decisions (Hossiep and Weiß 2017). An applicant who already has the right abilities for a role will generally find it easier to perform his job, and will perform at a higher level, than a person who has to act contrary to his natural tendencies. A personality-diagnostic analysis with ID37 can serve as a strategic instrument for companies to determine the degree to which a candidate meets the requirements of a role based on his personality, as well as indicating what targeted development measures he might need. Companies can thus base their staffing decisions on a well-founded system.
  - **Leadership**
    In our opinion, a good manager is someone who is familiar with his own personality and is able to exert conscious control over his actions. He is able to handle different situations and different people flexibly enough that he always remains capable of acting and is thus able to further the interests of employees and the company to the greatest degree possible. From our experience, there is no ideal constellation of motives for a manager, and therefore no ideal profile. Rather, the advantage of working with ID37 in the managerial context lies in the ability to decipher a manager's individual potential so he can gain a clear picture of his own personality, and so he can use this as advantageously as possible in his managerial role. Managers can also use ID37 as an instrument for individual leadership and team development.
  - **Team development**
    An ID37 team analysis shows how to build willing, high-performance teams, and how to lead them effectively. Team leaders can use the instrument to:
    - Increase the team's effectiveness and internal identification.
    - Identify similarities and differences within the team.
    - Create a vocabulary that enables the team to discuss similarities and differences.
    - Explain group dynamics and patterns of behavior.
    - Promote mutual understanding and respect.
    - Develop strategies to foster team strengths.
    - Identify and eliminate potential sources of conflict.
    - Create common team values and respect-based rules of behavior.
    - Adjust the distribution of roles and tasks.

Additional areas in which ID37 can be used include:

- **Competitive sports**
  Trainers and sport psychologists can use ID37 analysis to develop individual strategies for their athletes that are optimally attuned to their personalities. In doing so, they take a nuanced approach that distinguishes between the competition, training and recovery phases. Each phase requires different individual incentives in order to create exactly the right conditions for high performance, the further development of skills, or effective recovery. Trainers can additionally study their own motives profiles to determine where they might have blind spots that they might unconsciously be transmitting to their athletes. Through constant observation and careful, personalized direction, trainers can guide their athletes to greater mental strength. In team sports, the focus is additionally on team unity, increasing team spirit and developing the right appeal to push the team to a high level of performance.
- **Relationships**
  Opposites may attract in the short term. However, there is considerable research today indicating that relationships tend to be happier over the long term the more similar the people are, and the more they are able to adapt to one another. Relationship and couple counseling with ID37 draws on this insight, showing where couples have similar motives and where the sources of conflict might be.
- **Marketing and brand management**
  Why do people buy certain brands? The answer is, people don't buy brands, they buy what promises to satisfy them (or their motives) (Schreier et al. 2010, p. 86 f). Branding that works with human values brings the brand into a common frame of reference with the target group's values and can thereby trigger (purchasing) behavior. In this case, values correspond to motives. For example, the Volvo car brand specifically addresses people with a high need for security. By contrast, with its consistent positioning, Mercedes-Benz speaks primarily to drivers who have a strongly expressed STATUS motive (Chlupsa 2017, p. 63). Brands that implicitly and consistently convey the message that their products will give their consumers a feeling of satisfied motives will have a competitive advantage. ID37 provides a well-founded frame of reference for branding concepts of this kind.
- **Research**
  ID37 can also make contributions to basic psychological research and application-focused psychology, as it is able to capture the most important dispositional constructs within the dynamic personality. For example, it can be used to research motivations in the context of health and prevention.

> The ID37 personality model views people holistically. It can be used across sectors and disciplines.

Use of ID37 within companies – legal aspects
Due to the high-quality standards underlying the personality test (Sect. 4.2), as well as its practical applicability, ID37 is one of the psychological tests that are suitable

for use within a business context. ID37 Masters are experts in conducting the tests, and in analyzing and assessing the results professionally.

The following legal frameworks should be taken into account when using ID37 within companies (Hossiep and Weiß 2017):

- **Use of ID37 in the context of German companies**
  Of direct relevance here is the German Works Constitution Act (BetrVG), which regulates the functioning of works councils. According to Sections 94 and 95 (Section 94 on the issue of staff questionnaires in the workplace, and Section 95 on guidelines for selection), questionnaires given to staff members within a company generally require the consent of the works council. Professional users of ID37 should clarify at an early date how the works council needs to be involved in any work with the ID37 personality diagnostics instrument.
- **Data protection**
  - The prevailing labor-law framework applies to all regular employees. This includes all laws, regulations and binding provisions for the protection of workers, such as employee data-protection rules.
  - The European General Data Protection Regulation (GDPR) also covers the protection of the personal data of employees and job applicants. Even if employee data-protection is not itself included in the GDPR in the form of an independent regulation, this measure's requirements in some cases go well beyond those of the German Federal Data Protection Act (BDSG) – for example with regard to the employer's informational and disclosure obligations.
  - According to Section 32 paragraph 1 of the BDSG, the collection and use of an employee's personal data is permitted only if there is a direct connection with the job to be filled. Of course, this also applies in the case of job applicants. It is therefore necessary to ensure that the personality test is used only to assess traits relevant to a person's suitability for the (future) job's requirements. ID37 offers test variants that offer the ability to leave out the EROS motive, for example, thus avoiding any items that might touch on a person's private life.
  - For use of the personality test to be permissible, test takers must also receive an explanation regarding the nature, functioning and scope of the test, including a description of how the personality data will be used. Naturally, the test taker's consent to such use must also be secured. People taking the ID37 test provide their consent to the context-dependent use of their data by completing the questionnaire. These issues will also be explained further to them by the ID37 Master during a preliminary discussion. If ID37 is used in personnel-selection procedures, the written consent of the applicant is required.
  - The results of personality-oriented questionnaires constitute sensitive personal data; thus, if such results are retained, personal rights must also be respected. In addition, confidentiality must be maintained. The raw data associated with ID37 test takers is stored on European servers until the permission for such retention is revoked. If such a revocation does take place, the data is deleted without any possibility of later restoration.

- **Protection against discrimination**
  The ID37 procedure conforms with the provisions of Germany's General Act on Equal Treatment (AGG). The goal of the AGG is the prevention or elimination of disadvantages due to gender, age, disability status, sexual identity, religion, belief, race or ethnic background (§ 1 AGG).
- **DIN standard 33430**
  The DIN standard 33430 defines requirements for procedures and their use in the context of occupational suitability assessments. It is not a legal standard or norm. However, as a process norm, it establishes requirements and defines the allowable use of psychometric procedures within the occupational context. ID37 follows the quality standards of DIN Norm 33430. The norm is not binding for companies. Nevertheless, in the context of litigation, for example over a personnel-selection decision, it could prove beneficial for the company that the ID37 test follows these requirements.

Transparency, a willingness to educate, and open and trusting communication are requirements for successful work with the ID37 personality assessment within companies. At the beginning of any project, we recommend clarifying with the client which relevant departments and company representatives will be involved, and at what point.

6.2 The ID37 Assessment Session

The ID37 Master conducts the discussion of the test results after the test taker has completed the test, and once the computer-generated test results – that is, the individual motives profile – are available. The motives profile gives the ID37 Master a sense of who he will be talking with, thus allowing him to prepare the assessment session for optimal impact.

We recommend clearing some time at the beginning of the session so that both people can get to know one another, establishing an atmosphere of trust. With the knowledge about the client's personality, combined with the preliminary background information, the ID37 Master can always find a point of connection that he can use to welcome the client respectfully into his world.

This discussion of test results is of particular importance because the assessment is at this point supplemented by the test taker's personal context and life situation. The ID37 Master must thus listen very closely to the client, understand the entirety of the person's overall situation, and link this to the motives profile.

Goal of the assessment session
- Presentation of the value-free test results.
- Joint interpretation and reflection.
- Inclusion of the client's goals and context.

The ideal outcome of the assessment session is that the client comes to understand and accept his personal motives profile.

The aim of the ID37 personality assessment is to clearly describe the information that the motives profile reveals about the personality, identify patterns of behavior, and understand how the interactions between the 16 motives affect the individual's life situation.

6.2.1 Preparing for and Conducting the Assessment

During the assessment session, the ID37 Master immerses himself in the client's specific life circumstances, obtains a better overall understanding of the client, and helps explain processes and relationships between needs, motives and emotions. The client becomes consciously aware of his own feelings, thoughts and actions – the first step toward self-direction.

The assessment session: The fog clears

Before the assessment session, the ID37 Master sees in the motives profile that his client has a weakly expressed SAFETY motive (SAF –) and a very strongly expressed SOCIAL ACCEPTANCE motive (SAC ++). He knows that this person likes to take risks, is motivated by other people's esteem, and is very self-critical. Perhaps in previous sessions, the ID37 Master has frequently counseled people with a similar set of motive expressions who have found themselves in decisional conflicts when they have needed to assert themselves in new environments. He decides to ask specifically about this. During the assessment session, the client describes how he felt when he was offered a lead role on an innovation project. On the one hand, he looked forward to the challenging project, and to exciting new experiences (SAF –). On the other hand, he had doubts as to whether he was in fact up to the task (SAC ++). As a result, he felt a significant internal contradiction, feeling both fearless and anxious at the same time. In the end, he decided against accepting the project-lead position, without knowing exactly why. The ID37 Master is able to clarify this diffuse mix of feelings during the assessment session: Due to the client's very strongly expressed SOCIAL ACCEPTANCE motive, his worry that he would not be able to measure up to the high standards and expectations ultimately prevailed. This is likely to prove a valuable insight for the client as he ponders future decisions.

Due to its great explanatory power, the ID37 analysis often serves as the prelude to further coaching or counseling during which individualized intervention measures can be developed.

A period of 90 minutes is advised for the initial assessment session. We recommend the following procedure:

No matter what the original goal or inspiration in creating an ID37 motives profile, the person gains in self-awareness, which usually triggers an intensive process of reflection. This in turn can lead to further self-development approaches and measures.

Agenda for an ID37 assessment session

Getting started

- "Warm-up."
- Explanation of the discussion's goals.
- Brief presentation of the ID37 procedure.
- Introduction to the topic (e.g., "How did it go when filling out the questionnaire?", reminder that the results are value-free, explanation of the distinct character of the individual motives).

Discussion of the profile

- The ID37 Master discusses the motives profile in detail with the client.
- The analysis and interpretation of the motive expressions is based on the standardized descriptions of the results report.
- During the assessment session, the ID37 Master deals in a value-free way with each of the life motives, as well as the significance of their overall effect (e.g., interactions, motive conflicts).
- The ID37 Master addresses the issues of self-perception and the perception of others in order to point the client toward possible blind spots, and to explain emotionally foreign patterns of expression.
- The ID37 Master can provide the impetus needed to harness personal resources and individual potential for future growth.
- The ID37 Master is at all times respectful, listens carefully, and asks questions as necessary to ensure that he understands the client's life situation well and can take an overall view.

Conclusion

- Summing up: The ID37 Master allows enough time to answer all of the client's questions.
- The ID37 Master can reciprocate the client's trust by contrasting his own motives profile with that of the client. This is not absolutely necessary but has proved its worth in practice.

During the discussion of the assessment session, the ID37 Master respectfully and responsibly explains the motives profile. He can provide the impetus needed to harness personal resources and individual potential for future growth.

6.2.2 Interpretation Tips

As part of his training, the ID37 Master receives tools helping him to grasp the overall impact of the motives profile to be discussed. These include the test-results report; a set of guiding principles; instructions on how to deal with emotions, the perception of oneself and others, and item categorization; and the recommendation to compare or contrast his motives profile with that of the client. The motives profile constitutes an individual combination of motive expressions that describes the unique personality in a value-free manner. The ID37 philosophy does not allow for typologies, generalizations or ideal profiles. Even if certain motive constellations are helpful preconditions for certain requirements, there are no ideal profiles.

The individual motive expression not only provides information about which priority the person attaches to a motive, but also how strongly that priority is felt: How intensively does the person feel that he has to satisfy the motive? How often will a state of lack manifest itself? It is only in cases of a motive expression of ≤4 or ≥7 that we assume that it will significantly influence behavior.

Motive expressions that deviate strongly from the norm (≤3 and ≥8, or a difference of at least one standard deviation) are particularly revealing with regard to describing the client's personality and the individual needs, because they guide and influence his life and behavior most significantly. This means that the greater the deviation from the norm, the stronger the motive's impact within a person's life – both emotionally and with respect to behavior (for additional details on motive expressions, Sect. 4.3).

Excerpt from an assessment session, using a single motive as an example

The ID37 Master begins the profile analysis with the INFLUENCE motive, because it shows a very high value of 10 (INF ++). He starts by explaining the principle of a motive: "The INFLUENCE motive describes differences in the desire to influence people and processes and/or to exercise control over them. In colloquial terms, you could also say that it measures how much alpha leader you have in you." Then he addresses the client's specific motive expression: "Your self-assessment, with a score of 10, indicates that it feels very good for you when you can act as an alpha personality. You want to be a leader."

The ID37 Master observes the client's body language in response to this description, notes approval, and continues – confirmed in his analysis of the INFLUENCE motive. He then describes behavioral indicators associated with a weakly expressed INFLUENCE motive (INF –): "People who, unlike you, have a low score for the INFLUENCE motive do not need the feeling of control over others. On the contrary, they may try to avoid situations in which they have to exert influence. A typical behavior for a manager with a weakly expressed INFLUENCE motive might be to create an environment for his team in which they are empowered to make their own decisions. But to be clear, this does not mean that this manager is unable to make decisions. He simply doesn't need this feeling."

The client considers this briefly and tells the ID37 Master about a fellow executive in which he has recognized this behavior. Up to this point, he had been slightly contemptuous of this manager, writing him off as a weak, decision-shy leader.

The interplay of multiple motives enhances the accuracy of the behavioral prognosis. For example, two people with the same expression of the INFLUENCE motive can live out this motive expression completely differently depending on what other motives are active in them. Person A, with a very strongly expressed INFLUENCE motive (INF ++), but weak SOCIAL ACCEPTANCE (SAC –) and SAFETY (SAF –) expressions, will probably act very dominantly and self-confidently in decision-making situations, while also being quite willing to accept risks (Fig. 6.1a). Person B, who also has a very strongly expressed INFLUENCE motive (INF ++), but also has strongly expressed SOCIAL ACCEPTANCE (SAC +) and SAFETY (SAF +) motives, will probably make decisions cooperatively, seeking consent and relative security (Fig. 6.1b).

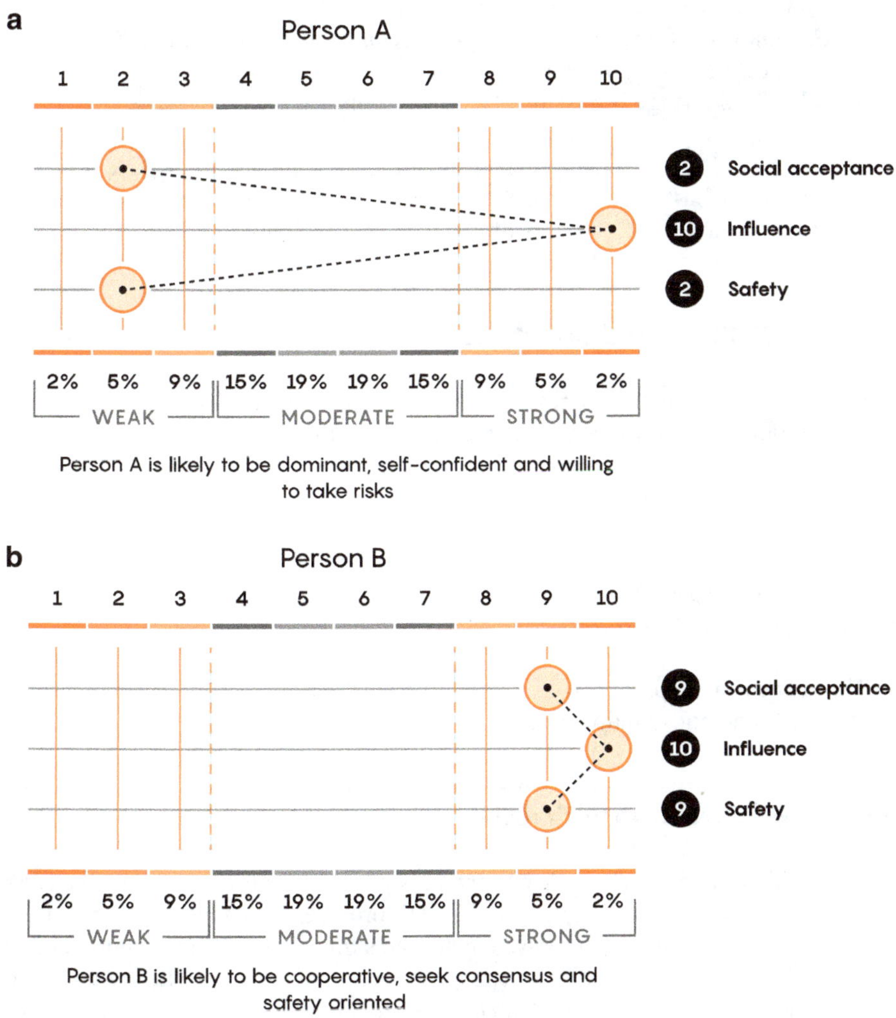

Fig. 6.1 The interplay of motives helps give precision to behavior prognoses. (**a**) Person A probably dominant, self-confident and risk-seeking. (**b**) Person B probably cooperative, consensus-seeking and safety-oriented

Strong motive expressions influence behavior, and thus also management behavior and leadership styles. The motive constellation alone provides no indication as to whether the person will be a good manager, or whether they can be successful. This depends on a number of different factors beyond personality alone, as well as on their interactions.

Reflection for ID37 Master

- The result is value-free – there are no strengths or weaknesses.
- ID37 does not identify skills or abilities; instead, it examines personal priorities on the basis of 16 motives.
- The analysis of test results is not a procedure for pleasing clients; that is, it's not about telling the client what he wants to hear.
- Behavioral change is possible, but only within the framework specified by the personal motives profile.
- Each ID37 Master should reflect on his own motives profile before going into a discussion of test results – even he is subject to blind spots and confirmation bias.
- Like any model, ID37 has its limits. It cannot explain every behavior.

6.2.3 ID37 Ethics and Quality Standards

When used professionally, the results of the ID37 personality assessment are delivered in conjunction with a personal assessment session, in order to exclude misinterpretations, overinterpretations and ambiguities.

The assessment session is:

- Free from judgment.
- Thoughtful, respectful and attentive.
- Open and self-reflective.

This ethos is an explicit part of the training for the ID37 Master. Scientific quality standards and consultation ethics set a high standard for work with ID37.

6.3 Self-Direction with ID37

Self-direction is a process by which users transfer the insights gained from the analysis of their motives into daily practice. ID37 provides guidance in helping individuals reach this point. With this systematic and simultaneously open approach, we offer a pathway by which to initiate change processes effectively. The method aims at the acquisition of effective self-direction skills in order to improve the personal quality of life. To this end, we combine the ID37 personality assessment with the research and applications associated with the Zurich Resources Model (ZRM®;

Krause and Storch 2014). We hope to stimulate effective practical work, and encourage everyone to supplement this approach with their own experiences.

Self-direction
Self-direction involves self-determined personal change processes in which desired behaviors become automatic. ID37 Masters can help their clients initiate, develop and ultimately implement these processes. In this regard, the knowledge of one's own personality is a crucial requirement in living a satisfied and successful life.

Our personality- and resource-oriented approach examines what people want and what is important to them. It focuses on recognizing, using and strengthening existing potential and resources. The 16 individually determined life motives are in this regard the most important elements.

On the basis of five distinct phases, we show how personal goals can be set and successfully implemented against the background of a person's own motive expressions.

Everyone acts according to their own personality. However, the ability to purposefully control one's actions enables a person to step out of the closed system of their self and actively intervene when necessary – for example, when someone wants to stick to a strict diet even though his FOOD ENJOYMENT motive is strongly expressed, when a teacher wants to enjoy a class trip even though his SOCIAL PARTICIPATION motive is weakly expressed, or when a person with a strongly expressed REVENGE motive wants to develop the capacity to stay calm.

At its heart, this is a matter of acquiring new behaviors on the basis of personal goals, and then of turning these into automatic behaviors. This increases the number of alternative actions that can be called upon spontaneously in difficult situations – and thus also the probability of living life in a more satisfied and less stressed way.

Self-direction gives people new options when acting.

The self-direction process take place in five phases:

- Phase 1: Clarifying personality details | Determining the person's life situation and their feelings about it (Sect. 6.3.1).
- Phase 2: Identifying and setting goals | Self-perception (Sect. 6.3.2).
- Phase 3: Activating resources | Self-motivation (Sect. 6.3.3).
- Phase 4: Anchoring goals | Turning intention into action (Sect. 6.3.4).
- Phase 5: Making behavior automatic | New habits (Sect. 6.3.5).

6.3.1 Phase 1: Clarifying Personality Details | Determining the Person's Life Situation and Their Feelings About It

The process begins with the ID37 personality assessment. The ID37 Master helps the client obtain a better understanding of the causes of his behavior and feelings.

The client is now familiar with his motive structure and knows why he behaves the way he does in certain situations. This is followed by a further diagnostic process designed to clarify the need for or the urgency of a change in the client's life. Where is there dissatisfaction in the current phase of life, where are the individual stressors, what barriers are preventing the realization of plans and intentions, and what patterns of thought are in place? With the motives profile and this deeper look into current circumstances, it becomes clear where the work can start. The client is provided with guidance regarding the resources available to him. In this reflexive analysis, the client also becomes aware that he can realize sustainable change only by taking responsibility for himself. Taking on the responsibility to steer one's own life succeeds as a result of factors that can be influenced, controlled and adjusted as needed: that is, with goals.

As soon as the individual motive patterns, life circumstances and basic attitude have been clarified, the process of goal-setting can begin. We can illustrate the process of self-direction with ID37 using the following example:

Example: Gaining confidence in front of an audience
In this example, we look at a manager whose motive structure includes the following expressions: SOCIAL ACCEPTANCE (SAC +), STATUS (STA +), AUTONOMY (AUT –), SOCIAL PARTICIPATION (SPA +). Fig. 6.2.

6.3.2 Phase 2: Identifying and Setting Goals | Self-Perception

Deciding what goals should be set depends as much on a person's pattern of motive expressions as on their personal life circumstances. These goals might be traceable

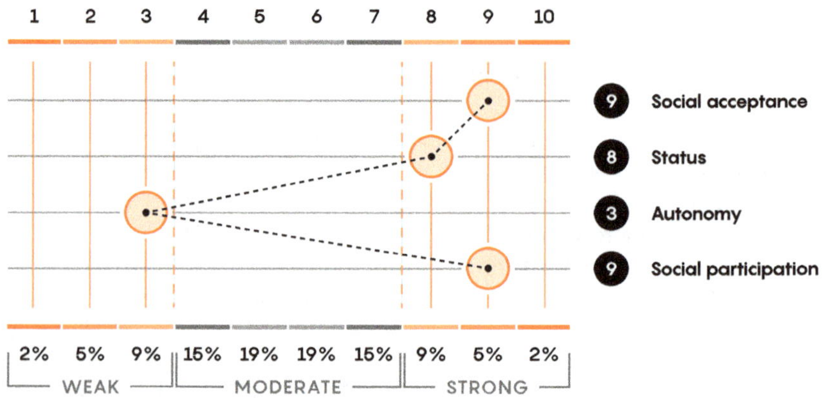

Fig. 6.2 Excerpt from the manager's motives profile

to a specific motive, or might alternately be related to patterns of behavior, such as the desire to be braver, more open or more resilient in times of stress.

Example: Gaining confidence in front of an audience
The manager finds that he radiates uncertainty when giving presentations. In the future, he wants to leave a confident and self-assured impression.

Many researchers and many studies have explored the issue of how goals must be formulated in order to be effective. Our work is based on the ZRM's® findings and approach (Krause and Storch 2014). According to this approach, formulating a specific action goal is useful only after an intention has been formed – that is, after the "crossing of the Rubicon" (Rubicon Model, Fig. 2.4). Before this point, a more general formulation of the goal is needed, referred to here as an attitude goal. We thus make a distinction between an attitude goal and an action goal.

Attitude goal
An attitude goal serves to provide orientation and is formulated in general terms. The criteria for a well-formulated attitude goal include the following:

- **The goal describes an attitude.** Attitude goals are formulated so that they are always valid. They describe an inner attitude rather than a specific, observable behavior. The following goal is thus not an attitude goal: "In the next presentation, I do not want to give the impression of uncertainty. I want to appear completely free of anxiety."
- **The goal is formulated in the present tense.** The goals relate to the present, with the implication that they can be achieved immediately – not only in the future.
- **The goal is described using imagery.** It can be beneficial to create an image of what one wants to achieve, as this helps to express the goal in clear language.

The attitude goal is chosen in such a way that it helps to activate the person's emotional memory, thus helping to prime the intention (volition).

Example: Gaining confidence in front of an audience
The manager might formulate the following attitude goal: "I radiate self-confidence."

This means formulating it so that it can become an automated action through the priming process.

A closer look: What is priming?
In the field of psychology, the concept of priming or canalization refers – simply put – to the triggering of behavioral reactions by subliminal stimuli.

Priming influences the way a stimulus is processed, allowing an earlier stimulus to activate implicit memory contents. This activation of specific associations within the memory of previous experiences takes place mostly on an unconscious level. A previously primed stimulus might be a word, a symbol, a gesture or anything similar (Wikipedia 2018).

For example, a research team led by psychologist Peter M. Gollwitzer asked subjects to read lists of words that were conceptually related to "cooperation," including words such as "fair," "share" and "collaborate." In so doing, the researchers activated an unconscious wish in the subjects to collaborate with others. Without being aware of it, the study subjects acted more cooperatively than did members of a control group who had not previously seen the word lists. Priming effects have been demonstrated in many experimental studies. Moreover, findings have shown that the brain's networks are activated more strongly as more senses are engaged. This means that smells, images, objects and sounds are all effective primes (Westerhoff 2009).

Action goal
Characteristics of effective action goals include:

- **Formulation as an approach goal (as opposed to an avoidance goal).** The person should not think about anything that is emotionally burdensome. When ordered not to think of a pink elephant, for example, it is precisely this thought that is triggered.
- **The goal is 100% under the person's own control.** If the person feels he is capable of attaining his goal through his own actions, this has a positive effect on his motivation. Moreover, the feeling of self-efficacy once the goal has been successfully achieved becomes correspondingly more powerful. This motivation is needed in order to "cross the Rubicon," and to form the necessary intention or willpower. It is of little use to formulate the goal in such a way that it contains elements that are outside of the person's control.
- **Positive affect.** The desired goal should be associated with positive affect. The more positive the associated feeling (the affect), the greater will be the motivation to carry out the action and reach the goal. In this regard, it is important to recall a similar situation in which the motive was activated, for instance in which the person acted self-confidently and thus experienced a positive feeling. In the

course of personal development, people are frequently encouraged to direct their perceptions to their sensations, and to pay attention to their feelings.

Example: Gaining confidence in front of an audience
The manager's refined action goal, which is based on the original attitude goal, might run: "I step self-confidently in front of my audience, and shine like the sun in South Africa."

Defining and formulating the goal precisely is very important with regard to ultimately achieving it. This goal-setting process will influence the way later actions are prepared. From a neurobiological perspective, the crucial task is to ensure that the goal serves as an effective guide for future action. For some time after the formulation of the goal, the neural connections supporting it remain quite weak. They become stronger as they are used more frequently – that is, they must be activated as often as possible in order to allow the desired behavior to be initiated automatically in the future (Krause and Storch 2014, p. 101 f.). ZRM researchers have found that it takes at least 4 weeks before goals can be translated into automated actions (Krause and Storch 2014, p. 186).

6.3.3 Phase 3: Activating Resources | Self-Motivation

Activation of the new neuronal network associated with the goal is tied closely to the activation of the client's inner resources. Everything the client does to motivate himself is resource activation. Thus, we must find these resources and make them accessible. There are a number of different kinds of resources that can be activated, including but not limited to motives. Coaches, counselors and even regular well-trusted people can help the client identify these resources. For example, the following resources can be repeatedly and persistently used to stimulate the desired new actions:

Activating motives What motives can I activate in order to achieve the goal? Every motive is capable of supporting self-motivation and the realization of desired action. The more strongly expressed the motive, the greater the likelihood that it will be linked with positive experiences and emotions, and thus the better suited it will be to support the realization of the goal.

Example: Gaining confidence in front of an audience
The manager could use his very strongly expressed SOCIAL PARTICIPATION motive as a resource. Before his talk, he could deliberately seek out small talk with the audience. This suits his natural inclination, he enjoys it, and he's good at doing it. The motive is an effective resource for reducing his anxiety and building up his self-confidence. He probably hasn't done this in the past, as he has been focused on his talk right up to the point of his appearance.

Identifying relevant capabilities, competences and interests A wide variety of existing capabilities, cognitive competences and interests can be connected to achievement of the goal. The idea here is that the client undertakes a purposeful inventory of his strengths, such as expert knowledge or existing talents. The systematic development of skills can also support the process.

Example: Gaining confidence in front of an audience
As an example, the manager could take a training course in mindfulness, presentation strategies or rhetorical techniques.

Establishing unconscious reminders Thanks to the priming process, people can set stimuli for themselves that they associate with their personal goal. In this way, they can consciously prime the desired behavioral reaction, enabling it to take place automatically. Unconscious reminders should trigger implementation of the goal. In this process, the personal goals are associated with positively regarded everyday objects, and thus literally "objectified."

Example: Gaining confidence in front of an audience
The manager has set himself the goal of radiating self-confidence. He could expand upon his goal with an image drawn from his store of experience: "grand as a giraffe." He has many positive associations with the idea of giraffes, including some from his exceptional experiences while on vacation in South Africa. This is where he came to understand the giraffe as a magnificent, self-confident animal that lives in closely connected groups (thus triggering his strongly expressed SOCIAL PARTICIPATION motive and weakly expressed AUTONOMY motive). The manager can fill his daily environment with images of giraffes in a variety of ways: for example, with a giraffe keychain, a T-shirt depicting a herd of giraffes, a mobile-phone screen background and a computer password. These memory aids could also serve as goal-triggering stimuli – for example, shortly before giving his talk, the manager could turn on his mobile phone, think about his goal and then begin the speech.

Using the body as support
The posture and motor processes can also be incorporated consciously into the efforts to achieve the goal. The idea of embodiment assumes that the body plays a key role in processing information. The body and psyche are constantly interacting with each other. The specialist literature contains numerous exercises that can serve as inspiration in this regard, often found under keywords such as "embodiment" or "body psychotherapy." However, when selecting suitable exercises, it is important to make sure they fit with the individual goal.

Make adjustments to the environment

It can also be beneficial to design one's everyday surroundings in such a way as to rid oneself of habits and automatic behaviors. In this regard, both the physical environment and ingrained processes can be changed.

Example: Gaining confidence in front of an audience

During a future speech, the manager could dispense with the lectern, which acts as a barrier between him and the audience.

Integrating the social environment

The social environment is a critical source of influence within everyone's personal life. We engage in constant interactions with family members, partners, friends and colleagues. It could be that our fellow human beings consciously or unconsciously stand in the way of our change processes. On the other hand, the social environment can also actively support the adjustment process. Thus, it makes sense to include the social environment in the plan for achieving the goal.

Example: Gaining confidence in front of an audience

After phase three is completed, the manager's newly refined goal might run: "Self-confident and grand as a giraffe, I step in front of my audience and shine like the sun in South Africa."

6.3.4 Phase 4: Anchoring Goals | Turning Intention into Action

In this phase, the intention to act is precisely formulated and linked to a suitable opportunity for action.

The wish, outcome, obstacle, plan (WOOP) method developed by Peter M. Gollwitzer und Gabriele Oettingen can be of use (Oettingen 2015) in this regard. In this method, one concretely imagines carrying out the action on the basis of four elements:

- A reachable goal (wish)
- A result (outcome)
- A potential barrier (obstacle)
- A strategy for overcoming the barrier (plan)

The resulting plan of action is formulated as an "if-then" statement: "If situation X occurs, then I will do Y." If-then plans associated with relevant personal motives become especially effective.

Figure 6.3 shows that in effective implementation, the specific occasion (obstacle) and a specific behavior (overcoming) are combined, with motivational resources also being engaged.

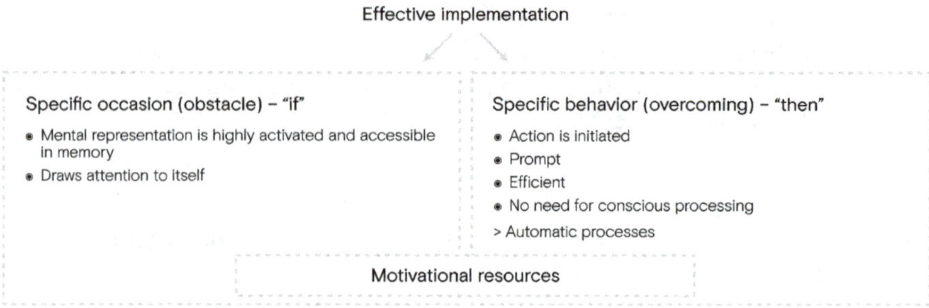

Fig. 6.3 How to anchor goals in if-then plans

Anchoring goals in a plan of action makes it easier to implement action-oriented intentions. This is in part because the action is carried out promptly, without further reflection, as soon as the occasion arises. In addition, the process helps people prepare mentally for obstacles and can make it easier to overcome them. Moreover, achieving the goal becomes fun, because the action satisfies the person's motives.

Example: Gaining confidence in front of an audience
The manager who wants to interact with the audience before giving his presentations in order to boost his self-confidence could face the following obstacle: Due to time constraints, there may be no opportunity for small talk with the public, because he arrives at the location at the last minute. Plan B could be: He opens his speech from the stage with a story about how he normally engages in small talk with the audience before he talks in order to reduce his nervousness. He can rehearse this plan B in such a way that he can carry it out with complete confidence. In this situation, a possible if-then plan might thus be: "If I can't engage audience members in small talk before my self-confident presentation, then I will use my well-rehearsed presentation opening." This approach is optimized by the use of primes, for example through this example's use of the giraffes.

The advantage of so-called if-then plans is that they trigger instant automatisms. The person can immediately seize the opportunity to engage in goal-oriented action. Studies have shown that intended behavior associated with if-then plans is implemented at a rate about 15–20% points higher than that of behavior lacking such associations (see, among other sources, the Bamberg 2002 study on environment-relevant consumer decisions, cited in Krause and Storch 2014, p. 177).

With if-then plans, desired behaviors can be immediately implemented and automated. They function best if they are combined with a person's personal motives.

6.3.5 Phase 5: Automatic Behavior | New Habits

A part of successful self-direction is a daily review of goals, progress along the path of change and opportunities for implementing the goal. The new behaviors can be primed – thus enabling them to run automatically even under stress or in unexpected situations – only through reflection and practice.

Example: Gaining confidence in front of an audience
The manager could keep a journal or use a mobile app to support his process of automation.

Visualizing the progress being made toward change and achievement of the goal is a critical step in the learning process. The brain needs this positive feedback to allow the action to be more easily activated and carried out the next time. In this regard, real, tangible rewards should be used – everyone knows what they are motivated by. A person can in this way learn self-regulation. He is able to bring both his behavior and his emotions under control.

The following example shows in abbreviated form how self-direction with ID37 can be a pragmatic means of effecting goal-oriented behavioral change in daily life.

Learning to say no
A young manager has set himself the goal of saying no more often. He finds it difficult to reject other people's requests. An explanation for this can be found in his ID37 personality assessment, which reveals a strongly expressed SOCIAL ACCEPTANCE motive, among other traits.

Previously, the young executive has accepted overtime hours because he has wanted to stand out, and because he was sure of receiving praise after the job was complete. However, the extra work has increasingly come at the expense of his private life. The manager feels he is being exploited and is unhappy. He decides to change his behavior, resolving not to take on additional projects in the future. His attitude goal is expressed as follows: "I delegate confidently." Drawing from this, he formulates his action goal: "Like a harbor master, I effortlessly manage the shipping traffic." The young executive has also found an analogy that he can use as a reminder: the estuary of a river. The main flow of the river branches into many side arms, all of which bring river water into the sea. He has distributed variations of this image within his environment both at work and at home.

With the help of his ID37 motives profile, he has come to understand why he tends to accede to other peoples' requests, and what obstacles need to be overcome. The young executive will not be able to prevent his employer and colleagues from continuing to ask him to carry out special tasks. However, he develops an if-then plan for such cases: "If someone comes to me with an

(continued)

additional task, then I break it into smaller jobs and confidently hand them off." It doesn't take long before someone comes to the manager with an internal project, and he utilizes his if-then plan. The manager delegates self-confidently, clearly displays his competence, and avoids alienating anyone. In this way, he even improves his reputation within the company. Without working significant overtime, he goes home satisfied and proud. The successful implementation of his goal gives him the recollection of having succeeded, and he experiences a sense of self-efficacy.

If the young manager uses this strategy to say no more often, the new behavior can become a habit that is initiated unconsciously. If there are setbacks on the way – perhaps because he doesn't succeed in rejecting the employer's first special request – he should reflect on and reappraise the situation. For example, he can identify disruptive patterns, break up his plan into steps of successively greater difficulty (starting with the smallest!) or draw on additional resources.

The initial inability to achieve a goal always provides an occasion for reflection. Analyzing the reasons for the setback can offer the opportunity to correct the goal or even develop an alternative goal. Regular reflection leads to improved self-perception.

6.3.6 What Does This Mean for My Professional Work?

The objective of the method described here, in which self-direction processes are implemented in five phases, is to lead people systematically to the point at which they can engage in effective self-direction.

A person who directs his own actions effectively is familiar with and understands his own personality and knows how to act in a self-determined way so as to achieve a state of well-being and satisfaction in his life. He is independent of external factors and other people such as colleagues, employers, coaches or life partners. That doesn't mean he won't utilize the support of others. On the contrary, social support can be very important in change processes.

Active self-direction is a conscious decision. Self-direction means having access to one's own resources, exploiting one's own potential, initiating personal changes and being able to act promptly without further thought. A self-directing person adjusts his actions to fit the environment and can thus act flexibly.

6.4 Case Studies from the Business World

The ID37 personality assessment offers a quick means of gaining knowledge about individual personalities. Despite the depth of information it provides, the motives profile is easy for the client to understand. The client receives an immediate assessment of his current situation and position in life, which serves as a reliable basis for further reflection. The ID37 Master is, in turn, able to grasp the core of his client's personality during the test-results assessment phase and can tailor his interventions accordingly from the very beginning.

For relatively simple questions, the information gleaned from the test-results discussion process may be able to deliver sufficient answers. For more complex situations, the analytical frame must be widened somewhat further. Because the personality diagnostic test itself takes relatively little time, coaches, counselors and managers can focus on developing individualized strategies and measures.

In the following, we describe specific cases from our own consulting practice in which the ID37 personality assessment made a successful contribution to self-direction, leadership behavior, the improvement of team performance or the management of human resources. In each of these case studies, the analysis of and reflection on the personality constituted the beginning of the solution.

6.4.1 Business Coaching

If business coaching is to be successful, integrating the client's personality into the process is of great importance. From nearly two decades of experience, we know that counseling is more effective when it is conducted on an individualized basis, tailored specifically to the client's personality. Only in this way can individually customized measures with lasting impact be developed.

6.4.1.1 Example: A Way out of the Dilemma

A self-employed business consultant had proved her competence and knack for large projects many times over. One day she received an inquiry from one of her most important clients. However, in her view, the offer was one of questionable morality. The job involved providing support to 100 executives as they laid off 10,000 employees. This rather short assignment, lasting about 15 consulting days, would be remunerated at a very high daily rate of pay. The consultant was not dependent on the financially attractive offer. However, it would give her the ability to focus on projects that were closer to her heart.

Challenge

The consultant felt torn when the inquiry arrived. She felt uncomfortable when thinking about the project and sought help in making the decision. She turned to us because we had carried out an ID37 analysis for her and had often afterwards helped her by serving as a sounding board.

Analysis of motives

The consultant's motives profile, which we ourselves revisited before the coaching call, showed strong expressions of the SOCIAL ENGAGEMENT (SEN) and PRINCIPLES (PRI) motives (Fig. 6.4). Thus, issues of social justice and morality were also very important to her. This led her to stop short of accepting the offer immediately. The motives profile additionally showed strongly expressed SOCIAL

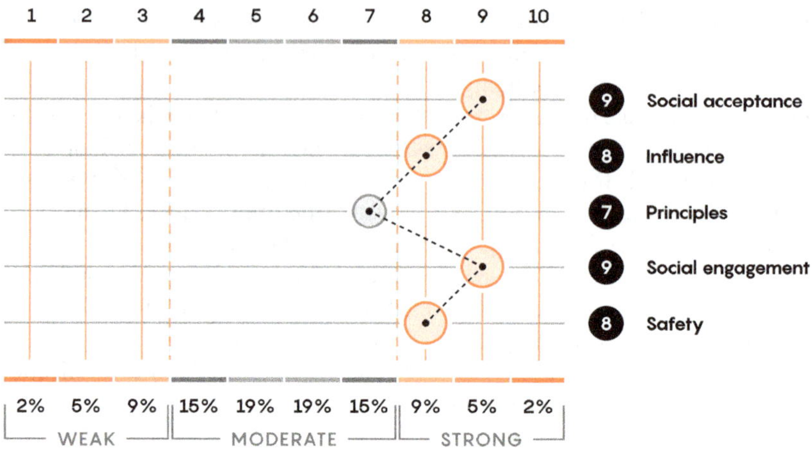

Fig. 6.4 Excerpt from the management consultant's motives profile

ACCEPTANCE (SAC) and INFLUENCE (INF) motives. The client's dilemma with regard to the proffered consulting offer was explainable on the basis of this motive conflict: On the one hand, she felt that her services were valued, given that the potential employer wanted to hire her for the project (SAC +). Moreover, the high level of responsibility associated with the project satisfied her need for influence (INF +). On the other hand, her high moral standards (PRI ±) and high level of idealism (SEN +) led her to reject the idea of profit-seeking at the workers' expense.

Solution

During the phone call, we were quickly able to uncover the source of her perceived inner turmoil. However, this was not enough to dispel the consultant's negative feelings. We suggested a thought experiment to her: "Imagine that you referred the project to other consulting colleagues and received a commission for doing so. "I couldn't do that," came her answer, quick as a pistol shot. "I'd be afraid I would never get the client back. That's exactly what happened to me once before, with another major customer. Besides, I don't like the idea that a colleague would be doing what is actually quite an exciting project."

Together we developed a second idea: The consultant could suggest that she leave after just 2 days, referring the client to an equally competent consulting colleague if she proved unable to deal with all the issues before that time." Now the consultant was enthused. With the proposal for an exit clause, she could conduct the discussions with a good feeling. She said this made her much happier. The consultant now had the feeling of working with a kind of safety net, a comforting sensation given her also strongly expressed SAFETY (SAF) motive.

Result

Within the course of a one-hour telephone call, we were able to clarify which motive constellation was the cause of the conflict, and help the client feel better about dealing with the situation. She regarded the solution we discussed as a psychologically valuable basis for her negotiations. She later told us that she had even enjoyed trying out the solution we had developed in our conversation. She was able to agree on an exit clause with the client and conducted the project in accordance with her ideas.

6.4.1.2 Example: Darth Vader Awakens

A young soccer player came to us with a request for a confidential conversation. Previously, we had conducted a team analysis for his professional club.

Challenge

The player was having a difficult time dealing with personal setbacks in the game. After making mistakes or sensing the slightest sign of criticism, he would fall into a mood of self-doubt that ultimately impaired his performance on the field. "If I get beat in the first one-on-one, and then again in another right afterward, and then make a few bad passes, the game's over for me." On some days, he said, he even wondered whether he was doing the right thing by playing professionally. "When the other team's fans boo me, it feels like I'm falling into a deep hole, and I ask myself if professional soccer is really the right place for me."

We suggested to the player, who was unquestionably an extremely talented athlete, that he work with his own resources and train himself in self-direction. We assured him that he could learn to reduce his on-field doubts. He agreed immediately.

Analysis of motives

The analysis of his motives profile confirmed that the soccer professional was highly sensitive with regard to his self-esteem (Fig. 6.5). His strongly expressed SOCIAL ACCEPTANCE motive (SAC +) had a direct impact on him exactly where it mattered most: on the field. Praise and recognition by important people, including the fans, soccer officials and supporters, gave him energy. By contrast, rejection, failures and the expectation of criticism inspired anxiety that undermined his performance on the soccer field. His strongly expressed SAFETY (SAF +) motive also helped increase his anxiety during the game.

Solution

Dealing with self-doubt became the primary subject of the consultation. Below, we describe some of the approaches used in our work together.

- The soccer player expressed the desire to be less vulnerable in the future. He already had a specific image in mind, which he formulated as the following attitude goal: "When I walk onto the field, I am the dark side of the Force."
- We helped him identify practical resources that would help him activate this positive attitude during the game. The Darth Vader character from Star Wars, who embodies the dark side of the Force, became his key prime. He even had a small Darth Vader symbol tattooed on his forearm; this could remind him of his goal at any time, such as when he needed a boost on the field. He also brought his parents

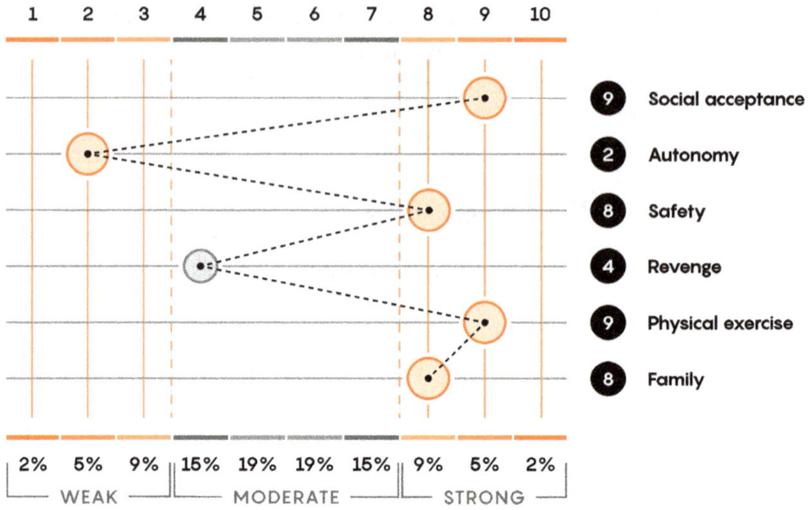

Fig. 6.5 Excerpt from the professional soccer player's motives profile

and sister into the conversation, as they had proved to be important resources in the past (FAM +). They accompanied him to his away games more often than previously and served as a point of reference in the stadiums during difficult situations.

- The professional soccer player also involved his coach, with whom he had a relationship built on trust. With the coach, we agreed on appropriate communications measures and actions, mainly revolving around the SOCIAL ACCEPTANCE, SAFETY and FAMILY motives. We provided the coach with tools he could use to give the player a boost before, during and after games (e.g., eye contact and thumbs-up gestures from the edge of the field).
- To ensure that the goals were properly anchored, the young pro athlete created an if-then plan simple enough to allow him to carry it out even in the hectic context of a game: "If I lose a one-on-one, I consciously breathe in deeply, and then let my breath out." He was able to practice this breathing technique during training sessions without the other players knowing anything about it. He called it his personal "Darth Vader awakening."

In our work with the player, we were continuously able to fine tune the intervention mechanisms. Together, we analyzed his emotional experiences in competition and practice settings. Although it took several weeks for his new attitude and the associated automatisms to take root, we were able to ensure even in the relatively early days that the young player felt himself to have an improved self-perception, and that his individual steps forward were producing a sense of self-efficacy.

Result

We didn't turn this person into a poker-faced, ice-cold "soccer warrior." Self-direction with ID37 is never aimed at changing the underlying personality. Rather, the soccer pro learned to deal with his fear of failure. He had the situation mostly under control, so that his on-field performance was less affected, and he could pursue his dream job as a professional soccer player with pleasure.

6.4.1.3 Example: Identifying and Activating Resources

A middle-aged architect had set up his own firm after completing his studies. His clients came predominantly from within the region. Good customer relationships were more important to him than expansion.

Challenge

During a period of economic crisis, the architect noted how difficult he found it to represent his own interests when dealing with his clients – especially when it came to negotiations over fees or supplementary payments, or when collecting late payments. He said he found it very difficult to refuse contracts or to justify saying “no” even to low-paying clients. The architect turned to us because he had the impression that something was wrong with him. In the interests of making a swift and precise diagnosis, we conducted an ID37 analysis with the architect. We also wanted to provide a fact-based demonstration that he had a normal personality.

Analysis of motives

During the assessment session, we were able to show why the architect found it difficult to say no to his clients or to demand payment from them (Fig. 6.6). His natural impulse was to avoid putting pressure on people (INFLUENCE –), and to try to eliminate any discord (REVENGE –). It was important to him to support people – preferably with good craftsmanship and the best possible architecture. This constellation, along with his weakly expressed AUTONOMY (AUT –) motive, showed how much he felt connected to people. He confirmed our analysis and stressed that he really was convinced that the only good business deal was one in which all sides were able to benefit. That’s what gave him the motivation he needed for his work. Against the background of this personality structure, it became clear why the architect was stressed if he had to turn down a contract that was attractive in terms of substantive content, but which would inevitably raise problems during the post-contract negotiations.

Solution

The architect was visibly relieved. He realized that while he certainly had a strong need for harmony, this was “normal” after all. He understood why his personality stood in the way of certain aspects of his work.

We agreed on three coaching sessions with the architect. In order to be able to fully live up to his responsibilities as the firm’s managing director, he would in the future have to draw on as-yet-untapped resources in his personality. To this end, we wanted to activate the SOCIAL ACCEPTANCE (SAC –) and PRINCIPLES (PRI –) motives.

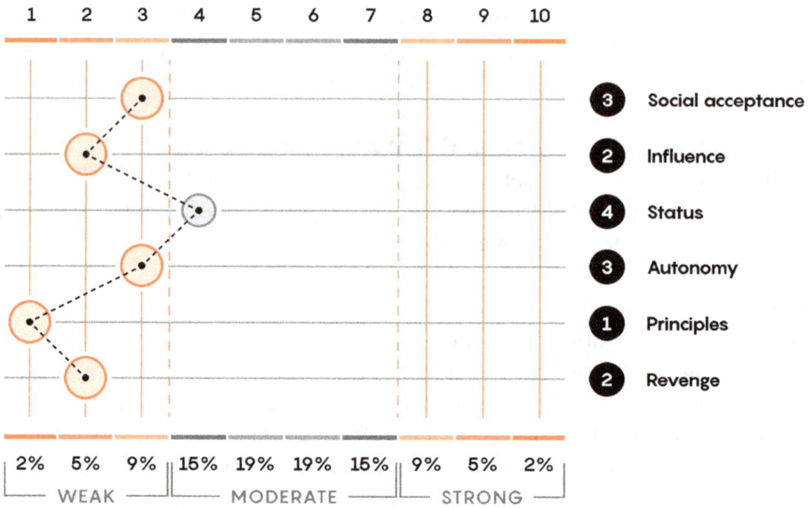

Fig. 6.6 Excerpt from the architect's motives profile

- Because the architect did not base his self-image on other people's opinions (SAC –), it was relatively easy for him to take clear stands. He had always handled himself this way when dealing with other professionals. Only with his customers, with whom he was always on close terms, was his self-confidence overshadowed by other, more strongly expressed motives.
- With his very weakly expressed PRINCIPLES (PRI –) motive, the architect showed a strong utilitarian orientation. Before every critical interaction with customers, he was able to prepare himself and clearly formulate the specific business-focused goal he wanted to pursue during the conversation.

With this focus, we developed a variety of mechanisms in the coaching sessions, refining them iteratively after he put them into practical use.

Result
When the client had approached us, he had prepared himself for long "therapy sessions" with an uncertain outcome, as he revealed at our last meeting. He was delighted with the swift and uncomplicated process of finding a solution that made a positive, sustainable change in the everyday course of his business. With the measures we developed together, the architect was able to work with a good feeling, and significantly more efficiently.

6.4.2 Managers and Leadership

Due to their executive function, managers have a high degree of responsibility for the survival of their organizations. Their task is to lead the company successfully into the future. Today, many executives face the challenge of exercising this responsibility in a dynamic and volatile business environment. As a result, they are more and more dependent on employees who act and make decisions on behalf of the company independently, with specialist responsibility increasingly distributed across many people with different skills and experience levels.

These demands require a modern understanding of leadership in which executives create the framework necessary for employees to be able to individually develop their performance potential. At the same time, they remain true to themselves – that is, to their personality.

Leadership cannot be viewed in isolation. It depends on a multiplicity of factors, including market conditions, company culture, the industry, the company's goals, the size of the company, and so on. The requirements associated with managerial roles are correspondingly diverse. Executive success depends on how one defines success; but this too depends on the context.

Thus, some successful managers are analytical, calculating and structured, while others are spontaneous, intuitive and volatile. Some are of outstanding intelligence, while others are simply average. Some are true workaholics, while others are more complacent. One may be open, approachable and extroverted, while the other is rather closed, shy and withdrawn. Effective managers are as different as people can possibly be. This in turn means that there can be no ideal leadership profile.

6.4.2.1 Example: Self-Reflection for Better Leadership Behavior

The owner and CEO of an automotive supply company contacted us, indicating that he wanted to work on his empathy. He briefly told us that in the last meeting with his managerial team, he had been the subject of some criticism. While extremely rare, statements such as "You put yourself above everybody, and don't bring anybody along with you," had led him to take this step.

Challenge

The company's owner embodied the third generation of family leadership for the company and headed the traditional firm alone. Within the company, he had adopted his predecessors' authoritarian leadership style. Rather than seeing himself as a monster, the CEO regarded himself as a man of clear words. Up until this point, he had seen no reason for a critical examination of his leadership style.

Analysis of motives

The motives profile showed a very weakly expressed SOCIAL ACCEPTANCE motive (SAC –) (Fig. 6.7). He was a self-confident person who was not used to questioning himself or imagining himself in another's position. His strongly expressed INFLUENCE (INF +), STATUS (STA +), AUTONOMY (AUT +) and REVENGE (REV +) motives further reinforced the dominant and distant impression he left with others. His position further led people to treat him as an authority figure, making it easy for him to accept these role-based expectations unquestioningly. The company owner had blind spots with regard to his personality and his understanding of leadership and performance.

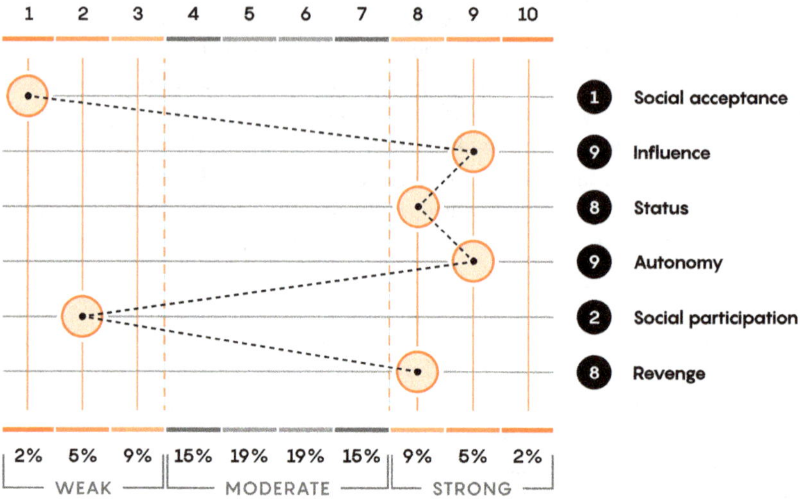

Fig. 6.7 Excerpt from the company owner's motives profile

Solution

During the assessment session, we were able to point out the businessman's blind spots to him. When we explained his SOCIAL ACCEPTANCE motive expression to him, he corroborated his weak motive expression, stating – for example – that "base flattery" had no place in the professional environment. He praised others by not criticizing them, he said. He was very satisfied with his assistant and was convinced that she herself also knew how good she was. After we talked to him about the self-perceptions of people with more strongly expressed SOCIAL ACCEPTANCE motives – for instance, explaining that they routinely compare themselves with their own aspirations, seek out and are willing to go to great efforts to get the appreciation of others, and are very sensitive to criticism – it became clear to him that his assistant often burst into tears because he had not praised her exceptional performance. He became thoughtful, and said that he needed good people, and didn't want to lose anyone. After the assessment session, we agreed on three coaching sessions, initially focused on deepening his ability to appreciate and recognize others. As an exercise, we gave the CEO text modules addressing the perception of self and others. In the subsequent sessions, we used role play to practice situations from daily managerial life and reflect on his motive expressions.

Result

At the end of the coaching sessions, the company owner offered this summary: "When I act in my comfort zone, others probably see me as the dominant, uncompromising and arrogant patriarch." A few sessions had been enough to make the executive aware of the impression he left with others, though he had not previously been aware of this. He realized that he could achieve more in his dealings with employees if he adapted his behavior to the situation, for example by praising his assistant's exceptional performance. He appreciated this insight a great deal. It took an outsider to identify his blind spots and patterns of behavior, and to point out their potential for conflict. With training, the company owner was successfully able to regulate his natural impulses. His reflective behavior made a significant contribution to improving the atmosphere at work.

6.4.2.2 Example: The Solution Lies in the Personality

Jordana, an executive who worked in the marketing division of an international corporation, was worried about her employee Tim. While capable of excellent professional work, the marketer seemed unmotivated and bored.

Challenge

After leading a large strategic international project, Tim had been back at his old job for more than 3 months. He was working on local campaigns, which required him to coordinate closely and in detail with colleagues from other departments. He was destructive and uncooperative with his colleagues. Jordana asked us what she should do to prevent Tim from becoming a problem for the marketing team, and how she could keep the highly skilled employee tied into the team. We discussed the situation with Jordana and suggested that Tim carry out an ID37 analysis. Just a few days later, Tim agreed.

Analysis of motives

Following the analysis of Tim's motives profile, it was clear that his emotional stressors concerned the SOCIAL ACCEPTANCE (SAC –), AUTONOMY (AUT +), STRUCTURE (STR –) and SAFETY (SAF –) motives (Fig. 6.8). His current job functions offered hardly any variety. He was learning nothing new and felt unchallenged. Tim was passive because he was working well beneath his ability level.

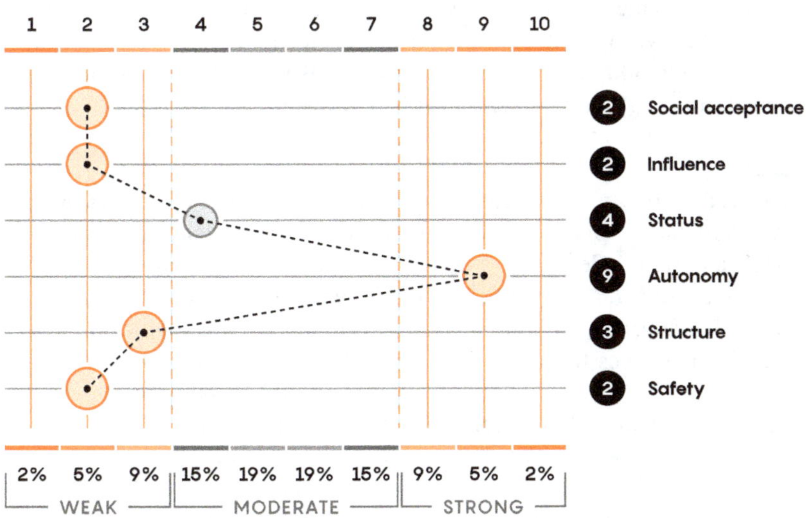

Fig. 6.8 Excerpt from the employee's motives profile

Solution

As Tim's manager, Jordana had to react and find Tim a challenging project as quickly as possible, or even find a way to expand his area of responsibility. As this can't be done overnight in an international corporation, we agreed with Jordana that she would show that she understood Tim's problem, and lay her cards clearly on the table. She should make clear to him that this situation would be no more than temporary, and that she would provide large projects or other opportunities for him. This perspective and the mention of a realistic time frame were important signals to Tim that she was taking her promises seriously.

Result

The ID37 analysis led Tim to examine his own personality and reflect on his current situation. He realized that he was an adventurer. For a long time, he had lived out this passion by traveling, and later on, in the job, had seized opportunities that suited him. He agreed with Jordana that he would take a six-month sabbatical. This time off gave Jordana the space needed to expand Tim's area of responsibility, and Tim was able to further satisfy his need for variety on his travels. Even before the details had been ironed out, Tim was noticeably more cooperative and invested, and tried to hide his boredom from the team. Because Jordana had recognized Tim's dissatisfaction with his unchallenging work at a relatively early date and had brought ID37 into use as an effective human-resources-development instrument, Tim did not leave the marketing team prematurely.

6.4.2.3 Example: Turning Skeptics into Allies

As a part of its digitalization process, a company was introducing agile working methods to its employees. In this context we were asked for advice by Jan, a manager at the firm. Jan had taken on the role of product owner. Among the team's members was Richard, who had formerly held a managerial position. Since the start of the company-wide change process, which had eliminated some levels of the executive hierarchy, Richard had no longer held a manager-level position. However, due to his considerable expertise in the area of software testing and quality assurance, he was an indispensable part of Jan's new team.

Challenge

After the team had worked together for a few weeks, Jan the product owner happened to overhear members of the team talking about Richard in a very negative way: "He's annoying! He's always complaining about something or other." Shortly thereafter, Richard and two members of his former team did not attend a review session. When Jan approached him, Richard blustered: "This whole transformation is a disaster. Nobody sees the big picture anymore, and it's only adding extra cost. I don't understand why this transformation is supposed to be a good thing … My former team … we were doing really well before all this started!"

Jan saw how frustrated Richard was by his loss of power. He also recognized the risk associated with Richard's declining performance levels, which could have potentially negative effects on the team's overall results and morale. He wanted to bring the former manager quickly back into the fold.

Analysis of motives

We agreed with Jan that he would ask Richard for a private conversation. Jan also set goals for himself, including:

- Respecting the former manager as an individual.
- Coming to agreement on conditions that would give Richard new motivation even in his new role.

To prepare for the conversation, Jan consulted Richard's ID37 motives profile. This was available to him thanks to an earlier joint leadership workshop (Fig. 6.9). The motives profile showed strongly expressed motives in the following areas: INFLUENCE (INF ++), STRUCTURE (STR +), SAFETY (SAF +).

Solution

Jan had identified the area of quality assurance as a sensitive point for the team. He thus wanted to steer the conversation with Richard in such a way that he could delegate this area to him, and ultimately entrust him with full responsibility for it. In this way, he could gratify two motives at once:

- Richard could once again feel that his INFLUENCE (INF ++) motive was being satisfied, and decide for himself whether he would make quick or thorough results available to the sales team, for example.
- Richard could also satisfy his strongly expressed SAFETY motive, and even utilize it as a valuable resource for the team. He had a fine sense for the point at which measurement results became risk factors, a talent that was very relevant for the full team's results. It was no accident that Richard was a specialist in the

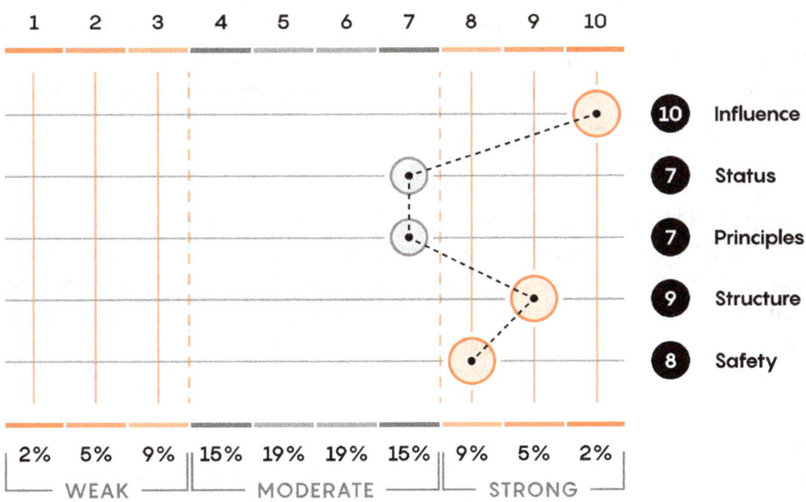

Fig. 6.9 Excerpt from the former manager's motives profile

area of quality assurance, as there was a high level of natural correspondence here (SAF +).

In preparation for the conversation, Jan also reviewed his own profile in order to reflect on possible blind spots. He recognized that his own weakly expressed STRUCTURE (STR –) motive was at odds with Richard's motive expression in this area. He therefore elected to make an effort to appear at the meeting on time and ensure that the conference table was clean. In addition, he resolved to make clear arrangements with Richard – as was important to Richard (STR +).

Result
Jan steered the conversation in such a way that he and Richard were able to work out a solution together. Jan promised to make the solution an agenda item for the next meeting, and to discuss it with the team. Jan's ability to act as a leader contributed to the successful outcome. The personality-oriented preparation of feedback discussions reveals relevant motives and interests, and allows them to be usefully addressed. This increases the likelihood of maintaining a mutually respectful atmosphere, while achieving a good, constructive outcome to the discussion. Jan had the ability to lead conversations skillfully and was very clear in his communication. He offered Richard an option that resonated both with the former manager's current situation and his personality. If Jan had not engaged with Richard's personality, the employee's resistant attitude would likely have persisted. Instead, Jan's proposed solution reinforced Richard's desired behavior. This sustainably increased Richard's self-motivation and willingness to perform, in turn improving the entire team's effectiveness and satisfaction levels.

6.4.2.4 Example: Understanding, Experiencing and Utilizing Team Diversity

A medium-sized international company was being restructured. A division with around 7000 employees was affected. A seven-person team was tasked with managing the change process, and leading it to a successful outcome. Within the new management team, a considerable amount of skepticism was evident, as the members did not know one another well.

Challenge
The company's top executives were aware of the new management team's potential. However, they were unsure how they could best unleash this potential. The team was expected to take up its work quickly – indeed, immediately after the official kick-off. Among other problems, there was still a lack of clarity with regard to the internal distribution of roles and tasks. We were commissioned to carry out a 2-day team-development session with ID37, to be held as part of the kick-off.

Solution
Because the team would have to work closely together and come to agreement in the future, it would be beneficial for them all to know from the beginning who they were working with. We formulated a number of goals for the workshop, including the following:

- Get to know each other better.
- Foster trust and a culture of open feedback.
- Clarify how the management team could exemplify a new project culture within the company at large.
- Activate the team members' resources.
- Explore possible future roles and responsibilities.

Three weeks before the workshop, we familiarized the participants with ID37, and showed how it could help in achieving goals. All participants were familiarized with the ID37 procedure before the workshop, and participated in discussions of their individual test results. All agreed to the disclosure of their profiles within the team. We then used the ID37 team overview, developed using the individual participants' profiles, as the basis for our workshop preparations (Fig. 6.10).

Excerpt from the workshop-design plan

Focus on similarities within the team

We analyzed the team composition and identified similar patterns of expression for the CURIOSITY (CUR) motive. No member of the team displayed a weak expression of this motive (Fig. 6.11).

	CUR	SAC	INF	STA	RET	AUT	SPA	PRI	SEN	STR	SAF	REV	PEX	FEN	FAM
P01	8	7	8	8	5	3	8	5	5	7	5	7	7	5	8
P02	9	5	9	8	8	3	8	5	5	9	9	8	8	10	5
P03	5	6	6	6	1	8	3	2	4	1	6	8	7	6	1
P04	6	8	6	6	9	4	2	3	2	4	4	7	8	5	6
P05	9	10	4	8	8	8	1	9	10	7	6	10	8	5	1
P06	8	3	5	7	1	5	5	1	3	4	5	3	6	2	1
P07	8	1	7	4	2	7	2	3	2	5	2	5	9	9	6

Fig. 6.10 Overview of all team members' motives profiles P01–P07. CUR curiosity, SAC social acceptance, INF influence, STA status, RET Retention, AUT autonomy, SPA social participation, PRI principles, SEN social engagement, STR structure, SAF safety, REV revenge, PEX physical exercise, FEN food enjoyment, FAM family

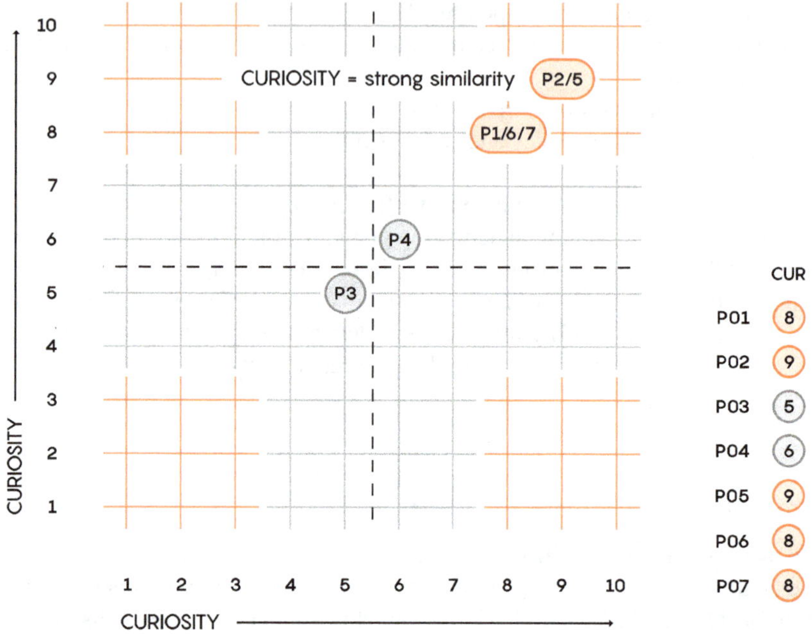

Fig. 6.11 Similarity across the team with regard to the CURIOSITY (CUR) motive

Exercise: Developing ways for the employees to talk to each other

- **Analysis result**
  The CUR motive represents a common resource for the team.
- **Exercise**
  The participants were given 10 seconds apiece to assess the following statement using a simple grid: "When contemplating the relationships between certain events, I find… ". The results were grouped in order to make trends clear.
- **Goal of the exercise**
  - To reflect on the team-analysis results for the CUR motive.
  - To help participants find a channel through which to understand and communicate with one another.

Expectation The members would presumably find a common platform for motivation in the CUR motive. For example, everyone could immerse themselves in specific topics, experience similar emotions in doing so, and find a common language through the development of knowledge and insights. However, the common platform also carried the risk of blind spots:

- During the course of daily work, the team could get caught up in endless discussions of their new insights; as a result, it could fail to make decisions in a timely manner, while coming to see itself as a knowledge elite.
- Possible self-perception by the team: "We are smart, interested and spirited."
- Possible external perception of the team: "Our new management team is overly intellectual, lacks basic common sense, and is both complicated and overly didactic."
- The team could come to regard other teams, such as operational units, as unintellectual and unintelligent.

During the workshop, the team agreed to take measures designed to ward off these possibilities.

Transfer into practice The team members decided to create a fixed agenda item for their meetings in which they would reflect on the issue of CURIOSITY.

- As a reminder that the CURIOUSITY motive might be weakly expressed in others, they developed a toolbox symbol that symbolized craftsmanship and an action orientation.
- Within this agenda item, each manager would report on how they had communicated and implemented decisions in practice.

Focus on internal team differences

The team analysis made clear that there could be a possible outsider on the leadership team, and that this could lead to conflicts and performance constraints (Fig. 6.12).

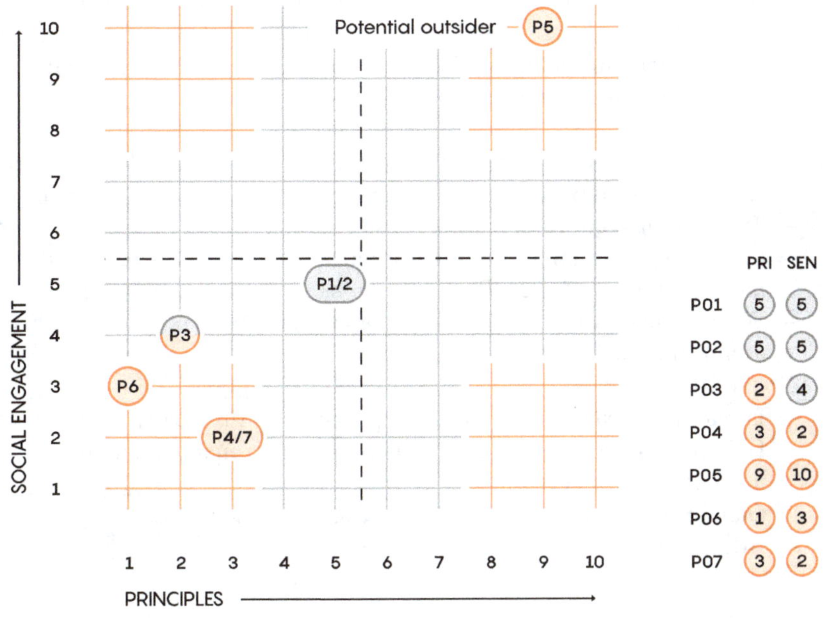

Fig. 6.12 Motive breakdown: PRINCIPLES (PRI) and SOCIAL ENGAGEMENT (SEN)

Exercise: Experiencing emotional distance

- **Analysis result**
  - With strongly expressed PRINCIPLES (PRI +) and SOCIAL ENGAGEMENT (SEN +) motives, team member P05 differs significantly from the others.
  - Given the variance in these motive constellations, P05 and the other managers live in different worlds with regard to those values.
- **Exercise**
  - The participants arrange themselves around a sufficiently large area according to the strength of their PRI and SEN motive expressions.
  - The group members talk among themselves (Fig. 6.12). In this way, it becomes clear that the "outsider" can't hear what is being said.
- **Goal of the exercise**
  - Make the outsider role symbolically clear.
  - Show what emotional distance feels like.

Exercise: Experiencing self-perception and external perceptions

- **Analysis result**
  - P04 and P05 have strongly expressed SOCIAL ACCEPTANCE motives (SAN + subgroup), while P06 and P07 show weak expressions (SAC – subgroup) in this area.
  - In a crisis situation, for example, P06 and P07 might take a harsh tone with fellow employees. By the same token, the weekly meeting could become uncomfortable for P04 and P05 due to the lack of mutually appreciative interactions.
- **Exercise**
  - Tandem pairs were assembled, each member of which differed significantly from the other with regard to the strength of their motive expressions.
  - The pairings talked about their strong and weak expressions, for instance by describing life situations in which they had perceived these motives at work, along with the emotions they had felt at the time.
  - We provided documents on self-perception and the perception of others as aids for the discussions.
- **Goal of the exercise**
  - Increase participants' awareness of self-perception versus external perceptions.
  - Help participants bring out aspects of their personalities that they had not previously perceived.
  - Gain insight into and respect for colleagues' value worlds.
  - Address differing emotional responses.

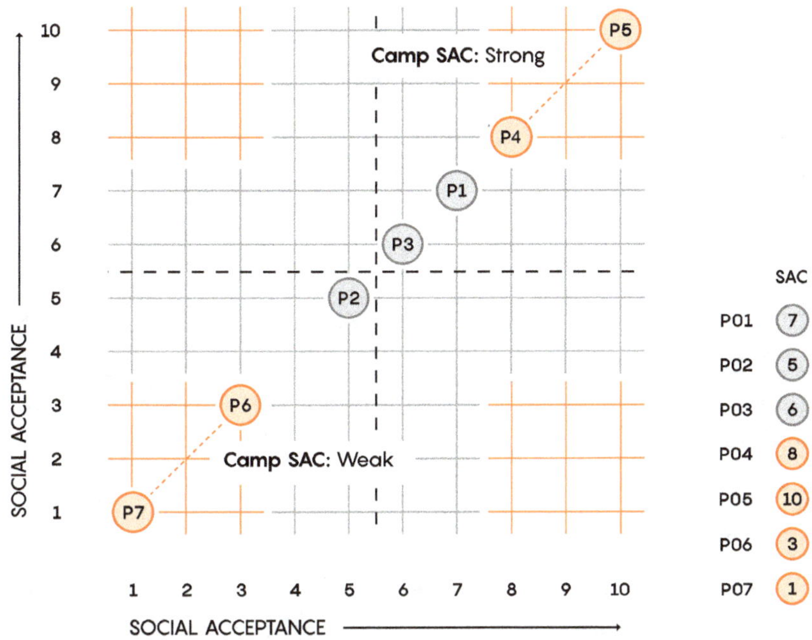

Fig. 6.13 Differences across team members: Possible factionalization between P04 & P05 vs. P06 & P07. SAC Social acceptance

Transfer into practice P05 has the greatest sensitivity to moral and social issues. The team decided that P05 could at any time initiate a "morals discussion" if he felt uncomfortable.

Focus on factionalization

The team profile also indicated a risk of a possible factionalization, or division into internal groups. The expectation was as follows: There could be problems with regard to issues of feedback, criticism handling, and the development of a failure-tolerant culture (Fig. 6.13).

Transfer into practice P04 and P05 should always show a literal yellow card when they feel their colleagues' tone with other employees is out of bounds, making them feel uncomfortable. In addition. P02 and P03, with their middling-strength motive expressions, should act as mediators.

Focus on diversity as a strength

We considered how the team's diversity of motive expressions could be used as a strength. We identified SAFETY (SAF) as the motive with the greatest potential in this regard (Fig. 6.14). Here, P02 and P07 showed the greatest distance between the strength of their motive expressions.

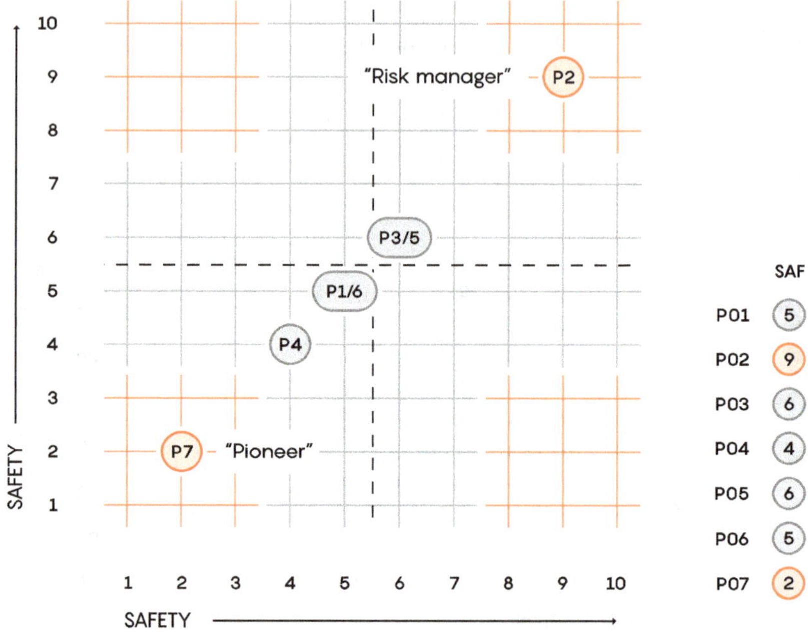

Fig. 6.14 Cross-team diversity in the SAFETY (SAF) motive

Transfer into practice P02 and P07 were assigned two different roles:

- P02 became the "risk manager," because he was quite sensitive to possible risks (SAF +).
- By contrast, P07 became the "pioneer," because he was open-minded and had what amounted to a radar for new opportunities (SAF –).

Because P02 and P07 were two very different personalities, we created a profile comparison that visualized this for the purposes of practical work activity (Fig. 6.15).

Result

The skepticism toward one another was transformed into acceptance over the course of the workshop. The experience of transparency regarding the team's diversity created a lasting openness among the participating managers. The team's members came to understand different behavior and different leadership styles. Through the workshop, the team of executives developed a shared language for feedback and conflicts, and they created an initial set of mechanisms for respectful interaction. Regular reflection became a fixed routine. Following the workshop, the team's work together developed into an effective collaborative operation and had a positive impact on the entire organization. The example shows that a team's ability to work together depends significantly on how openly the members deal with one another. Moreover, it demonstrates that mutual understanding can be trained.

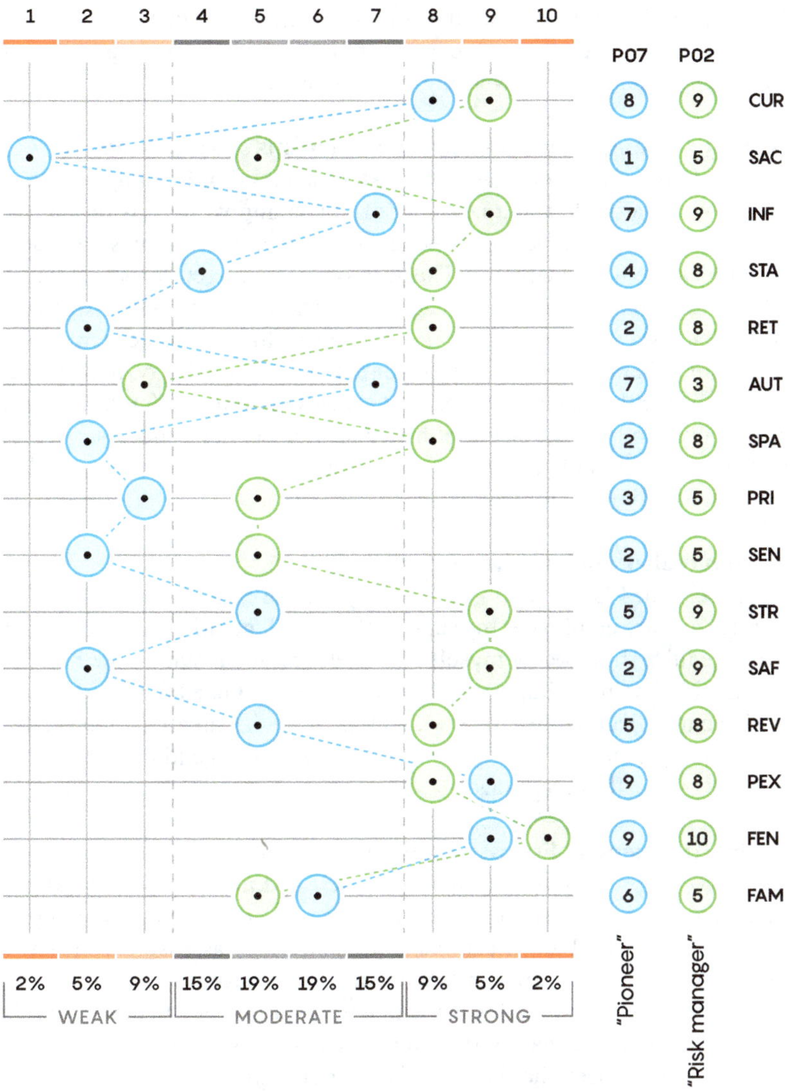

Fig. 6.15 Comparison between the "risk manager" and the "pioneer"

6.4.2.5 Interview: Heavier on the Support, Lighter on the Instructions

In the summer of 2020, we conducted a conversation with consultant Michael Kloss about the use of the ID37 personality assessment as a leadership instrument. We wanted him to tell us how he uses the analytical tool in the course of his daily life as a manager. Kloss is a partner at IT consultancy Conciso. In this position, he holds managerial responsibility within the company. For clients, he generally serves as an agile coach, supporting teams that are introducing and optimizing agile working practices. Before joining Conciso, the computer-science graduate held a variety of agile leadership roles. As a result, he is very familiar with the requirements of effective team management in new working environments.

You've been working in agile working environments since 2006 and have helped shape them. How would you define the task of leadership in an agile context?
Agility is both an attitude and a new way of organizing work. It is primarily about having direct contact with the client and engaging in rapid learning so that the entire organization can remain adaptable. This mindset has a direct impact on the character of teamwork and the job of management: The manager acts as the so-called servant-leader. As a service provider for employees, the servant-leader creates conditions enabling them to develop their potential in an optimal way. In this regard, no two employees are the same, and everyone needs something different. As a servant-leader, it is my job to identify these differences, provide the necessary resources, and do everything possible to allow every employee to do their job as well as possible while developing their potential.

How do you realize your role as leader?
As an agile coach, I help teams continuously improve themselves. As a manager, I'm there to give my employees the support they need, not to give them instructions. Both roles require that I know myself very well and understand how I affect other people. The first and most important thing is therefore: I need to start with me. This means I have to reflect on myself as well, along with the situations I experience. To do this, it is important that I can identify what perspectives and hypotheses are arising from my own self-perceptions.

How is the ID37 personality assessment useful in this process?
For one, ID37 helps me remain aware of myself and my own perceptual filters. It also helps me get a good sense for what makes individual employees tick – and quickly. If I know who I am, I can make a much better assessment of how others differ from me and how we are similar. Having the opportunity to look at a situation through someone else's eyes helps me with my consulting practice every day, allowing me to get right to the heart of the client's issues. This opens numerous doors. In this way, we can replace what is otherwise just an ominous gut feeling with a language that helps us reach our goal faster through dialogue.

And what does that mean for team management?
This is particularly exciting for work with teams, because I can help reveal the group's many facets. The ID37 work I've previously done with teams shows that the basic level of tolerance shown by team members rises when we conduct a team analysis beforehand, and then work openly with the findings. The benefits are clear: Everyone becomes aware of blind spots – both their own and those of others. This allows people to deal with them more consciously, which in turn reduces unnecessary friction. This applies even when dealing with experts or customers. In such cases, a person can get advice from team members with other motive constellations,

who may be able to understand a situation emotionally or simply better. In the IT world, it is quite a new thing to attach value to communication and dealing openly with emotions. As our lives become increasingly digitalized, the tasks and challenges we face are becoming increasingly complex and thus require more coordination and joint action. The degree to which a team is functional or dysfunctional often plays a critical role in a product's ultimate market success. This question is thus also a vital one for many companies. That doesn't mean that tools like ID37 are immediately accepted. However, my experience is that people increasingly open up as soon as they have experienced the associated benefits – that is, when they find it easier to communicate and feel that they're being understood.

What experiences with the instrument have impressed you the most?
A key experience for me was the discussion of ID37 test results with a client whose strongly expressed INFLUENCE and REVENGE motives had entirely overshadowed his equally strongly expressed SOCIAL ACCEPTANCE motive during the course of his daily work. I had known this client for some time, but it had never occurred to me that this person needed recognition. Only during the assessment session did it become clear to me that a lack of recognition also helped explain why he was dissatisfied with his job. No one ever said to him, "That was really good work." His managers gave him no praise. We worked out a way in which the client himself could take action when he needed recognition. He later told me that the analysis had made a number of things clear to him, and that it constituted a genuine turning point in his life.

What added value does ID37 bring to Conciso?
We can better understand and support employees for whom we have carried out personality assessments. Of course, it's up to each person whether they want to create their own motives profile or not. However, we've noticed that interest in the topic is increasing. Personally, I think this approach is well-suited to the members of Generation Y that we look for as employees. Take the example of an employee with a strongly expressed FAMILY motive. Nothing could be worse than sending this employee to a client located 500 kilometers away for 5 days out of the week. Knowledge about our employees' individual life preferences helps us to create an environment that suits them to the greatest degree possible. It's especially important in the consulting business to have satisfied employees. The more satisfied our consultants are, the more energy they have, and the more well-adjusted they are. Customers appreciate this too.

How does it benefit you personally?
In order to train in something or improve myself, I have to know what my shortcomings are. Thanks to my ID37 personality profile, I know that I have a very weakly expressed STRUCTURE motive, for example. If someone tells me I ought to be more orderly and less volatile, I can respond less emotionally than I have in the past, because I know that structure is probably much more important for them than it is for me. I've come to understand where I have to begin work and can train myself to

recognize this kind of situation. This allows me to rein in my initial response, and instead adjust my response to the situation – especially since I'm meant to act as a role model in my position as a manager.

How long have you worked with ID37?
I've been an ID37 Master since the very beginning, since I switched over as a Reiss Motivation Profile Master. Altogether, I've been working with personality diagnostics on a continuous basis for nearly a decade. For me, the most important thing about ID37 is its ability to render the multifaceted dimensions that express our individuality. I'm also convinced that this tool – which was developed with the University of Luxembourg – will remain relevant well into the future.

Last but not least: Is there anything else you'd like to add?
The agile working method is based on three key pillars: transparency, inspection and adaptation. That means you make a careful inspection of what happens, and then adapt your subsequent processes based on what you've learned. This requires embracing transparency to make sure you're seeing the whole picture. If we want to apply this in the context of our work, how can we avoid doing it with ourselves? The three principles can be applied wonderfully to ourselves: Above all, ID37 provides me with transparency and helps me – on the basis of these three principles – to develop continuously, thereby strengthening my flexibility and adaptability as a person.

6.4.3 Human-Resources Management

In the competition for skilled workers, personality diagnostics tools constitute a key factor in the development of an effective human-resources (HR) strategy. For example, personality diagnostics can be integrated in the HR strategy in order to place talent management on a more objective basis: from attracting the right skilled workers and executives to facilitating their personal development and retaining them as employees once they're in the fold.

6.4.3.1 Example: The Candidate Is King: Successful Employer Branding

A growing company specializing in IT consulting and software development was desperately looking for experts in highly sought-after specializations. The competition for IT architects, experienced programmers and software developers was intense. The quickly growing consulting company was a newcomer to the market and was thus not widely known.

Challenge
The consulting company had to convince and inspire potential candidates from the very first minute. The founders of the company placed great value on making sure that every contact, even in the application submission and processing phases, was

very professional and positive, thus communicating the young company's respect-oriented internal culture.

Solution

The company understood that it could use the recruiting process as an advantage for itself. This started even before applications were submitted. In order to establish good contacts with potential employees and maintain the number of qualified applications at a high level, the company worked closely with the local technical university. It awarded projects and student jobs, and was an active sponsor of in-house fairs. Potential candidates thus had early good experiences with the company.

The application process itself was quite fast and took place online. Candidates were able to get to know the consultants on the company's website, giving them a picture of the people who were doing the consulting. Internally, the company's philosophy was that company culture constituted an essential aspect of recruitment. If a candidate was invited to an interview, he met with one of the company founders as well as with various project teams. The technical discussions were carried out using a team-interview approach. On the one hand, this was intended to let the candidates experience the company as transparently as possible; on the other, it allowed the consultants to get an impression of the candidate and provide feedback.

The consultancy has used the ID37 personality assessment since the company's founding. Particularly during the introductory training phase, it had proved itself with respect to helping new employees integrate into the quickly growing company as swiftly as possible, and had helped optimize collaboration within teams. This issue was thus specifically addressed during the face-to-face interview. If the recruitment process proved successful, the new hire was given the opportunity to create his own ID37 personality profile. This was a voluntary measure. However, it had proved to be a valuable means of giving people a smooth start in the company. It allowed every consultant to be authentic from the beginning, and it facilitated integration into existing project teams. Using the personality profile, performance reviews could be individually designed, with development and support measures tailored to the individual.

Result

The hiring process, including the onboarding phase, was very professional, and helped employees become familiar with the organization's culture very quickly. Similarly, it helped outsiders come to perceive the company as an attractive employer at an early phase of the process. Over time, a custom developed in which unsuccessful applicants who had visited the office in person remained in contact with the consultancy through a "talent community." The message implicit in this process, that employees were valued and treated as individual personalities, ultimately got around. The application and employee-integration process developed into an important employer-branding instrument for the young consulting company.

6.4.3.2 Example: Staff Recruitment and Development: Choosing the Right Candidate in an Unbiased Way

When new candidates are hired or employees promoted, sensitivity and professionalism are required. According to human-resources consultant Claudia, however, hiring interviews are not always prepared and conducted professionally. Claudia can look back on a 25-year career in various HR positions, and was one of the first ID37 Masters that we trained.

Challenge

From the HR consultant's point of view, several aspects of the employee search and selection process are challenging. "Many of those in charge of these processes fail to think beyond the competences and soft skills a candidate needs to have. What's missing is a holistic picture of the desired personality, especially if selection interviews aren't going to be held. In addition, as someone making decisions about future employees, I have to understand myself and my blind spots. What do I tend to particularly focus on? Otherwise, I'm a slave to my own biases, and unconsciously prefer candidates who have a stable full of kids just because I'm also a family-oriented person. Or I disqualify someone because they're not as interested in sports as I am. These factors have absolutely nothing to do with the job. But no one can ever really shake their first impressions – even HR professionals like us," said Claudia, explaining the difficulties of hiring interviews to us.

Solution

"I advise my clients to have a clear strategy, and to use personality diagnostics tools when choosing new employees." In this regard, Claudia recommends creating a personality profile not for the candidates, but for those who are making the staff-selection decisions. "When the decision-makers are familiar with themselves and their preferences, they are better able to free themselves of the influence of their first impressions. This allows them to remain more open during the interview, and focus on the real requirements," Claudia said. Claudia herself works with ID37.

The knowledge gained through examination of one's own person is also valuable with regard to being better able to assess the candidates, he said. For example, an applicant's statements can be used to check whether he really worked closely with his employees as a manager in the past, and to determine what kind of leadership he would be likely to show in the future. The question of what traits a candidate should have can also be clarified through the use of a personality diagnostics procedure.

From the HR consultant's point of view, the most important factors in making good staff-selection decisions are well-thought-out job-requirement profiles, interviews that are well prepared and HR decision-makers that are able to reflect on themselves. ID37 is a very useful tool for the preparation and conduct of interviews, she said.

Result

Choosing the right employees is a critical task, with every hiring decision demanding a high level of confidence. Every wrong decision produces expense for the company, may lead to conflict within specialist teams or with customers, and is unpleasant for the new hire. Thus, the work with ID37 has proved its value for the HR consultant's clients. They appreciate the well-founded information that the procedure produces. Unfortunate staffing decisions can happen anyway, but the use of personality diagnostics instruments reduces their likelihood. This is because the use of such a tool requires those in charge of human resources to think extensively in advance about what they are looking for, and to ask themselves where they themselves may have blind spots. Claudia reported that this new approach has helped give her a high referral rate as an HR consultant.

6.5 How to Recognize when Working with ID37 Is Successful

The results of the ID37 personality assessment rarely leave anyone unmoved.

Work with ID37 is successful when the person receiving the profile:

- Recognizes himself in his motives profile and accepts it.
- Has gained self-knowledge with regard to his own thinking, experience and actions.
- Is willing to engage in self-reflection.
- Understands that other people think and feel differently.
- Engages in more nuanced and unbiased thinking about other people.
- Gives more attention and respect to people as individuals.

Working with ID37 is beneficial if only because of the reflexive processes it triggers. Without self-knowledge, no self-reflection is possible. Without self-reflection, individually tailored goals cannot be set. And without goals, no personal development is possible.

However, it takes some practice to clarify and formulate truly tailor-made personal goals.

6.6 The Path to ID37

The ID37 personality diagnostic offers a scientifically sound approach that can be integrated into existing consulting, coaching or training concepts, while also opening new opportunities. Ideally, the motive-oriented ID37 analysis would represent the beginning of a personal-development process. Professional ID37 users must purchase a license, the so-called ID37 Master license.

Prerequisites for purchase of an ID37 Master license

Professionals with training in coaching, consulting, psychology or related fields, as well as HR managers, executives and team leaders can expand their qualifications by becoming ID37 Masters.

The use of ID37 has proved its practical value for:

- **Coaches** – who help people cultivate equanimity and find balance in their lives or achieve greater satisfaction in life.
- **Consultants and business coaches** who help people navigate change and transformation processes.
- **Trainers** involved in vocational training and personal development.
- **HR managers and personnel developers** – who work on creating new recruiting processes and are responsible for talent management.
- **Executives** who want to deepen their knowledge about people, because they are creating new organizational structures, introducing new roles in their companies or are themselves contemplating a career change.
- **Teams** that want to organize themselves so that overall team performance is optimized on the basis of individual traits.

Certification as an ID37 Master

Through the training process, the ID37 Master gains the requisite knowledge and the license that allows him to work professionally with the ID37 personality diagnostics instrument and integrate this instrument into his own business model. Prior to the training, we conduct a personal ID37 analysis with each participant in order to make them aware of their motive architecture and drive structure. This then allows them to reflect on this information in the context of their professional role.

Thematic modules in the ID37 Master certification course

- Basics of motivational psychology: How motives, motivation and behavior function.
- In-depth insight into the theory of motives, based on the findings of the University of Luxembourg, as well as on background research.
- Effect and impact of the individual personality in daily life and in work processes.
- Analysis of personality profiles based on case studies.
- Understanding the interaction of motives in individual contexts, identifying behavioral patterns.
- Usage formats and areas of application: Employee management, leadership, teams, agile working environments.
- Holistic self-direction: Effective self-management
- Structuring the assessment session and training for this process.

ID37 Master training

ID37 Masters have the opportunity to train further with us on a regular basis, while exchanging ideas and experiences with other personality experts within our network. Currently, there is a network of around 900 Masters in Germany who are working with the University of Luxembourg's personality diagnostics instrument (data valid as of 2018).

Get your personal motives profile
On the website www.ID37.io, any interested person can create their own personal ID37 motives profile.

References

Chlupsa, C. (2017). *Der Einfluss unbewusster Motive auf den Entscheidungsprozess*. Wiesbaden: Springer.

Hossiep, R., & Weiß, S. (2017). Testverfahren II: Persönlichkeit und personenbezogene Attribute. In D. E. Krause (eds.), *Personalauswahl* (pp. 159–180). Wiesbaden: Springer.

Krause, F., & Storch, M. (2014). *Selbstmanagement – ressourcenorientiert* (5th ed.). Bern: Huber.

McKinsey Germany, Project Management, Raabe, N., & Holleben, K. V. (2011). Wettbewerbsfaktor Fachkräfte. https://www.mckinsey.de/files/fachkraefte.pdf Accessed 25 Mar 2018.

Oettingen, G. (2015). *Die Psychologie des Gelingens*. Munich: Pattloch.

Schreier, C., et al. (2010). *Die geheime Sprache der Produkte*. Freiburg: Haufe.

Westerhoff, N. (2009). Könnte, müsste, wollte. *Gehirn & Geist, 10*, 20–26.

Wikipedia. (2018). Priming. https://de.wikipedia.org/wiki/Priming_(Psychology). Accessed 25 Mar 2018.

7 Epilogue

We have taken a deep look into the topics of drive, satisfaction and success, and explained how this trio of factors interrelates to achieve optimum interaction within a person. It is impossible to grasp the uniqueness of any given individual in its entirety. But exploration of an individual personality is absolutely worthwhile, whether for the purposes of personal development and acquiring the ability to self-direct, or in order to support others in this goal.

Those who understand people on an individual level can help them reach greater levels of self-direction, performance and life satisfaction.

We regard the following takeaways as particularly important:

1. Every person is unique – their distinct personality shapes their thought, feelings and actions.
   - Everyone behaves as their personality determines. Interaction between a person and their environment also influences their behavior.
   - Behavior is observable, but it does not allow precise conclusions to be drawn about the personality.
   - People differ significantly with regard to their priorities and goals in life. This can lead to interpersonal conflicts.
   - All people are striving toward a state that they perceive as positive.
2. Motives, emotions and motivations are the drives that produce action.
   - Motives are the driving forces behind individual behavior. They explain why a person acts.
   - People develop patterns of behavior in order to satisfy their motives.
   - Motive expressions reveal people's priorities in life and indicate how intensively they want to satisfy them.
   - Positive emotions verify that a motive has been temporarily satisfied.
   - Negative emotions indicate a state of deficiency.
   - Intrinsic motivation arises from the pursuit of personal goals.

T. Staller, C. Kirschke, *Personality Assessment with ID37*,
https://doi.org/10.1007/978-3-030-53921-4_7

3. The ID37 personality assessment provides an accurate and empirically driven analysis of the personality on the basis of 16 motives.
   - The complex interplay of the 16 motives captures the uniqueness of a personality.
   - ID37 identifies the motives structure and individual life priorities on the basis of motive expressions. In addition, it:
     - Makes behavioral patterns visible.
     - Reveals potential intra- and interpersonal conflicts.
     - Identifies the potential for development and higher performance levels.
     - Illustrates how motives influence an individual's life situation.
     - Supports a person in defining individual strategies for personal development.
4. Knowledge of one's own personality is the prerequisite for self-direction.
   - Those who know themselves and are prepared to engage in reflection understand that other people are different from them.
   - Self-awareness helps people recognize their own motives, set suitable goals and initiate any necessary changes.
   - Overcoming obstacles to action requires self-direction.
5. Self-direction is the process of actively shaping one's life in order to achieve greater levels of satisfaction and success.
   - Purposeful regulation of one's own actions is possible. Anyone can learn to adapt their behavior situationally, as circumstances demand.
   - Satisfaction arises when the 16 motives are brought into alignment with one's personal goals.
   - Success is the achievement of personal goals.

Self-direction is about understanding yourself better, recognizing your own behavioral patterns on the basis of your motives and remaining able to act even in difficult situations. This includes having respect for others and maintaining an appreciation of their realities.

As a scientific model and pragmatic tool, the ID37 personality assessment serves as a starting point for people who want to develop self-awareness and learn self-direction. We want to inspire consultants, trainers, coaches, human-resources managers and executives to integrate ID37 into their work. ID37 makes it possible to respond appropriately to individual problems and demands. The goal of ID37-based consulting work isn't to change people, but rather to offer them support in their personal development. We want to encourage everyone to get to know themselves better, accept their individual personalities and lead the lives best suited to them.

> "One of the most notable characteristics of the ID37 personality assessment is the great respect it shows for the individuality of each person."

Individuality is something very beautiful. Exploring one's own personality is always worthwhile, as it is the key to greater satisfaction and success.

Glossary[1]

Action (→ Behavior) refers to goal-oriented behavior. The person and the situation are each decisive factors in the initiation of an action. The assessment of the emotional benefit promised by a situation can trigger an action or not.

Action goal (→ Automatization, → Attitude goal, → Intention) An action goal is formulated so that it can become an automatic action. An action goal is formulated as an approach goal, must be 100% under the person's own control, and must be associated with positive affects. Ideally, action goals will be defined only after an attitude goal has been formulated, and once sufficient will has been formed with regard to the goal (intention).

Affect (→ Emotion, → Feeling) Affects are a person's simplest emotions. They are either positive or negative, and provide information as to whether something is good (resulting impulse signal: repeat) or not (resulting impulse signal: avoid). Feelings, emotions and moods can develop from affects.

Affective (synonym: emotional) means marked or characterized by emotion.

Affect regulation s. Emotion regulation

Ant-Colony Optimization Algorithm (ACO) The Ant-Colony Optimization Algorithm is an algorithm for approximating the solution of complex optimization problems. The procedure is based on the behavior of ants as they forage for food.

Approach (synonym: Appetence; → Avoidance) Attraction or affinity A person engages in specific behavior because he wants to achieve a positive emotional state. According to motivation psychology, human behavior is driven by efforts

[1] This glossary explains terms that are frequently used throughout the book, and which are thus important to understand. It does not provide dictionary-style definitions. Explanation of abbreviations and symbols:

s. = the term is explained under another keyword's entry;
(→) = indication of a conceptual relationship to another concept;
(synonym) = reference to another common term with the same meaning.

T. Staller, C. Kirschke, *Personality Assessment with ID37*,
https://doi.org/10.1007/978-3-030-53921-4

to strive toward something positive (approach) or avoid something negative (avoidance). An approach-approach conflict refers to a conflict in which a person has the choice between two goals that appear equally important, for example, but which cannot be achieved at the same time.

Assessment session s. ID37 assessment session

Attitude goal (→ Automatization, → Action goal) An attitude goal is a goal that serves to provide orientation. It is generally formulated and is chosen so as to activate a person's memory of emotional experience. To automatize desired behaviors, it has proven useful to define an attitude goal first, and then translate this into a specific action goal as soon as the will to accomplish the goal has been generated.

Automatization In neuroscience, behavioral patterns are said to be automatic when they have been primed in the brain. They then become a habit, because synaptic connections between neurons have been strengthened through frequent activation. New behaviors can be trained so that they become automatisms, and can be performed unconsciously as a part of daily life. This is a useful tactic in situations defined by change. The ID37 personality profile makes motive expressions visible. These can be used as resources for targeted behavioral change.

Avoidance (→ Approach) The act of avoiding or withdrawing. A person engages in specific behavior because he wants to avoid a negative emotional state. According to motivation psychology, human behavior is driven by efforts to strive toward something positive (approach) or avoid something negative (avoidance). An avoidance-avoidance conflict refers to a conflict in which a person has the choice between two options that are both perceived as unfavorable, for example.

Behavior (→ Disposition, → Action) is observable. In most cases, this refers to a motor activity. Behavior varies from second to second, and unlike a behavioral disposition, does not allow precise conclusions to be drawn regarding the personality.

Behavioral pattern s. Disposition

Blind spot (→ Self-centeredness) refers to the phenomenon in which people are virtually blind to one or more characteristics within their own personality. Blind spots often lead to misjudgments of situations and cause inappropriate behavior. Through the use of motive profiles, ID37 Masters can help their clients become aware of possible blind spots and encourage self-reflection.

Confirmation bias (→ Self-centeredness) is the natural tendency by people to continually reconfirm their existing opinions and prejudices instead of seeking to question these. As a result, people mainly believe what they want to believe. This can produce perceptual distortions that may in turn lead to misunderstandings and conflicts.

Construct A construct is a state of affairs that can be deduced on the basis of observable data. For example, a motive is a construct in the context of the ID37 test procedure. Motives can be deduced through behavior.

Continuum A continuum is something that is seamlessly connected, such as a motive scale.

Disposition (→ Behavior) is a behavioral regularity or individual pattern of behavior shown by a person. Dispositions are based on relatively stable personality traits, and unlike behavior in a more simplistic sense, are suitable for the purpose of distinguishing or characterizing a personality. Individual patterns of behavior can be identified using the ID37 motive profile.

Drive (→ Need, → Emotion, → Motive, → Motivation) Drives have the objective of remedying a perceived state of lack or of satisfying needs. Motives, emotions and motivations are the primary drives that produce action. The ID37 personality profile makes some of an individual's important drives – their motives – visible. Knowing these facilitates the process of understanding that person's actions, identifying their individual life priorities and formulating behavioral predictions.

Dynamic perspective on personality (→ Personality) Personality is not a fixed construct; rather, it is dynamic and subject to constant change. Every person can change, but only within his frame of reference. The 16 motives describe the personal framework within which an individual personality can develop.

Emotion (→ Affect, → Drive, → Feeling) Emotions are short-lived states with both psychological and physiological components that play a vital role in the process of evaluation. They accompany the entire process of acting. Among other tasks, they guide a person's actions with regard to the satisfaction of needs and motives. For example, emotions indicate whether motives have in fact been satisfied (positive evaluation) or not (negative evaluation). The field of psychology makes a distinction between feelings and emotions.

Emotion regulation (→ Self-regulation) is the ability to regulate one's own emotions and moods. People who can regulate their emotions can influence what emotions they have, when they have them, and how these are experienced. Emotion regulation plays an important role in self-regulation.

Explicit motives (→ Implicit motives, → Motive, → Intrinsic motivation) are motives that are conscious and articulable. They are learned in childhood in the course of engagement with the social environment, represent the self-concept, and can be directly assessed, for instance through the use of questionnaires. A correspondence between implicit and explicit motives increases intrinsic motivation. The ID37 personality assessment identifies explicit motives.

Extrinsic motivation (→ Intrinsic motivation, → Motivation) is motivation that is triggered by external factors such as a material reward. The incentive to do something lies primarily in the consequences of the action.

Factor analysis Factor analysis is a procedure used in multivariate statistics. Factor analysis generally checks whether the statistical relations among the items from a test or questionnaire can be sufficiently explained by the anticipated factors.

Failure (→ Success) means that personally set goals are not realized. Failure is individual and will be experienced differently from person to person. One person might learn from their failures to do better the next time. Over the course of a long lifespan, the achievement of personal goals generally entails an alternation between success and failure. The ID37 personality profile offers clues as to how people deal with failure. This enables the development of individualized measures for handling failure.

Feeling (→ Affect, → Emotion) Psychology makes a distinction between feelings and emotions, but without offering a precise definition. However, a feeling is a pleasant or unpleasant state, and is a more complex form of affect. Feelings influence the organism in the sense that they trigger emotions. Emotions are perceptible as physical signals, while feelings are not or are only diffusely perceptible in this way. Moods arise when feelings persist over a long period of time.

Flow (→ Intrinsic motivation) In the flow state, a person is intrinsically motivated, and there is a high degree of fit between the activity and the requirement. In this state, a person is entirely immersed in the activity. He performs it without effort and is both satisfied and productive. Flow research and the concept itself were developed by psychologist Mihály Csíkszentmihályi, who explored how people can achieve happiness by establishing control over their own inner lives.

Goal Goals are the reasons why people decide at a certain point in time to initiate, carry out and terminate an action. Without goals, actions are unthinkable. When acting – for example when one wants to develop oneself further – a goal is necessary, or an idea of what one wants to achieve. The ID37 motive profile allows goals to be set that are self-congruent.

ID37 (synonym: ID37 personality assessment) ID37 is a psychological model and test procedure that describes a person's individuality on the basis of 16 distinctive motives. This is a new concept, developed at the University of Luxembourg in 2017. ID37 is based on current research findings. The 16 motives are: CURIOSITY, SOCIAL ACCEPTANCE, INFLUENCE, STATUS, RETENTION, AUTONOMY, SOCIAL PARTICIPATION, PRINCIPLES, SOCIAL ENGAGEMENT, STRUCTURE, SAFETY, REVENGE, PHYSICAL EXERCISE, FOOD ENJOYMENT, FAMILY and EROS. ID37 is a registered trademark of the ID37 Company.

ID37 assessment session (→ ID37 Master) The assessment session takes place after a test taker has completed the ID37 questionnaire and has received the computer-generated test results in the form of the individual motive profile. An ID37 Master conducts the assessment session. At its core, this is a matter of clearly describing the personality, identifying patterns of behavior, and understanding how the interaction of the 16 motives affects the individual's life situation. The discussion of test results is of particular importance in this regard, as the evaluation is supplemented by the test taker's personal context, life situation and emotions. The ideal outcome of the assessment discussion is that the test taker comes to understand and accept his personal motive profile. The individual usually develops new aspects of self-awareness, and is induced to engage in self-reflection. The ID37 Master can provide the impetus needed to harness personal resources and individual potential.

ID37 Master ID37 Masters are certified experts who have acquired relevant knowledge as well as their ID37 Master's license through a process of training, enabling them to work professionally with the ID37 personality assessment tool. ID37 Masters are personality-assessment experts in the area of motives, motivation and behavior. All professionals with training in coaching, consulting, psychology or related fields, as well as HR managers, executives and team leaders can expand their qualifications by becoming ID37 Masters. Information on available training and further-education sessions can be found at www.ID37.io.

ID37 Master license s. ID37 Master

ID37 motives profile (→ Motive expression) The totality of the 16 motive expressions produces the characteristic ID37 motives profile. It constitutes a personal combination of motive expressions, describes the unique personality in a value-free manner, and is always to be considered solely within the individual context. Only in the individual context does the image of the personality become complete.

Identity (→ Individual, → Personality) Identity is formed through a balance between the personal and social dimensions. It requires individuals to generate their own values, needs, motives and interests, while at the same time engaging with the requirements and expectations of the environment.

"If-then plan" (→ Automatization) is a mechanism used for the purposes of self-direction. In doing so, an intention to act is precisely formulated, and associated with a suitable occasion for action with the goal of automating new behaviors. The advantage of an "if-then plan" is that desired behaviors can be implemented immediately. The concept of the "if-then plan" was developed by psychologists Peter M. Gollwitzer and Gabriele Oettingen. "If-then plans" function best if they are combined with a person's personal motives.

Implicit motives (→ Explicit motives, → Intrinsic motivation, → Motive) are motives that are unconscious and cannot be represented through language. They entail a sensitivity to certain stimuli that is developed early in childhood. Implicit motives are affect-based, associated with physiological parameters (e.g., hormones) and are only indirectly ascertainable, for instance through the use of projective measurement procedures. A correspondence between implicit and explicit motives increases intrinsic motivation.

Individual (→ Identity, → Personality) refers to the single being. The term reflects the uniqueness of each human being, as the word "individual" derives from the verb "dividere" (Latin: to divide), and literally means "that which is indivisible." An individual becomes a personality by taking possession of the achievements of the culture from which they come; however, they define themselves through personal characteristics and independent action, interests and idiosyncrasies, resulting in the development of an individual identity. People differ significantly with regard to their life priorities and goals. The ID37 personality assessment makes this expression of individuality visible.

Intellect The intellect is used to guide action when feelings and experiences are not sufficient for doing so. This is the case in new situations, for example, when a person has not yet been able to gather experience. He must then consciously think and gather information before acting.

Intention The determination to act in a certain manner. Intention is a phase in the course of motivated action. It is the process of will aimed at carrying out the determination to act. After the will has become clear, the person develops an intention; that is, he has the fixed determination to translate the goal into an action, and to systematically pursue the goal. The motivation critical for the realization of the goal arises during the intention phase. Despite the presence of motivation, it may come to pass that an action does not unfold as intended (e.g., due to postponement or distraction). People can learn to minimize problems in the implementation of action, for example through self-control or self-regulation.

Interpersonal (→ Intrapersonal) means between two or more individuals. As an example, interpersonal conflicts are conflicts that exist between team members.

Intrapersonal (→ Interpersonal) means within an individual. As an example, intrapersonal conflicts are motive conflicts experienced by a person.

Intrinsic motivation (→ Extrinsic motivation, → Flow) The incentive to act lies within the activity itself (self-motivation). There is no need for an external instrument of control in order to carry out an activity gladly and consistently. An intrinsically motivated activity can function as its own reward for a long period of time, as it serves a variety of the person's needs, motives, feelings and goals in a positive manner. If other aspects also come into play, intrinsic motivation can develop into a state of flow.

Item is a self-descriptive statement in a questionnaire paired with a set of potential responses (response scale) indicating a graduated level of agreement or disagreement. In the ID37 test procedure, items are used to determine the test taker's motive expressions. Each motive is defined by nine items. An example of an item on the ID37 questionnaire would be: "I often try to please others."

Life satisfaction s. Satisfaction

Motive (→ Motivation, → Motive expression) Motives are orientation-providing, situationally independent drivers of action. They are deeply rooted in the personality, are partially genetically determined, and are expressed to different degrees from person to person. As such, they are useful as indicators of personality, because they are relatively stable and allow us to identify behavioral patterns. People seek to satisfy their motives or the underlying needs by developing patterns of behavior and habits aimed at achieving this goal. The ID37 personality assessment assesses 16 motives and makes behavioral patterns visible in the form of the motives profile. However, the image of the personality becomes complete only in the individual context.

Motivation (→ Motive, → Extrinsic motivation, → Intrinsic motivation) is a state in which the motives have been excited. It triggers an action in the direction of a positive expected target state. Motivation to engage in a certain behavior arises through the interplay of factors associated with the person, the environment and their interaction.

Motive expression (→ Motive) Motive expressions reveal a person's priorities in life and indicate how intensively he wants to satisfy them. People behave differently depending on the expression of a given motive. They have different emotional sensitivities, think differently and perceive the world differently. The more significant the deviation from the norm, the stronger the motive's impact within a person's life – both emotionally and with respect to behavior.

Motive dimension (→ Construct) is the theoretical construct that sits behind different but thematically related behaviors. For example: CURIOSITY.

Motive conflict (→ Approach, → Avoidance, → Intrapersonal) Motive conflicts are conflicts experienced by a person when efforts to satisfy his own motives appear contradictory or incompatible. They are perceived by the person as stressors, paradoxes or dilemmas, and often lead to decisional conflicts (e.g., avoidance-avoidance conflicts). If a person experiences a motive conflict, the objective and/or the alternatives with regard to action are not in keeping with their motives. A decisional dilemma can usually be resolved if the personal motive profile is available and can be consulted. Conversely, conflicts cannot be inferred solely from the motive profile. A test taker or client typically indicates during the discussion of test results whether he perceives a motive conflict.

Motive constellation The interplay of motives plays a critical role in the explanation of individual behavior. A combination of multiple motives, for example, may enable a behavioral regularity (disposition) to become an eye-catching character trait, or render it barely perceptible. An ID37 Master will pay special attention to motive constellations in order to explain the person's behavior with greater precision, and to be able to suggest appropriate interventions.

Motive profile s. ID37 motive profile

Need (→ Drive) is a mostly unconsciously experienced state of lack, that is linked to the desire to eliminate this state (that is, a discrepancy between the actual state and the desired state). Needs are so deeply embedded in a person that they can be satisfied only temporarily, and reoccur over and over again. Psychological needs must be satisfied in order to give meaning to life. In contrast to this, there are also physical needs that must be satisfied in order to survive (e.g., sleep).

Objectivity (→ Reliability, → Validity) is one of the primary quality criteria for a scientific test. Objectivity is intended to ensure that results are comparable between two people. Objectivity may be said to exist when the results of a test do not depend on whether test administrator A or test administrator B oversees, evaluates and interprets the testing process and results.

Personality (→ Dynamic perspective on personality, →Identity, → Individual) Personality is to be understood as encompassing the entirety of an individual's traits; that is, the individual specificities of physical appearance as well as the regularity and consistency of behavior and experience across situations and time periods.

Personality profile s. Motive profile

Personality test (→ ID37) A personality test identifies an individual's trait expressions. In colloquial terms, it is said that a personality test "measures" the personality. However, because the concept of "test" is associated in everyday speech with a grade or assessment, other concepts are often used instead, such as personality assessment. The results of a personality test are always value-free. The ID37 personality test is an online questionnaire consisting of 144 self-descriptive statements about everyday behaviors, attitudes and habits.

Personality trait (→ Trait, → State) A personality trait is an identifiable feature that distinguishes one person from another. When analyzing the dimensions of personality, personality scholarship distinguishes between traits, which are generally stable, and states, which are subject to change.

Priming In psychology, the concept of priming refers to the triggering of behavioral reactions by subliminal stimuli. This is the automatic activation of memory content through the presentation of other content associated with it. In studies, for example, people have been shown to be more cooperative if they have previously engaged unknowingly with words from within the general field of meaning of "cooperation." In such a case, they have created an association with the topic of cooperation, and the corresponding automatic actions have been activated.

Reality is the totality of the experienced world. This reality is only an interpretation by the brain. Each person constructs their own reality and evaluates situations and people on the basis of this reality. This limited perceptual space often leads to misunderstandings and conflicts that make it more difficult to live and work together. With the individual motive profile, an ID37 Master can think himself into another person's reality. Looking out from within this reality, he can help him expand his field of perception.

Reliability (→ Objectivity, → Validity) is one of the primary quality criteria for a scientific test. Reliability describes the degree of precision with which a test measures a particular characteristic. A measurement is precise if it is carried out without measurement errors to the greatest degree possible.

Resource Resources refer to everything on which a person can repeatedly draw in order to activate actions promising a positive result and an emotional benefit. This includes motives and emotions, as well as abilities, skills and interests. The ID37 personality assessment reveals the test taker's motivational resources. The ID37 Master can help make these resources accessible.

Satisfaction Psychology describes satisfaction quite generally as the result of a comparison between expectation and the actual occurrence of what has been expected. The smaller the experienced discrepancy, the more satisfied a person is. Even the impression of being well on the way to achieving the goal can be satisfying. Every person strives for satisfaction. Each individual defines, achieves and experiences satisfaction differently. There are a number of well-founded concepts that lead to higher levels of satisfaction and performance. Life satisfaction refers to a comparatively long period of time and is closely tied to the personality. Life satisfaction is a person's own assessment of his general situation in life.

Self-awareness (→ Script) refers to one's own knowledge regarding oneself and one's internal processes. Self-awareness depends on one's willingness and capability to absorb knowledge and new insights about oneself. Self-awareness is required for effective self-direction. There are various means by which one can gain self-awareness (e.g., observation of one's own behavior, or feedback from other people). The individual ID37 motives profile and the associated knowledge regarding personal motivators is one such means.

Self-centeredness (→ Confirmation bias, → Blind spot, → Value tyranny) refers to people's natural inclination to think that their own set of values are correct. One's own set of standards becomes a standard for all values and actions. Conflict-producing consequences of self-centeredness can include blind spots, value tyranny or confirmation bias. In the ID37 personality profile, self-centeredness tends to appear with greater frequency in cases of strong and weak motive expressions.

Self-congruence (→ Motive, → Goal) is the experience of a fit between personal motives and goals.

Self-control (→ Self-regulation) is conscious regulation of action that relies on the intellect. It entails a focus on what is the most important goal at that moment. This is extremely demanding and energy-consuming. Self-control is largely effective as a short-term measure (e.g., when studying for a final exam, instead of going to the beach with friends).

Self-direction encompasses a person's attempts and efforts to initiate, develop and implement personal, self-determined processes of change with the aim of improving their quality of life. It essentially creates a greater freedom of action and keeps the person from being entirely dependent either on their inner script or on external factors. The knowledge of one's own personality is the key element in this process. The concepts of "self-direction," "self-management" and "self-guidance" are often used as synonyms. ID37's five-phase self-direction method is one means of initiating change processes.

Self-efficacy is a person's subjective assessment that he can influence the realization of goals through his own actions and can in the future overcome challenges on his own. Self-efficacious people show perseverance and flexibility when pursuing action goals. The experience of self-efficacy has been shown to have a positive effect with regard to the reduction of stress and the general feeling of well-being.

Self-motivation s. Intrinsic motivation

Self-regulation (→ Emotion regulation, → Self-control) In the process of self-regulation, regulatory processes are adapted to the personality, and synchronized with the action goal. Unlike self-control, the guiding influence over one's actions comes virtually without effort. Self-regulation is suitable for carrying out long-term behavioral changes. Emotion regulation plays an important role in self-regulation.

Self-responsibility A person wants to actively steer and shape his own life, rather than allowing himself to be shaped by factors external to himself. He is willing to take responsibility for his attitudes and behaviors and does in fact do this. Self-responsibility is a requirement for effective self-direction.

Scale (→ Item) refers to a set of items that can be consolidated according to statistical and theoretical analysis. ID37 has 16 self-description scales. These are unipolar.

Script (→ Self-awareness) The patterns that determine a person's experience and behavior can be understood as a personal basic program – in the sense of a computer program – or script. People are generally unaware of their internal scripts. When engaged in a change-oriented project or self-direction training program, it can be useful to analyze one's own internal script.

Standardization is a quality criterion for a scientific test. Standardization is carried out based on a set of tests completed by members of a representative sample (normative sample), which are subjected to statistical analysis. They serve as a means of comparing the test results for an individual person with a representative comparative population. For instance, does the test taker show above- or below-average expression of a given motive, or does he broadly correspond with the statistical norm? The normative sample must be up-to-date and representative. According to the DIN 33430 standard, a normative sample must not be more than 8 years old. The normative sample used for ID37 is from 2017 and includes 1001 participants.

State (→ Personality trait, → Trait) refers to a temporary or passing mental or emotional condition, such as anxiety.

Stimulus (synonym: Trigger) A stimulus is something that incites or activates a behavior.

Success (→ Failure) is the achievement of personal goals. Setting suitable goals is a prerequisite for this. Success is highly individual; that is, success is simply what each person individually defines as success for themselves. Over the course of a long lifespan, the achievement of personal goals generally entails an alternation between success and failure. The ID37 motive profile provides information regarding what goals may suit the given individual.

Test item s. Item

Test scale s. Scale

Trait s. Personality trait

Trait (→ Personality trait, →State) refers to a stable human characteristic, such as being "fearful."

Trigger s. Stimulus

Validity (→ Objectivity, → Reliability) is one of the primary quality criteria for a scientific test. Validity determines whether the test in fact measures what it is intended to measure. A high degree of validity is always dependent on a high degree of both objectivity and reliability. There are various avenues by which to determine validity, such as content validity, construct validity and criterion validity.

Value (→ Motive) Values are judgment-laden thoughts and attitudes regarding important things, one's own person, friends or society. A person's values become their standard of measure for the world at large. They are relatively constant. Unlike motives, values are not innate, but are created in the process of socialization within systems. Behind every set of values are motives that push the individual to live according to these values.

Value tyranny (→ Self-centeredness) People tend to think that their own set of values are correct (self-centeredness). When they repeatedly try to convince others to adopt their own values and the underlying motives, this is termed value tyranny. This usually leads to recurring disputes.

Index

T. Staller, C. Kirschke, *Personality Assessment with ID37*,
https://doi.org/10.1007/978-3-030-53921-4

CPSIA information can be obtained
at www.ICGtesting.com
Printed in the USA
BVHW010157171120
593508BV00001B/1